THE ULTIMATE CROCK POT COOKBOOK 800

Hot & Hearty Classic Slow Cooker Recipes for Any Taste and Occasion, Easy and Foolproof Recipes for Every Day

William E. Klein

Copyright ©2020 By William E. Klein

All rights reserved.

No part of this guide may be reproduced in any form without permission in writing from the publisher except in the case of brief quotations embodied in critical articles or reviews.

Legal & Disclaimer

The information contained in this book and its contents is not designed to replace or take the place of any form of medical or professional advice; and is not meant to replace the need for independent medical, financial, legal or other professional advice or services, as may be required. The content and information in this book has been provided for educational and entertainment purposes only.

The content and information contained in this book has been compiled from sources deemed reliable, and it is accurate to the best of the Author's knowledge, information and belief. However, the Author cannot guarantee its accuracy and validity and cannot be held liable for any errors and/or omissions. Further, changes are periodically made to this book as and when needed. Where appropriate and/or necessary, you must consult a professional (including but not limited to your doctor, attorney, financial advisor or such other professional advisor) before using any of the suggested remedies, techniques, or information in this book.

Table of Content

Introduction ··· 1
  The Features and Functions of the Crock Pot ··· 1
  The Digital Control Panel ··· 2
  Tips for Better Experience with Crock Pot ··· 2
  About the Recipes ··· 2

Chapter 1 Breakfasts and Brunches ··· 3
  Basic Oatmeal ··· 3
  Almond and Date Oatmeal ··· 3
  Maple Cranberry Granola ··· 3
  Fish Congee ··· 3
  Sweet Potato and Corn Scramble ··· 4
  Cheese Grits with Collard Greens ··· 4
  Potato and Prosciutto Breakfast Strata ··· 4
  Green Chili Cheddar Crustless Quiche ··· 5
  Sausage Hash Brown Breakfast Casserole ··· 5
  Mango Yogurt with Honey and Cardamon ··· 5
  Sausage and Waffle Breakfast Bake ··· 6
  Chorizo Egg Casserole ··· 6
  Almond and Raisin Granola ··· 6
  Ham Egg Cheese Casserole ··· 7
  Peanut Butter Oatmeal Granola ··· 7
  Pear and Chai Oatmeal ··· 7
  Eggs in Tomato Purgatory ··· 7
  Sausage Casserole ··· 8
  Potato, Parsnip, and Carrot Hash ··· 8
  Apple Cobbler ··· 8
  Quinoa and Cherry Porridge ··· 8
  Potato and Tomato Strata ··· 8

Chapter 2 Appetizers ··· 9
  Beef and Cheese Dip ··· 9
  Lemony Chicken Wings ··· 9
  Crab Dip ··· 9
  Grape Jelly Meatballs ··· 9
  Chex Mix ··· 10
  Glazed Hawaiian Kielbasa Bites ··· 10
  BBQ Party Starters ··· 10
  Tomato Salsa ··· 10
  Cranberry Swedish Meatballs ··· 11
  Sweet and Spicy Peanuts ··· 11
  Sweet and Spicy Chicken Wings ··· 11
  Barbecued Smokies ··· 11
  Pizza Bites ··· 11
  Cheese Pulled Pork Crostini ··· 12
  Marinated Wings ··· 12
  Lush BBQ Sausage Bites ··· 12
  Turkey Teriyaki Sandwiches ··· 13
  Tequila Sausage Queso ··· 13
  Glazed Chicken Wings ··· 13
  Broccoli Dip ··· 14
  Catalina Marmalade Meatballs ··· 14
  Chili Dip ··· 14
  Sweet Smoked Chicken Wings ··· 14
  Crunchy Snack Mix ··· 14

Chapter 3 Stocks and Sauces ··· 15
  Fish Stock ··· 15
  Vegetable Stock ··· 15
  Chicken Stock ··· 15
  Salsa Mexicana ··· 16

Berry Sauce	16
Shallot and Red Wine Sauce	16
Buffalo Wing Sauce	16
Classic Bolognese Sauce	17
Basil Tomato Sauce	17
Alfredo Sauce	17
Salsa Verde	18
Vegan Garlic Pasta Sauce	18
Nacho Cheese Sauce	18
Italian Meat Gravy	18

Chapter 4 Desserts · · · 19

Black and Blue Berry Cobbler	19
Creamy Pumpkin Pie Pudding	19
Pineapple Tapioca	19
Raisin Rice Pudding	19
Chocolate Fondue	20
Chocolate Chip Graham Cracker Cookies	20
Fallen Chocolate Soufflé Cake	20
Fruity Cake with Walnuts	20
Stewed Dried Apricots	21
Strawberry Rhubarb Compote	21
Fudgy Brownies	21
Pecan-Crusted Blueberry Crisp	21
Lemon Blueberry Cornmeal Cake	22
Chocolate Snack Cake	22
Carrot Cake with Cream Cheese Frosting	23
Sour Cream Cheesecake	23
Pumpkin Spice Cheesecake	24
Ultimate Chocolate Cheesecake	24
Coconut Key Lime Pie	25
Ginger Peach Crumble	25
Apple Crisp with Oat Topping	26
Hearty Apricot Cheesecake	26
Rhubarb and Strawberry Compote	27
Cherry and Hazelnut Stuffed Apples	27
Vanilla Creme Brûlée	27
Spiced Applesauce Cake	28
Mixed Fruit Curry	28
Sweet Cherry Grunt	28
Apple Crumble	29
Posh Fruit Compote	29
Apple and Walnut Pie	29
Flan	29
Baked Raisin Stuffed Apples	30
Pumpkin Pie Custard	30
Self-Frosting Chocolate Cake	30
Super Lemony Rice Pudding	30
Pineapple and Mango Crisp	31
Chocolate Brownie Cake	31
Vanilla Chocolate Cake	31
Cherry Molton Cake	32
Pot De Crème	32
Pumpkin and Mixed Berry Compote	32
Cinnamon Applesauce	32
Almond Cake	33
Gingerbread	33
Almond and Sour Cream Cheesecake	33
Almond and Peanut Butter Cheesecake	34
Pound Cake	34
Raspberry and Lime Custard Cake	34

Chapter 5 Classic Comfort Foods · · · 35

Chili Mac and Cheese	35
Mushroom Macaroni and Cheese	35
Broccoli and Three-Cheese Lasagna	36
Baked Ziti with Sausage	36
Ham and Potato Casserole	37
Italian Meatball Stew	37
Grape-Nuts Custard Pudding	37
Chicken and Red Potato Stew	37
Caramelized Onion Pot Roast	38
Smothered Pork	38
Thai Red Curry Chicken with Vegetables	38
Chicken and Wild Rice Soup	39

Cheesy Sausage Lasagna · 39
Super Bean Soup · 40
Chicken and Carrot Fricassee · 40

Chapter 6 Soups, Stews, and Chilies · 41

Cream of Zucchini Soup · 41
Nutmeg Carrot Soup · 41
Beef Alphabet Soup · 41
Ham and Vegetable Soup · 42
Mushroom and Bacon Soup · 42
Italian Beef Minestrone · 42
Ground Beef Macaroni Soup · 42
Thyme Onion Soup · 43
Butternut Squash Soup with Thyme · 43
Creamy Cheddar Potato Soup · 43
Garbanzo Bean Soup · 44
Rosemary White Bean Soup · 44
Pork Veggie Soup · 44
Red Pear and Pumpkin Soup · 45
Creamy Carrot and Broccoli Soup · 45
Sausage Cabbage Soup · 45
Leek and Potato Soup · 45
Classic Gyro Soup · 46
Mushroom Tofu Soup · 46
Vegetable Beef Soup · 46
Spanish Beef and Rice Soup · 47
Beef and Parsnip Soup · 47
Red Pepper and Lentil Soup · 47
Kale and White Bean Soup · 48
Authentic Zuppa Bastarda · 48
Beef and Pumpkin Stew · 48
Sausage and Kale Soup · 49
Leek and Potato Soup · 49
Onion and Tomato Soup · 49
Tangy Carrot Bisque · 49
Pork and Butternut Squash Stew · 50
Vegetable and Black-Eyed Pea Chili · 50
Corn and Beef Chili · 50
Creamy Butternut Squash Soup · 51
Curried Vegetable Soup · 51
Beef and Barley Soup · 51
Black Bean and Turkey Sausage Stew · 51
Turkey Sausage and Navy Bean Stew · 52
Macaroni Bean Stew · 52
Veggie and Brown Rice Stew · 52
Fennel and Leek Soup · 52
Vegetable and Rice Stew · 53
Beef and Kidney Bean Stew · 53
Southern Brunswick Stew · 53
Chickpea and Lentil Stew · 53
Beef and Pearl Barley Stew · 54
Brown Sugar Beef Chili · 54
Brown Rice and Black Bean Chili · 54
Sweet Potato and Sirloin Stew · 54
Beef Chili · 55
Veggie and Cashew Chili · 55
Hamburger Chili with Beans · 55
Potato and Beef Chili · 55
Bacon and Beef Chili · 56
Indian-Style Chili · 56
Brown Lentil Chili · 56
Beef Chili with Cilantro Cream · 57
Hominy and Turkey Thigh Chili · 57
Veggie Bulgur Wheat Chili · 58

Chapter 7 Side Dishes · 59

Cider Butternut Squash Purée · 59
Braised Butternut Squash with Pecans · 59
Acorn Squash with Maple Orange Glaze · 59
Sake-Cooked Asparagus · 60
Garlic Mushrooms with Crème Fraîche · 60
Braised Peas with Lettuce and Onions · 60
Thyme Garlic Tomatoes · 61
Garlic Collard Greens and Kale · 61
Buttered Parsley Red Potatoes · 61

Shoepeg Corn Casserole	61
Black-Eyed Peas with Ham	62
Balsamic Fresh Shell Beans with Herbs	62
Cowboy Calico Beans with Ground Beef	62
Spanish Hominy	62
Green Beans and Potatoes with Bacon	63
Zucchini Stuffed Sweet Onions	63
Maple Baked Beans with Bacon	63
Root Vegetable Medley	63
Coconut Curried Butternut Squash	64
Cheesy Red Potatoes	64
Zucchini Tomato Casserole	64
Creamed Broccoli	64
Jalapeño Creamed Corn	65
Warm Fruit Salad	65
Cinnamon Glazed Acorn Squash	65
Spinach and Cheese Casserole	65
Bacon Hash Brown Casserole	65
Garlicky Braised Kale with Chorizo	66
Leeks Braised in Cream	66
Thyme Root Veggies	66
Root Veggie Gratin with Barley	66
Mashed Squash with Garlic	67
Leafy Greens with Onions	67
Garlicky Balsamic Glazed Onions	67
Green Bean and Mushroom Casserole	67
Cauliflower-Bacon Casserole with Pecans	68
Citrus Carrots with Leek	68
Orange Cauliflower with Herbs	68
Honey Parsnips and Carrots	68
Carrot Cheese Casserole	68
Mexican Corn with Pimentos	69
Barbecue Collard Greens with Tofu	69
Spicy Corn-Ham Pudding	69
Garlic Squash Curry	69
Pumpkin-Carrot Pudding	70
Pecan-Stuffed Acorn Squash	70
Greek Yogurt Mashed Pumpkin	70
Acorn Squash with Shallots and Dates	70
Garlic Button Mushrooms	71
Thai-Flavored Green Vegetables	71
Lemon-Rosemary Beets	71
Peppery Broccoli with Sesame Seeds	71
Basil Potato and Corn	71

Chapter 8 Vegetarian Mains 72

Black Bean Spinach Enchiladas	72
Spinach Mushroom Cheese Quiche	72
Seitan Tikka Masala with Green Beans	72
Tempeh and Vegetable Shepherd's Pie	73
Tempeh and Corn Stuffed Bell Peppers	73
Potato Stuffed Peppers	73
Veggie Tofu Stir-Fry	74
Indian Spiced Potatoes and Cauliflower	74
Vegetarian Bean Cassoulet	74
Beans and Couscous Stuffed Peppers	75
Curried Coconut Quinoa	75
Eggplant and Potato Curry	75
Spice Stuffed Baby Eggplants	76
Roasted Cauliflower with Tomato Cashew Sauce	76
Almond Vegetable Korma	77
Red Tofu Curry and Green Beans	77
North African Pumpkin and Cauliflower Stew	77
Cauliflower and Zucchini Vindaloo	78
Braised Eggplant and Lentils	78
Summer Vegetable Mélange	78
Caponata	79
Barley-Stuffed Cabbage Rolls	79
Tofu with Greens	79
Sumptuous Chinese Vegetable Mix	79

Chapter 9 Poultry 80

Chicken Parmesan	80
Hawaiian Huli Huli Chicken	80
Lemon Garlic Chicken	80
Apple Balsamic Chicken	81

Mango Pineapple Chicken Tacos	81
Mushroom Chicken Alfredo	81
Jamaican-Inspired Brown Chicken Stew	82
Lemon-Dill Chicken	82
Cornbread Chicken Bake	82
Thai Sesame Chicken Thighs	83
Chicken with Apple and Chardonnay Gravy	83
Sour Cream Chicken Enchiladas	83
Rotisserie-Style Chicken with Carrots	84
Mushroom Chicken Cacciatore	84
Tandoori Chicken	84
Ginger Peach Glazed Chicken Thighs	85
Orange-Hoisin Chicken	85
Filipino Chicken Adobo	85
Jerk Chicken	86
Whole Roasted Mexican Chicken	86
Tarragon Chicken Marsala	86
Garlicky Lemon-Thyme Turkey Legs	87
Turkey Teriyaki Thighs	87
Apricot Glazed Turkey with Herbs	87
Tea Smoked Turkey Legs	88
Mexican Turkey	88
Turkey Taco Salad	88
Stuffed Turkey Cutlets with Artichokes	89
Duck Breasts with Port and Orange Sauce	89
Italian-Style Braised Chicken and Veggies	90
Chicken Cacciatore	90
Classic Chicken Casablanca	90
Authentic Con Pollo	91
Chicken and Turkey Sausage Jambalaya	91
Chicken Cheese Parmigiana	91
Chicken Chili	91
Chicken Tamales	92
BBQ Chicken Legs	92
Garlicky Chicken	92
Chicken Olé Casserole	93
Chicken Breast with Peas	93
Chicken Tetrazzini	93
Veggie Ketchup Chicken	93
California Chicken	94
Tex-Mex Chicken and Rice	94
Tender Chicken with BBQ-Soda Sauce	94
Turkey Macaroni with Corn	94
Southwestern Chicken with Corn	95
Greek Chicken with Potatoes	95
Red Pepper Chicken with Black Beans	95
Mediterranean Chicken with Artichokes	95
Peanut Butter Chicken Thighs	96
Toasted Sesame Chicken Wings	96
Chicken Wings in Plum Sauce	96
Sweet and Sour Chicken Wings	96
Turkey-Broccoli Supreme	97
BBQ Turkey Cutlets	97
Ground Turkey with Potatoes	97
Turkey Loaf	97
Turkey Sloppy Joes	97

Chapter 10 Red Meat 98

Cabbage and Beef Stew	98
Beef and Baby Carrot Stew	98
Beer-Braised Beef Brisket	98
Sweet and Sour Tomato Brisket	99
Lamb with Artichokes	99
Vinegary Steak with Green Chilies	100
Pork Chops with Plum Sauce	100
Flank Steak Fajitas	100
Asian Baby Back Ribs	101
Maple Pork Chops in Bourbon	101
Mediterranean Beef Roast	101
Asian-Flavored Braised Spareribs	102
Balsamic Beef with Cranberry Gravy	102
Mexican Beef Enchilada	102
Beef Roast Sandwiches	103
Beef Ragoût with Veggies	103
Pork Loin with Cran-Orange Sauce	103
Smoked Sausages with BBQ Sauce	104

Cider Pork Loin	104
Pork Tenderloin with Mango Sauce	104
Sausage and Peppers in Wine	105
Sweet and Spiced Pork Loin	105
Teriyaki Pork Tenderloin	105
Country-Style Spareribs	106
Braised Lamb with Eggplant	106
Mediterranean Lamb and Lentils	106
Lamb Chops and White Beans	107
Leg of Lamb with Pinto Beans	107
Indian Tandoori Lamb	107
Sweet and Savory Brisket	108
Leg of Lamb and Cabbage	108
Corned Beef Braised in Riesling	108
Brisket Braised with Dried Fruits	109
Chicago-Style Flank Steaks	109
BBQ Short Ribs	110
Osso Buco	110
Texas-Style Smoked Beef Brisket	110
Mexican Beef Brisket	111
Onion Beef Short Ribs	111
Zinfandel-Braised Beef Short Ribs	111
Sweet and Sour Pork	112
Garlicky Veal Stew	112
Beef Roast with Stewed Tomatoes	112
German Sauerbraten	113
Chinese-Style Cumin Lamb	113
Apple and Cranberry Pork Roast	114
Pork-Beef Patties with Cabbage	114
Pork Roast in Apricot Glaze	114
Sumptuous Pork with Veggies	114
Beef Roast with Tangy Au Jus	115
Texas-Style Pork Burritos	115
Pork Wraps with Hoisin Sauce	115
Oregano Lamb Chops	116
Pork and Butternut Stew	116
Italian Pork Sausage Lasagna Soup	116
Garlic Braised Lamb Shanks	117
Pork Shoulder Chili Con Carne	117
Hungarian Pork Paprikash	117
Lamb Goulash au Blanc	118
Irish Lamb Stew	118
Soy-Honey Lamb and Brown Rice	118

Chapter 11 Fish and Seafood 119

Basil Perch with Potatoes	119
Herbed Braised Flounder	119
Red Snapper Feast	119
Five-Ingredient Tuna Loaf	119
Salmon with Chili-Garlic Glaze	120
Spinach-Stuffed Sole	120
Halibut Tacos	121
Swordfish with Tomato and Olive Relish	121
Salmon and Mushroom Bake	122
Cod with Garlic Edamame	122
Cheddar Salmon Soufflé	122
Sweet and Sour Tuna	122
Tuna and Veggie Casserole with Almonds	123
Fish Tagine with Artichokes	123
Salmon with White Rice Salad	123
BBQ Tuna	124
Halibut with Green Bean Salad	124
Shrimp and Ham Jambalaya	124
Tuna and Egg Casserole	125
Shrimp and Crab Gumbo	125
Crab Angel Hair Pasta	125
Shrimp Spaghetti with Marinara	125
Seafood Medley	126
Thai Green Curry Shrimp	126
Creamy Shrimp Curry	126
Citrus Swordfish Fillets	126
Asian Shrimp and Rice Casserole	127
Green Chile and Shrimp Tacos	127
Scallops with Creamy Leeks	127
Monterey Jack Seafood Pasta	127
Moroccan Sea Bass with Bell Pepper	128

Foil Pack Garlic Butter Tilapia　128
Poached Tuna with Olives　128
Fruit Salsa Mahi Mahi with Lentils　129
Lime Buttered Salmon　129
Crayfish Creole　129
Poached Turbot　130
Lemon-Dijon Salmon　130
Coconut Halibut with Eggplant Relish　130
Honeyed Worcestershire Salmon　131
Branzino and Potato Bake　131
White Fish Curry　131
Shrimp, Quinoa, and Corn Salad　132
Barbecue Shrimp and Scallops　132
Mushroom and Tomato Mussels　133
Spanish Herbed Octopus　133
Marinara Shrimp　134
Shrimp Polenta　134

Chapter 12 Rice, Grains, and Beans　135

Kedgeree (Spiced Rice with Smoked Fish)　135
White Beans with Pancetta and Carrot　135
Creamy Saffron Rice　136
Wild Rice, Bacon, and Cherries　136
Almond-Mushroom Wild Rice　136
Cranberry Sweet Potato and Wild Rice　136
Butternut Squash Risotto with White Wine　137
Wild Rice and Fruit Pilaf　137
Mexican Pinto Beans　137
Aromatic Vegetable Pulao　138
Lemon Thyme Pearl Barley Risotto　138

Brown Rice Risotto with Starch Vegetables　138
Pine Nut Pilaf　139
Barley and Mushroom Risotto　139
Barley Risotto Primavera　139
Tex-Mex Quinoa Salad　139
Ratatouille Quinoa Casserole　140
Boston Baked Beans　140
Buckwheat with Lush Mushrooms　140
Barley Pilaf with Dates　141
Quinoa with Corn　141
Tuscan-Style White Beans with Herbs　141
Grits Casserole　142
Rice, Farro, and Barley Medley　142
Basil Parmesan Polenta　142
Bean and Pea Medley　142
Refried Beans　143
Lentils with Escarole and Cheese　143
Mexican Black Bean and Pork Stew　143
Molasses Baked Soybeans　144
Rosemary Lentils with Ham and Carrot　144
Black-Eyed Peas and Greens and Sausage　144
Herbed Black Beans with Onions　145
Puy Lentils with Leek　145
Southwestern Bean and Ham Pot　145
French White Beans　145
Rosemary Northern Beans　145

Appendix 1 Measurement Conversion Chart　146

Appendix 2 Recipe Index　147

Introduction

One of my most common kitchen utensils is my crock pot. I love making soups, stews, roasts, etc., especially in the fall and winter. Many of you have probably always assumed that a crock pot and a slow cooker are the same. However, it turns out that while a crock pot is a type of slow cooker, not all slow cookers are crock pots.

Let's take a closer look at the crock pot first. The first model was presented to us in 1970 and sold exclusively in a bean container. Over time, the brand has expanded its cooking repertoire to include many different types of dishes. The company then redesigned their bean pot by modifying it and adding handles and a glass lid.

The product was subsequently registered under the trade name "Crock-Pot", which is now marketed under the rival brand. Now, of course, the word "slow cooker" has become an umbrella term for every type of slow cooker.

With a true crock pot, the crock itself is a container with heating elements all along the sides as well as on the bottom. The device has two heat settings, high (typically 300°F) and low (200°F), with most models now coming with a "Keep Warm" setting. It cooks food slowly at a low temperature, with the heat surrounding the food and bringing it up to a safe temperature quickly.

The Features and Functions of the Crock Pot

Its Size: On the recommendation of my mom, I bought a 6 litter crock pot. It looked huge (too much) when it arrived, but I've appreciated her advice ever since. You can handle a whole chicken, place a large pallet for my beloved pulled pork, or make enough slow cooker cuisine to feed a crowd. When I was making my first dinner, slow cooker meals saved my life - I was a stressful flight attendant, but I knew there would at least be one delicious stew for my guests. Even though it's just my husband and I, I still love making great slow cooker meals.

Programmed Cooking Times: As this was my first (and only) crock pot, I didn't even realize that other models hadn't programmed a cooking time! Mine allows me to set the exact cooking time I want, which means the heating process will be on when I'm not there. It keeps me from panicking if I'm late or distracted by trifles.

The "Warm" Setting: Not only did I save my sanity from running errands to finish the slow cooker, but I also learned to appreciate the "Warm Up" feature for its original best intention of keeping food warm at a party. Whether it's muffins for Thanksgiving dinner or a jar of beans at a party, I love using this setting for the slow cooker and saving the stove burners (or my host's) for other things.

Insert Is Easy to Clean: I'm a lazy dishwasher. Very lazy. As such, I appreciate that no matter what I put my slow cooker through, it always cleans with just a few swipes of a soapy rag. I very rarely even need to soak it. The insert is made of enamel stoneware, similar to enamel-lined Dutch ovens, and somehow this this translates into "lazy girl's best friend."

The Digital Control Panel

It's a little thing, but I like being able to just touch a button to turn on the slow cooker and set the cooking time. This display is also much easier to clean.

You adjust the pre-set times by using the "+" and "-" time select buttons.

Pre-set Times:

Steam – 10 minutes is the pre-set time. You can change it from 3 minutes to 1 hour. 3 minutes is the shortest cook time available on the Crock-pot pressure cooker. If you want to cook something less than 3 minutes, you'll need to set a timer and press the stop button after the desired number of minutes.

Soup – 30 minutes. Range from 5 minutes to 2 hours

Poultry – 15 minutes. Range from 15 minutes – 2 hours

Beans/Chili – 20 minutes. Range from 5 minutes to 2 hours

Meat/Stew – 35 minutes. Adjustable range from 15 minute to 2 hours

Multigrain – 40 minutes. Range from 10 minutes to 2 hours

Rice/Risotto – 12 minutes' low pressure. Range from 6 minute to 30 minutes

Dessert – 10 minutes' low pressure. Range from 5 minutes to 2 hours

Yogurt – not a pressure cooker function – low temperature for 8 hours. Range from 6 hours to 12 hours

Slow Cook – not a pressure cooker function – high temperature for 4 hours. Range from 30 minutes to 20 hours. Temperature adjusts to low and high.

Brown / Saute – not a pressure cooker function – high temperature for 30 minutes. Range from 5 minutes to 30 minutes. Temperature adjusts to low and high.

Keep Warm – not a pressure cooker function – warm temperature for 4 hours. Range from 30 minutes – 4 hours.

You'll want to keep the pre-set times handy so you know before selecting a button what the cook time and pressure level will be.

Tips for Better Experience with Crock Pot

· For easy clean-up and care of your slow cooker, rub the inside of the stoneware with oil or spray it with non-stick cooking spray before using it. Slow cooker liners also ease clean-up.

· Fill the crock pot no less than half full and no more than two-thirds full. Cooking too little or too much food in the slow cooker can affect cooking time, quality and the safety.

· Because vegetables cook slower than meat and poultry, place the vegetables in the crock pot first. Place the meat on top of the vegetables and top with liquid, such as broth, water or a sauce.

· Add the liquid, such as broth, water or barbecue sauce suggested in the recipe. Because liquids do not boil away in a slow cooker, in most cases, you can reduce liquids by one-third to one-half when converting a non-slow cooker recipe for crock pot use.

· Keep the lid in place during cooking. Removing the lid slows cooking time. Every time the lid is lifted, about 15-20 minutes of cooking time is lost.

· Add grains such as pasta at the end of the cooking process or it will become mushy. You may want to cook pasta or another grain such as rice separately and add it just before serving.

· Add milk, cheese and cream during the last hour to prevent curdling.

· Very soft vegetables such as tomatoes, mushrooms, and zucchini may be added during the last 45 minutes of cooking time

About the Recipes

Now you have known the features of Crock Pot and how to make most of it, so, you can start to cook with your Crock Pot. In this cookbook, I provided about 800 recipes for you. No Matter what you want to eat, you can find it. Now, go ahead and try the delicious recipes next.

Chapter 1 Breakfasts and Brunches

Basic Oatmeal

Prep time: 5 minutes | Cook time: 6 hours | Serves 4

1⅓ cups dry old-fashioned rolled oats
2½ cups plus 1 tablespoon water
Dash of salt

1. Mix together cereal, water, and salt in a crock pot. Cook on low for 6 hours.
2. Stir and serve.

Almond and Date Oatmeal

Prep time: 5 minutes | Cook time: 4 to 6 hours | Serves 8

2 cups dry rolled oats
½ cup dry Grape-Nuts cereal
½ cup slivered almonds
¼ cup chopped dates
4 cups water

1. Combine all ingredients in a crock pot. Cook on low for 4 to 6 hours.
2. Serve with fat-free milk, if desired.

Maple Cranberry Granola

Prep time: 5 minutes | Cook time: 5½ to 7½ hours | Makes about 10 cups

Wet Ingredients:
¾ cup pure maple syrup
½ cup water
¼ cup firmly packed light brown sugar
¼ cup canola oil or sunflower seed oil
Dry Ingredients:
6 cups old-fashioned rolled oats
1 cup raw sunflower seeds
½ cup raw pumpkin seeds
½ cup raw oat bran
1 cup honey-toasted wheat germ
1½ cups sweetened dried cranberries
½ cup chopped dried apricots
3 tablespoons raw sesame seeds

1. Put the wet ingredients in a crock pot and set on high. Stir with a whisk to combine well.
2. In a large bowl, combine all the dry ingredients and stir to evenly distribute. Add one-third of the dry ingredients to the warm mixture, stirring until evenly moistened with a spatula or wooden spoon. slowly add the remaining dry ingredients, stirring constantly so that all of it is evenly moistened. Continue to cook on high, uncovered, for exactly 1½ hours, stirring every 30 minutes.
3. Turn the crock pot to low, cover, and cook until the granola is dry and a very light golden color, 4 to 6 hours, stirring every hour or so for even cooking. When done, it will slide off a spatula or spoon.
4. While the granola is hot, stir in the wheat germ, dried cranberries, apricots, and sesame seeds. Let cool completely (the mixture will become crispier as it cools). Serve immediately.

Fish Congee

Prep time: 10 minutes | Cook time: 4⅓ hours | Serves 6

1½ cups long-grain white rice
1 (1-inch) piece fresh ginger, peeled and grated
3 quarts boiling water
12 ounces (340 g) firm white fish fillets, such as flounder or cod, skin removed, thinly sliced
Coarse salt, to taste
Sliced scallions, for serving

1. Place the rice and ginger into the crock pot. Add the boiling water and stir. Cover and cook on low until congee reaches consistency of loose porridge, about 4 hours (or on high for 2 hours).
2. Add fish and cook on low until fish falls apart, about 20 minutes more (or on high for 10 minutes). Season to taste with salt and serve with the sliced scallions.

Sweet Potato and Corn Scramble

Prep time: 10 minutes | Cook time: 8 hours | Serves 2

1 teaspoon butter, at room temperature, or extra-virgin olive oil
4 eggs
½ cup 2% milk
⅛ teaspoon sea salt
½ teaspoon smoked paprika
½ teaspoon ground cumin
Freshly ground black pepper, to taste
1 cup finely diced sweet potato
1 cup frozen corn kernels, thawed
½ cup diced roasted red peppers
2 tablespoons minced onion

1. Grease the inside of the crock pot with the butter.
2. In a small bowl, whisk together the eggs, milk, salt, paprika, and cumin. Season with the freshly ground black pepper.
3. Put the sweet potato, corn, red peppers, and onion into the crock pot. Pour in the egg mixture and stir gently.
4. Cover and cook on low for 8 hours or overnight. Serve warm.

Cheese Grits with Collard Greens

Prep time: 10 minutes | Cook time: 3 hours | Serves 8

2 cups white hominy grits (not quick-cooking)
4½ cups hot water, divided
4 cups milk
Coarse salt, to taste
4 ounces (113 g) cotija or feta cheese, crumbled
2 tablespoons extra-virgin olive oil
1 small onion, thinly sliced
6 garlic cloves, thinly sliced
¼ teaspoon red pepper flakes
1 bunch collard greens (about 1 pound / 454 g), tough stems and ribs removed, leaves coarsely chopped
Fried eggs, for serving
Hot sauce, for serving

1. Stir to combine grits with 4 cups of hot water, milk, and 2 teaspoons of salt in the crock pot. Cover and cook, stirring occasionally, on high until grits are creamy, 3 hours (or on low for 6 hours). Stir in cheese and season with salt.
2. Meanwhile, heat oil in a large skillet over medium heat. Add onion and cook until translucent, about 3 minutes. Add garlic and cook, stirring often, until golden, about 3 minutes. Stir in red pepper flakes and cook until fragrant, about 30 seconds.
3. Stir in collard greens and 1 teaspoon of salt. Reduce heat to medium-low. Add remaining ½ cup of hot water, cover, and steam until greens are just tender and water evaporates, about 10 minutes. (If greens are ready but there is still water in the pan, raise heat to medium-high, and cook, uncovered, until completely evaporated.)
4. Serve grits with greens, fried eggs, and hot sauce.

Potato and Prosciutto Breakfast Strata

Prep time: 10 minutes | Cook time: 8 hours | Serves 2

1 teaspoon butter, at room temperature, or extra-virgin olive oil
4 eggs
½ cup 2% milk
1 tablespoon minced fresh rosemary
⅛ teaspoon sea salt
Freshly ground black pepper, to taste
2 medium russet potatoes, peeled and thinly sliced
2 ounces (57 g) prosciutto

1. Grease the inside of the crock pot with the butter.
2. In a small bowl, whisk together the eggs, milk, rosemary, salt, and a few grinds of the black pepper.
3. Layer one-third of the potatoes in the bottom of the crock pot and top that layer with one-third of the prosciutto. Pour one-third of the egg mixture over the prosciutto. Repeat this layering with the remaining ingredients.
4. Cover and cook on low for 8 hours or overnight. Serve warm.

Green Chili Cheddar Crustless Quiche

Prep time: 15 minutes | Cook time: 3 to 4 hours | Serves 6

3 corn tortillas
2 (4-ounce / 113-g) cans whole green chilies
1 (15-ounce / 425-g) can chili con carne
1½ cups shredded Cheddar cheese, divided
4 large eggs
1½ cups 2% milk
1 cup biscuit mix
¼ teaspoon salt
¼ teaspoon pepper
1 teaspoon hot pepper sauce (optional)
1 (4-ounce / 113-g) can chopped green chilies
2 medium tomatoes, sliced
Sour cream (optional)

1. In a greased crock pot, layer tortillas, whole green chilies, chili con carne and 1 cup of cheese.
2. In a small bowl, whisk the eggs, milk, biscuit mix, salt, pepper, and hot pepper sauce (if desired) until blended, then pour into a crock pot. Top with chopped green chilies and tomatoes.
3. Cook on low, covered, for 3 to 4 hours or until a thermometer reads 160°F (71°C), sprinkling with remaining ½ cup of cheese during the last 30 minutes of cooking.
4. Turn off crock pot and let stand for 15 minutes before serving. If desired, top with sour cream.

Sausage Hash Brown Breakfast Casserole

Prep time: 15 minutes | Cook time: 3 hours | Serves 6 to 8

2 tablespoons unsalted butter
2 tablespoons all-purpose flour
¾ cup low-sodium chicken broth
½ cup milk
Coarse salt and freshly ground pepper, to taste
1 pound (454 g) sweet Italian sausage, casings removed
3 sweet peppers, such as Cubanelle, thinly sliced
2 pounds (907 g) russet potatoes, peeled and grated
1 cup grated Cheddar cheese
6 scallions, finely chopped
Fried eggs, for serving
Chopped fresh chives, for garnish

1. Melt butter in a saucepan over medium heat. Whisk in flour and cook for about 1 minute. Add broth and milk and bring to a boil, whisking constantly. Remove from heat and season with salt and pepper. Transfer sauce to a bowl.
2. Heat the saucepan over medium-high heat. Add sausage and cook, breaking up meat with a spoon, until browned, about 5 minutes. Add peppers and continue to cook until peppers are soft, about 5 minutes. Season with salt and pepper. Transfer to a crock pot, spreading into an even layer.
3. Add potatoes, cheese, and scallions to milk mixture and mix well. Transfer to crock pot and spread into an even layer. Cover and cook on high until hot and bubbly, about 3 hours (or on low for 6 hours). Serve warm, with fried eggs and topped with chives.

Mango Yogurt with Honey and Cardamon

Prep time: 5 minutes | Cook time: 2 hours | Serves 4

4 cups 2% milk
¼ cup plain yogurt
2 mangoes, cut into chunks
1 tablespoon honey
¼ teaspoon ground cardamom

1. Pour the milk into the crock pot. Cover and cook on low for 2 hours.
2. Turn off the crock pot and stir in the yogurt. Cover with the lid and wrap the outside of the crock pot housing with a bath towel to help insulate it. Allow it to rest for 8 hours or overnight.
3. For a thick yogurt, strain the mixture in a medium bowl through a few layers of cheesecloth for 10 to 15 minutes. Discard the whey remaining in the cheesecloth or save it for making smoothies.
4. To serve, stir in the mango chunks, honey, and cardamom.

Sausage and Waffle Breakfast Bake

Prep time: 10 minutes | Cook time: 5 to 6 hours | Serves 12

2 pounds (907 g) bulk spicy breakfast pork sausage
1 tablespoon rubbed sage
½ teaspoon fennel seed
1 (12.3-ounce / 349-g) package frozen waffles, cut into bite-sized pieces
8 large eggs
1¼ cups half-and-half
¼ cup maple syrup, plus additional for serving
¼ teaspoon salt
¼ teaspoon pepper
2 cups shredded Cheddar cheese
Cooking spray

1. Fold two 18-inch-long pieces of foil into two 18×4-inch strips. Line the sides around the perimeter of a crock pot with foil strips. Spray with cooking spray.
2. In a large skillet, cook and crumble sausage over medium heat, about 4 minutes. Drain. Add the sage and fennel seed.
3. Place waffles in the crock pot and top with sausage. In a bowl, mix eggs, half-and-half, syrup, and seasonings. Pour over the sausage and waffles. Top with cheese. Cook on low, covered, for 5 to 6 hours or until set.
4. Let stand, uncovered, for 15 minutes. Serve with additional maple syrup.

Chorizo Egg Casserole

Prep time: 15 minutes | Cook time: 4 to 4½ hours | Serves 8

1 pound (454 g) fresh chorizo or bulk spicy pork sausage
1 medium onion, chopped
1 medium sweet red pepper, chopped
2 jalapeño peppers, deseeded and chopped
1 (30-ounce / 850-g) package frozen shredded hash brown potatoes, thawed
1½ cups shredded Mexican cheese blend
12 large eggs
1 cup 2% milk
½ teaspoon pepper
Chopped avocado, minced fresh cilantro, and lime wedges (optional)

1. In a large skillet, cook chorizo, onion, red pepper, and jalapeños over medium heat until cooked through and vegetables are tender, 7 to 8 minutes, breaking chorizo into crumbles. Drain and let cool slightly.
2. In a greased crock pot, layer a third of the potatoes, chorizo mixture and cheese blend. Repeat layers twice. In a large bowl, whisk the eggs, milk, and pepper until blended, then pour over top.
3. Cook on low, covered, for 4 to 4½ hours or until the eggs are set and a thermometer reads 160ºF (71ºC). Uncover and let stand for 10 minutes before serving. If desired, top servings with avocado, cilantro, and lime wedges.

Almond and Raisin Granola

Prep time: 10 minutes | Cook time: 4 to 5 hours | Makes 9 cups

5 cups old-fashioned rolled oats
2 cups whole almonds, chopped
½ cup vegetable oil
1⅓ cup maple syrup
1⅓ cup honey
1⅓ cup packed light brown sugar
4 teaspoons vanilla extract
1 teaspoon ground cinnamon
½ teaspoon salt
2 cups raisins
Cooking spray

1. Spritz the crock pot with cooking spray. Combine oats and almonds in the prepared crock pot. Whisk oil, maple syrup, honey, sugar, vanilla, cinnamon, and salt together in a bowl.
2. Drizzle oil mixture over oat mixture and gently toss until evenly coated. Cover and cook, stirring every hour, until oat mixture is deep golden brown and fragrant, 4 to 5 hours on high.
3. Transfer oat mixture to a rimmed baking sheet and spread into even layer. Let cool to room temperature, about 30 minutes. Transfer cooled granola to large bowl, add raisins, and gently toss to combine. Serve.

Ham Egg Cheese Casserole

Prep time: 15 minutes | Cook time: 3 to 4 hours | Serves 6

6 large eggs
1 cup biscuit mix
2⅓ cup 2% milk
1⅓ cup sour cream
2 tablespoons minced fresh parsley
2 garlic cloves, minced
½ teaspoon salt
½ teaspoon pepper
1 cup cubed fully cooked ham
1 cup shredded Swiss cheese
1 small onion, finely chopped
1⅓ cup shredded Parmesan cheese

1. In a large bowl, whisk the first eight ingredients until blended. Stir in remaining ingredients. Pour into a greased crock pot.
2. Cook on low, covered, for 3 to 4 hours or until eggs are set. Cut into wedges and serve.

Peanut Butter Oatmeal Granola

Prep time: 10 to 15 minutes | Cook time: 1½ hours | Serves 16 to 20

6 cups dry oatmeal
½ cup wheat germ
½ cup toasted coconut
½ cup sunflower seeds
½ cup raisins
1 cup butter
1 cup peanut butter
1 cup brown sugar

1. Combine oatmeal, wheat germ, coconut, sunflower seeds, and raisins in the crock pot.
2. Melt together butter, peanut butter, and brown sugar in a small bowl. Pour them over oatmeal mixture. Mix well.
3. Cover. Cook on low for 1½ hours, stirring every 15 minutes.
4. Allow to cool in crock pot, stirring every 30 minutes, or spread onto cookie sheet. When thoroughly cooled, break into chunks and store in airtight container. Serve chilled.

Pear and Chai Oatmeal

Prep time: 5 minutes | Cook time: 8 hours | Serves 2

¾ cup steel-cut oats
⅛ teaspoon ground cardamom
⅛ teaspoon ground nutmeg
⅛ teaspoon ground ginger
¼ teaspoon cinnamon
⅛ teaspoon sea salt
1 ripe pear, cored, peeled, and diced
3 cups unsweetened almond milk

1. Put the oats, cardamom, nutmeg, ginger, cinnamon, and salt in the crock pot and stir to combine. Stir in the pear and the almond milk.
2. Cover and cook the oatmeal on low for 8 hours or overnight.
3. Serve warm.

Eggs in Tomato Purgatory

Prep time: 15 minutes | Cook time: 7¹⅓ to 8¹⅓ hours | Serves 8

2½ pounds (1.1 kg) Roma tomatoes, chopped
2 onions, chopped
2 garlic cloves, chopped
1 teaspoon paprika
½ teaspoon ground cumin
½ teaspoon dried marjoram leaves
1 cup vegetable broth
8 large eggs
2 red chili peppers, minced
½ cup chopped flat-leaf parsley

1. In the crock pot, mix the tomatoes, onions, garlic, paprika, cumin, marjoram, and vegetable broth, and stir to mix. Cover and cook on low for 7 to 8 hours, or until a sauce has formed.
2. One at a time, break the eggs into the sauce, then do not stir.
3. Cover and cook on high until the egg whites are completely set and the yolk is thickened, about 20 minutes. Sprinkle the eggs with the minced red chili peppers.
4. Sprinkle with the parsley and serve.

Chapter 1 Breakfasts and Brunches | 7

Sausage Casserole

Prep time: 15 minutes | Cook time: 4 hours | Serves 8

1 pound (454 g) loose sausage
6 eggs
2 cups milk
8 slices bread, cubed
2 cups shredded Cheddar cheese

1. In a nonstick skillet, brown the sausage for 15 to 20 minutes. Flip the sausage halfway through. Pat the sausage dry with paper towels after cooking.
2. Mix the eggs and milk in a large bowl. Stir in the bread cubes, cheese, and cooked sausage. Refrigerate overnight.
3. Place the mixture in the greased crock pot. Cook on low for 4 hours.
4. Serve warm.

Potato, Parsnip, and Carrot Hash

Prep time: 20 minutes | Cook time: 7 to 8 hours | Serves 8

4 Yukon Gold potatoes, chopped
2 russet potatoes, chopped
3 large carrots, peeled and chopped
1 large parsnip, peeled and chopped
2 onions, chopped
¼ cup vegetable broth
2 garlic cloves, minced
1 teaspoon dried thyme leaves
½ teaspoon salt
2 tablespoons olive oil

1. In the crock pot, mix all the ingredients. Stir to combine well. Cover and cook on low for 7 to 8 hours.
2. Stir the hash well and serve.

Apple Cobbler

Prep time: 20 minutes | Cook time: 2 to 3 hours | Serves 8 to 10

8 medium, tart apples
½ cup sugar
2 tablespoons fresh lemon juice
1 to 2 teaspoons lemon zest
Dash of ground cinnamon
1½ cups natural fat-free cereal mixed with fruit and nuts
¼ cup butter, melted
Cooking spray

1. Spritz the crock pot lightly with cooking spray.
2. Core, peel, and slice apples into the crock pot.
3. Add sugar, lemon juice and zest, and cinnamon.
4. Mix cereal and melted butter together, then add to the ingredients in the crock pot. Mix thoroughly.
5. Cover. Cook on low for 6 hours, or on high for 2 to 3 hours.
6. Serve warm.

Quinoa and Cherry Porridge

Prep time: 5 minutes | Cook time: 8 hours | Serves 2

¾ cup quinoa
½ cup dried cherries
⅛ teaspoon sea salt
1 teaspoon vanilla extract
3 cups almond milk

1. Put the quinoa, cherries, and salt in the crock pot. Pour in the vanilla and almond milk, and stir them together.
2. Cover and cook on low for 8 hours or overnight.
3. Serve warm.

Potato and Tomato Strata

Prep time: 20 minutes | Cook time: 6 to 8 hours | Serves 8

8 Yukon Gold potatoes, peeled and diced
1 onion, minced
2 red bell peppers, stemmed, deseeded, and minced
3 Roma tomatoes, deseeded and chopped
3 garlic cloves, minced
1½ cups shredded Swiss cheese
8 eggs
2 egg whites
1 teaspoon dried marjoram leaves
1 cup 2% milk

1. In the crock pot, layer the diced potatoes, onion, bell peppers, tomatoes, garlic, and cheese.
2. In a medium bowl, mix the eggs, egg whites, marjoram, and milk well with a wire whisk. Pour this mixture into the crock pot.
3. Cover and cook on low for 6 to 8 hours, or until a food thermometer inserted in the mixture registers 165°F (74°C) and the potatoes are tender.
4. Scoop out of the crock pot to serve.

Chapter 2 Appetizers

Beef and Cheese Dip

Prep time: 15 minutes | Cook time: 2 hours | Makes about 6 cups

1 pound (454 g) ground beef
1 onion, chopped
1 (2-pound / 907-g) box Velveeta cheese, cubed
1 (10¾-ounce / 305-g) can cream of mushroom soup
1 (14½-ounce / 411-g) can diced tomatoes with green chilies

1. Brown beef and onion in a skillet over medium heat, about 6 to 8 minutes. Drain meat mixture and place in a crock pot.
2. Add all remaining ingredients into a crock pot and combine.
3. Cover and cook on low for 2 hours, or until cheese is melted, stirring occasionally.
4. Serve over baked potatoes or with tortilla chips, if desired.

Lemony Chicken Wings

Prep time: 15 minutes | Cook time: 6 to 8 hours | Makes about 4 dozen

5 pounds (2.3 kg) chicken wings (about 25 wings)
1 (12-ounce / 340-g) bottle chili sauce
¼ cup lemon juice
¼ cup molasses
2 tablespoons Worcestershire sauce
6 garlic cloves, minced
1 tablespoon chili powder
1 tablespoon salsa
1 teaspoon garlic salt
3 drops hot pepper sauce

1. Cut chicken wings into three sections, discarding wing tips. Place the wings in a crock pot.
2. In a small bowl, combine the remaining ingredients. Pour over chicken and stir to coat. Cover and cook on low for 6 to 8 hours or until chicken is tender. Serve warm.

Crab Dip

Prep time: 20 minutes | Cook time: 1½ to 2½ hours | Makes 2¹⅓ cups

1 (8-ounce / 227-g) package cream cheese, softened
2 green onions, chopped
¼ cup chopped sweet red pepper
2 tablespoons minced fresh parsley
2 tablespoons mayonnaise
1 tablespoon Dijon mustard
1 teaspoon Worcestershire sauce
¼ teaspoon salt
¼ teaspoon pepper
2 (6-ounce / 170-g) cans lump crab meat, drained
2 tablespoons capers, drained
Dash hot pepper sauce
Assorted crackers, for serving

1. In a crock pot, combine the first nine ingredients. Add crab and stir well.
2. Cover and cook on low for 1 to 2 hours. Stir in capers and pepper sauce and cook for 30 minutes longer to allow the flavors to blend. Serve with crackers.

Grape Jelly Meatballs

Prep time: 10 minutes | Cook time: 4 to 5 hours | Makes about 10½ dozen

1 cup grape juice
1 cup apple jelly
1 cup ketchup
1 (8-ounce / 227-g) can tomato sauce
1 (64-ounce / 1.8-kg) package frozen fully cooked Italian meatballs

1. In a small saucepan, combine the juice, jelly, ketchup, and tomato sauce. Cook and stir over medium heat until jelly is melted.
2. Place the meatballs in a crock pot. Pour the sauce over the top and gently stir to coat. Cover and cook on low for 4 to 5 hours or until heated through. Serve warm.

Chex Mix

Prep time: 5 minutes | Cook time: 1 to 1½ hours | Makes about 3 quarts

4 cups Wheat Chex
4 cups Cheerios
3 cups pretzel sticks
1 (12-ounce / 340-g) can salted peanuts
¼ cup butter, melted
2 to 3 tablespoons grated Parmesan cheese
1 teaspoon celery salt
½ to ¾ teaspoon seasoned salt

1. In a crock pot, combine cereals, pretzels, and peanuts. Combine the butter, cheese, celery salt, and seasoned salt in a bowl. Drizzle over cereal mixture and mix well.
2. Cover and cook on low for 1 to 1½ hours, stirring every 20 minutes. Serve warm or at room temperature.

Glazed Hawaiian Kielbasa Bites

Prep time: 15 minutes | Cook time: 2½ to 3½ hours | Serves 12

2 pounds (907 g) smoked kielbasa or Polish sausage, cut into 1-inch pieces
1 (20-ounce / 567-g) can unsweetened pineapple chunks, undrained
½ cup ketchup
2 tablespoons brown sugar
2 tablespoons yellow mustard
1 tablespoon cider vinegar
¾ cup lemon-lime soda
2 tablespoons cornstarch
2 tablespoons cold water

1. Place sausage in a crock pot. Drain pineapple, reserving ¾ cup juice; set pineapple aside. In a small bowl, whisk the ketchup, brown sugar, mustard, and vinegar. Stir in soda and reserved pineapple juice. Pour over sausage and stir to coat. Cover and cook on low for 2 to 3 hours or until heated through.
2. Stir in pineapple. In a separate bowl, combine cornstarch and water until smooth. Whisk into a crock pot. Cover and cook for 30 minutes more, or until sauce is thickened. Serve with toothpicks.

BBQ Party Starters

Prep time: 15 minutes | Cook time: 2¼ to 3¼ hours | Serves 16

1 pound (454 g) ground beef
¼ cup finely chopped onion
1 (16-ounce / 454-g) package miniature hot dogs, drained
1 (12-ounce / 340-g) jar apricot preserves
1 cup barbecue sauce
1 (20-ounce / 567-g) can pineapple chunks, drained

1. In a large bowl, combine beef and onion, mixing lightly but thoroughly. Shape into 1-inch balls. In a large skillet over medium heat, cook the meatballs in two batches until cooked through, turning occasionally.
2. Using a slotted spoon, transfer the meatballs to a crock pot. Add the miniature hot dogs, apricot preserves, and barbecue sauce, stirring well. Cover and cook on high for 2 to 3 hours or until heated through.
3. Stir in the pineapple chunks. Cook, covered, for 15 to 20 minutes longer or until heated through. Serve warm.

Tomato Salsa

Prep time: 15 minutes | Cook time: 2½ to 3 hours | Makes about 2 cups

10 plum tomatoes
2 garlic cloves
1 small onion, cut into wedges
2 jalapeño peppers
¼ cup cilantro leaves
½ teaspoon salt (optional)

1. Core tomatoes and cut a small slit in two tomatoes, then insert a garlic clove into each slit. Place tomatoes and onion in a crock pot.
2. Cut stems off jalapeños and remove seeds if a milder salsa is desired. Place jalapeños in the crock pot.
3. Cover and cook on high for 2½ to 3 hours or until vegetables are softened (some may brown slightly). Allow to cool for 10 minutes.
4. In a blender, combine the tomato mixture, cilantro, and salt (if desired). Process until blended. Refrigerate until ready to serve.

Cranberry Swedish Meatballs

Prep time: 10 minutes | Cook time: 3 to 4 hours | Makes about 5 dozen

2 envelopes brown gravy mix
1 (32-ounce / 907-g) package frozen fully cooked Swedish meatballs
2⅓ cup jellied cranberry sauce
2 teaspoons Dijon mustard
¼ cup heavy whipping cream

1. Prepare the gravy mix according to the package directions. In a crock pot, combine the meatballs, cranberry sauce, mustard, and gravy. Cover and cook on low for 3 to 4 hours or until heated through, adding cream during the last 30 minutes of cooking. Serve warm.

Sweet and Spicy Peanuts

Prep time: 10 minutes | Cook time: 1½ hours | Makes 4 cups

3 cups salted peanuts
½ cup sugar
1⅓ cup packed brown sugar
2 tablespoons hot water
2 tablespoons butter, melted
1 tablespoon Sriracha Asian hot chili sauce or hot pepper sauce
1 teaspoon chili powder

1. Place peanuts in a greased crock pot. In a small bowl, combine the sugars, water, butter, hot sauce, and chili powder. Pour over peanuts and stir to coat. Cover and cook on high for 1½ hours, stirring once.
2. Spread on waxed paper to cool. Serve warm.

Sweet and Spicy Chicken Wings

Prep time: 15 minutes | Cook time: 5 to 6 hours | Makes about 2½ dozen

3 pounds (1.4 kg) chicken wings
1½ cups ketchup
1 cup packed brown sugar
1 small onion, finely chopped
¼ cup finely chopped sweet red pepper
2 tablespoons chili powder
2 tablespoons Worcestershire sauce
1½ teaspoons crushed red pepper flakes
1 teaspoon ground mustard
1 teaspoon dried basil
1 teaspoon dried thyme
1 teaspoon pepper

1. Cut wings into three sections, discarding wing tip sections. Place the chicken in a crock pot.
2. In a small bowl, combine the remaining ingredients. Pour over chicken and stir until coated. Cover and cook on low for 5 to 6 hours or until chicken juices run clear. Serve warm.

Barbecued Smokies

Prep time: 5 minutes | Cook time: 5 to 6 hours | Serves 8

1 (1-pound / 454-g) package miniature smoked sausages
1 (28-ounce / 794-g) bottle barbecue sauce
1¼ cups water
3 tablespoons Worcestershire sauce
3 tablespoons steak sauce
½ teaspoon pepper

1. In a crock pot, combine all ingredients. Cover and cook on low for 5 to 6 hours or until heated through. Serve warm.

Pizza Bites

Prep time: 10 minutes | Cook time: 1 hour | Serves 8

1 pound (454 g) ground beef
1 pound (454 g) bulk Italian sausage
1 pound (454 g) Velveeta cheese, cubed
4 teaspoons pizza seasoning
½ teaspoon Worcestershire sauce

1. In a large nonstick skillet, brown beef and sausage until crumbly. Drain and place in a crock pot.
2. Add remaining ingredients to the crock pot and stir to combine. Cover and cook on low for 1 hour. Serve warm.

Cheese Pulled Pork Crostini

Prep time: 30 minutes | Cook time: 6 to 8 hours | Makes 32 appetizers

1 boneless pork shoulder butt roast (about 2 pounds / 907 g)
½ cup lime juice
2 envelopes mesquite marinade mix
¼ cup sugar
¼ cup olive oil
Salsa:
1 cup frozen corn, thawed
1 cup canned black beans, rinsed and drained
1 small tomato, finely chopped
2 tablespoons finely chopped deseeded jalapeño pepper
2 tablespoons lime juice
2 tablespoons olive oil
1½ teaspoons ground cumin
1 teaspoon chili powder
½ teaspoon salt
¼ teaspoon crushed red pepper flakes
Sauce:
1 (4-ounce / 113-g) can chopped green chilies
1⅓ cup apricot preserves
⅛ teaspoon salt
Crostini:
32 slices French bread baguette (¼ inch thick)
¼ cup olive oil
2⅓ cup crumbled queso fresco or feta cheese
Lime wedges, for serving (optional)

1. Place roast in a crock pot. In a small bowl, whisk lime juice, marinade mix, sugar, and oil until blended. Pour over roast and stir until well coated. Cook on low, covered, for 6 to 8 hours or until meat is tender.
2. For salsa, in a small bowl, combine corn, beans, tomato, and jalapeño. Stir in lime juice, oil, and seasonings. Set aside.
3. In a small saucepan, combine sauce ingredients. Cook and stir over low heat until blended. Set aside.
4. For crostini, preheat broiler. Brush bread slices on both sides with oil and place on baking sheets. Broil for 1 to 2 minutes on each side or until golden brown.
5. Remove roast from the crock pot and let cool slightly. Shred pork with two forks. To serve, layer toasts with salsa, pork, and cheese. Top with sauce. If desired, serve with lime wedges.

Marinated Wings

Prep time: 5 minutes | Cook time: 3 to 4 hours | Serves 20

20 whole chicken wings (about 4 pounds / 1.8 kg in total)
1 cup soy sauce
¼ cup white wine or chicken broth
2 garlic cloves, minced
1 teaspoon ground ginger
3 tablespoons sugar
¼ cup canola oil

1. Cut chicken wings into three sections, then discard wing tips. Place in a large resealable plastic bag. In a small bowl, whisk remaining ingredients until blended. Add to chicken, then seal bag and turn to coat. Refrigerate overnight.
2. Transfer chicken and marinade to the crock pot. Cook, covered, on low for 3 to 4 hours or until chicken is tender.
3. Using tongs, remove wings to a serving plate.

Lush BBQ Sausage Bites

Prep time: 10 minutes | Cook time: 2½ to 3 hours | Serves 12 to 14

¾ pound (340 g) smoked kielbasa or Polish sausage, cut into ½-inch slices
¾ pound (340 g) fully cooked bratwurst links, cut into ½-inch slices
1 (1-pound / 454-g) package miniature smoked sausages
1 (18-ounce / 510-g) bottle barbecue sauce
2⅓ cup orange marmalade
½ teaspoon ground mustard
⅛ teaspoon ground allspice
1 (20-ounce / 567-g) can pineapple chunks, drained

1. In the crock pot, combine the sausages. In a small bowl, whisk the barbecue sauce, marmalade, mustard and allspice. Pour over sausage mixture, then stir to coat.
2. Cover and cook on high for 2½ to 3 hours or until heated through. Stir in pineapple. Serve using toothpicks.

Turkey Teriyaki Sandwiches

Prep time: 20 minutes | Cook time: 5¾ to 6¾ hours | Serves 20

2 boneless skinless turkey breast halves (2 pounds / 907 g each)
2⅓ cup packed brown sugar
2⅓ cup reduced-sodium soy sauce
¼ cup cider vinegar
3 garlic cloves, minced
1 tablespoon minced fresh ginger
½ teaspoon pepper
2 tablespoons cornstarch
2 tablespoons cold water
20 Hawaiian sweet rolls
2 tablespoons butter, melted

1. Place turkey in a crock pot. In a small bowl, combine the brown sugar, soy sauce, vinegar, garlic, ginger, and pepper. Pour over turkey and stir to coat. Cover and cook on low for 5 to 6 hours or until meat is tender.
2. Remove turkey from the crock pot. In another bowl, mix cornstarch and cold water until smooth. Gradually stir the mixture into cooking liquid. When cool enough to handle, shred meat with two forks and return meat to a crock pot. Cook on high, covered, for 30 to 35 minutes or until sauce is thickened.
3. Preheat the oven to 325°F (163°C). Split rolls and brush cut sides with butter, then place on a baking sheet, cut side up. Bake for 8 to 10 minutes or until toasted and golden brown. Spoon 1⅓ cup turkey mixture on roll bottoms. Replace tops and serve.

Tequila Sausage Queso

Prep time: 10 minutes | Cook time: 2¼ hours | Serves 4 to 6

8 ounces (227 g) chorizo sausage
1 tablespoon olive oil
½ cup diced poblano pepper, seeds removed and discarded
¼ cup diced onion
1⅓ cup tequila
2 cups shredded Monterey Jack
Salsa, chopped fresh cilantro, and diced tomatoes, for serving

1. Cook the chorizo in a nonstick skillet over medium-high heat, breaking up the sausage with a spoon, for 3 to 4 minutes, or until fully cooked. Remove from the heat. Place the cooked sausage on a plate lined with paper towels to drain.
2. Drain the fat from the skillet, add the oil to it, and warm it over medium-high heat. Add the poblano pepper and onion and sauté for 2 to 3 minutes until the onion is light and translucent. Remove from the heat.
3. Return the pan to medium-high heat and carefully add the tequila. Reduce the heat to low and simmer for 2 minutes, or until the tequila evaporates. Remove from the heat.
4. Combine the chorizo and sautéed poblano pepper–onion mixture in the crock pot. Add the cheese, cover, and cook, stirring occasionally, on low for 2 hours.
5. Reduce the setting to warm. Garnish with the salsa, cilantro, and tomatoes and serve warm.

Glazed Chicken Wings

Prep time: 1½ hours | Cook time: 3 to 4 hours | Makes 4 dozen

5 pounds (2.3 kg) chicken wings
2½ cups hot ketchup
2⅓ cup white vinegar
½ cup plus 2 tablespoons honey
½ cup molasses
1 teaspoon salt
1 teaspoon Worcestershire sauce
½ teaspoon onion powder
½ teaspoon chili powder
½ to 1 teaspoon liquid smoke, optional

1. Cut the chicken wings into three sections, then discard wing tip sections. Place wings in two greased baking pans. Bake, uncovered, at 375°F (190°C) for 30 minutes, then drain. Turn wings, then bake for 20 to 25 minutes longer or until juices run clear.
2. Meanwhile, in a large saucepan, combine the ketchup, vinegar, honey, molasses, salt, Worcestershire sauce, onion powder and chili powder. Add liquid smoke if desired. Bring to a boil. Reduce heat and simmer, uncovered, for 25 to 30 minutes.
3. Drain the wings, then place a third of wings in the crock pot. Top with about 1 cup of sauce mixture. Repeat layers twice. Cover and cook on low for 3 to 4 hours. Stir before serving.

Chapter 2 Appetizers | 13

Broccoli Dip

Prep time: 15 minutes | Cook time: 2 hours | Makes 5½ cups

1 pound (454 g) ground beef
1 pound (454 g) process cheese (Velveeta), cubed
1 (10¾-ounce / 305-g) can condensed cream of mushroom soup, undiluted
3 cups frozen chopped broccoli, thawed
2 tablespoons salsa
Tortilla chips, for serving

1. In a large skillet, cook beef over medium heat until no longer pink, then drain. Transfer to the crock pot. Add cheese, soup, broccoli and salsa, then mix well.
2. Cover and cook on low for 2 to 3 hours or until heated through, stirring after 1 hour. Serve with chips.

Catalina Marmalade Meatballs

Prep time: 10 minutes | Cook time: 4 to 5 hours | Makes 5 dozen

1 (1-pound / 454-g) bottle Catalina salad dressing
1 cup orange marmalade
3 tablespoons Worcestershire sauce
½ teaspoon crushed red pepper flakes
1 (2-pound / 907-g) package frozen cooked meatballs, thawed

1. In the crock pot, combine the salad dressing, marmalade, Worcestershire sauce and pepper flakes.
2. Stir in meatballs. Cover and cook on low for 4 to 5 hours or until heated through.
3. Serve warm.

Chili Dip

Prep time: 5 minutes | Cook time: 1 to 2 hours | Makes 2 cups

1 (24-ounce / 680-g) jar salsa
1 (15-ounce / 425-g) can chili with beans
2 (2¼-ounce / 64-g) cans sliced ripe olives, drained
12 ounces (340 g) process cheese (Velveeta), cubed
Tortilla chips, for serving

1. In the crock pot, combine the salsa, chili and olives. Stir in cheese.
2. Cover and cook on low for 1 to 2 hours or until cheese is melted, stirring halfway through.
3. Serve with chips.

Sweet Smoked Chicken Wings

Prep time: 20 minutes | Cook time: 3¼ to 3¾ hours | Makes 2½ dozen

3 pounds (1.4 kg) chicken wingettes (about 30)
½ teaspoon salt, divided
Ground black pepper, to taste
1½ cups ketchup
¼ cup packed brown sugar
¼ cup red wine vinegar
2 tablespoons Worcestershire sauce
1 tablespoon Dijon mustard
1 teaspoon minced garlic
1 teaspoon liquid smoke

1. Sprinkle chicken wings with a dash of salt and pepper. Broil from the heat for 5 to 10 minutes on each side or until golden brown. Transfer to a greased crock pot.
2. Combine the ketchup, brown sugar, vinegar, Worcestershire sauce, mustard, garlic, liquid smoke, and remaining salt in a bowl. Stir to mix well. Pour the mixture over wings. Toss to coat.
3. Cover and cook on low for 3¼ to 3¾ hours or until chicken juices run clear.
4. Serve warm.

Crunchy Snack Mix

Prep time: 10 minutes | Cook time: 2½ hours | Makes 2½ quarts

4½ cups crispy chow mein
4 cups Rice Chex cereal
1 (9¾-ounce / 276-g) can salted cashews
1 cup flaked coconut, toasted
½ cup butter, melted
2 tablespoons soy sauce
2¼ teaspoons curry powder
¾ teaspoon ground ginger

1. In the crock pot, combine the chow mein, cereal, cashews and coconut. In a small bowl, whisk the butter, soy sauce, curry powder and ginger, then drizzle over cereal mixture and mix well.
2. Cover and cook on low for 2½ hours, stirring every 30 minutes. Serve warm or at room temperature.

Chapter 3 Stocks and Sauces

Fish Stock

Prep time: 15 minutes | Cook time: 8 hours | Makes 4 to 5 quarts

2 pounds (907 g) fish bones (from non-oily, firm fish, such as snapper, sole, and bass), rinsed
1 onion, quartered
2 celery stalks, chopped
2 leeks, split lengthwise, rinsed well, and chopped
1 carrot, chopped
2 garlic cloves
3 thyme sprigs
5 flat-leaf parsley sprigs
4 quarts boiling water

1. Place all ingredients, except boiling water, in a crock pot. Add the boiling water (it should cover the ingredients by 3 inches). Cover and cook on low for 8 hours.
2. Remove from heat and strain stock through a fine-mesh sieve (discard solids). Let stock cool completely. (Stock can be refrigerated in an airtight container for up to 1 week, or frozen for up to 6 months.)

Vegetable Stock

Prep time: 20 minutes | Cook time: 8½ hours | Makes 4 to 5 quarts

3 onions, quartered
5 celery stalks, chopped
3 carrots, chopped
1 head garlic, halved
1 fennel bulb, chopped
5 white mushrooms
2 leeks, split, rinsed well, and chopped
2 tablespoons olive oil
4 quarts boiling water
1 dried bay leaf
1 teaspoon black peppercorns
3 thyme sprigs
5 flat-leaf parsley sprigs

1. Preheat the oven to 425ºF (220ºC).
2. Combine onions, celery, carrots, garlic, fennel, mushrooms, and leeks in a large bowl, tossing with oil. Spread in a single layer on a rimmed baking sheet and roast until golden, tossing halfway through, about 30 minutes.
3. Transfer vegetables to a crock pot. Add the boiling water, bay leaf, peppercorns, thyme, and parsley. Cover and cook on low for 8 hours. Remove from heat and strain stock through a fine-mesh sieve (discard solids). Let stock cool completely. (Stock can be refrigerated in an airtight container for up to 1 week, or frozen for up to 6 months.)

Chicken Stock

Prep time: 10 minutes | Cook time: 8 hours | Makes 12 cups

4 pounds (1.8 kg) mixed chicken bones
2 large onions
3 celery stalks, cut into large chunks
8 garlic cloves, unpeeled
2 bay leaves
½ bunch parsley, stems and leaves
1 teaspoon dried thyme
2 tablespoons peppercorns
1 teaspoon kosher salt, plus more for seasoning
12 cups or more cold water, enough to submerge meat and vegetables

1. Bring a large stockpot filled with water to a boil over high heat. Add the chicken bones and boil for 10 minutes. Drain the bones into a colander and rinse thoroughly with cold water.
2. Put the chicken bones into the crock pot along with the onions, celery, garlic, bay leaves, parsley, thyme, peppercorns, salt, and water. Cover and cook on low for 8 hours.
3. Using a fine-mesh sieve or cheesecloth-lined colander, strain the broth and discard the solids. Season with additional salt, if needed. If using the stock right away, use a ladle or large spoon to skim and discard the fat that rises to the top. Otherwise, cover and store the stock in the refrigerator for up to 3 days and skim the solidified fat before using.

Salsa Mexicana

Prep time: 20 minutes | Cook time: 5 to 6 hours | Makes about 3 cups

3 tablespoons olive oil
1 large yellow banana chile, peeled, deseeded, and chopped
2 small white onions, chopped
2 cloves garlic, chopped
1 (28-ounce / 794-g) can tomato purée
2 tablespoons tomato paste
1½ cups chicken broth
2 tablespoons chopped fresh cilantro
1 tablespoon chili powder, or more to taste
½ teaspoon ground cumin
½ teaspoon dried Mexican oregano or marjoram
Salt, to taste

1. In a medium-size skillet over medium heat, heat the oil, then cook the chile, onions, and garlic, stirring, until softened, about 5 minutes. Transfer to the crock pot and add the tomato purée and paste, broth, cilantro, chili powder, cumin, and oregano. Stir to combine, then cover and simmer on low for 5 to 6 hours.
2. Use a handheld immersion blender to partially purée the sauce right in the crock pot or transfer to a blender to purée. Season with salt. The sauce will keep, refrigerated, for 5 to 7 days and frozen for up to a month.

Berry Sauce

Prep time: 10 minutes | Cook time: 4 hours | Makes about 10 cups

2 pints fresh blackberries
2 pints fresh strawberries, hulled, cut into quarters if large
2 pints fresh blueberries, picked over for stems
1 to 1½ cups sugar (depending on the sweetness of the berries)
2 tablespoons fresh lemon juice
Grated zest of 1 lemon
2 tablespoons cornstarch

1. Mix all the ingredients together in a crock pot. Cover and cook on low for 4 hours, stirring twice during the cooking time.
2. Allow the sauce to cool before removing from the crock pot. Store in airtight containers in the refrigerator for up to 1 week or in the freezer for up to 3 months.

Shallot and Red Wine Sauce

Prep time: 5 minutes | Cook time: 5 hours | Makes about 10 cups

½ cup (¼ stick) unsalted butter, melted
½ cup finely chopped shallots
2 teaspoons dried thyme
2 cups full-bodied red wine
8 cups beef broth
½ teaspoon freshly ground black pepper
¼ cup all-purpose flour

1. Combine ¼ cup of the butter, shallots, thyme, red wine, broth, and pepper in a crock pot. Cook, uncovered, on high for 4 hours, until the mixture is reduced by one-third.
2. Stir the remaining melted butter and flour together, then whisk into the sauce. Cover and cook for an additional 45 minutes, until the sauce is thickened.
3. Serve immediately or refrigerate until ready to serve.

Buffalo Wing Sauce

Prep time: 5 minutes | Cook time: 6 hours | Makes enough for 3 pounds of wings

1 (12-ounce / 340-g) bottle hot sauce
½ cup (1 stick) unsalted butter
2 tablespoons Worcestershire sauce
2 teaspoons garlic powder
2 teaspoons onion powder
¼ teaspoon cayenne pepper
¼ teaspoon kosher salt, plus more for seasoning
Freshly ground black pepper, to taste

1. To the crock pot, add the hot sauce, butter, Worcestershire sauce, garlic powder, onion powder, cayenne, and salt. Stir to combine. Cover and cook on low for 6 hours.
2. Season with additional salt and pepper as needed before serving.

Classic Bolognese Sauce

Prep time: 15 minutes | Cook time: 6 to 7 hours | Makes 10 cups

1 tablespoon unsalted butter
2 tablespoons olive oil
1 large sweet onion, such as Vidalia, finely chopped
1 cup finely diced carrot
1 cup finely diced celery
1 clove garlic, minced
1 pound (454 g) lean ground pork
8 ounces (227 g) ground veal
8 ounces (227 g) lean ground beef
⅛ teaspoon ground nutmeg
⅛ teaspoon ground cinnamon
1 cup whole milk
1 cup dry white wine or vermouth
3 (32-ounce / 907-g) cans crushed plum tomatoes
Salt and freshly ground black pepper, to taste

1. Melt the butter in the oil in a large skillet over medium heat. Add the onion, carrot, celery, and garlic and sauté until the vegetables are softened. Add the meats and sauté until no longer pink, breaking up any large chunks with a wooden spoon.
2. Spoon off any fat or water from the pan until the pan is dry. Add the nutmeg and cinnamon and sauté for another 2 minutes to allow the flavors to blend. Stir in the milk and boil until the milk has just about evaporated.
3. Transfer the contents of the skillet to a crock pot. Add the wine and tomatoes and stir to blend. Cover and cook the sauce on high for 6 to 7 hours. Season with salt and pepper.
4. Serve immediately or refrigerate until ready to serve.

Basil Tomato Sauce

Prep time: 15 minutes | Cook time: 2½ to 3 hours | Makes about 5 cups

2 tablespoons unsalted butter
2 tablespoons olive oil
1 medium-size yellow onion, finely chopped
1 to 2 cloves garlic, minced
2 (28-ounce / 794-g) cans whole plum tomatoes, drained (if packed in purée, don't drain) and coarsely chopped
2 tablespoons dry red or white wine
Pinch of sugar
¼ cup shredded fresh basil, divided
Pinch of dried thyme or oregano
Salt and freshly ground black pepper, to taste
2 tablespoons chopped fresh flat-leaf parsley

1. In a medium-size skillet over medium heat, melt the butter in the olive oil. Cook the onion, stirring, until softened, about 5 minutes. Add the garlic and cook, stirring, for 2 minutes.
2. Transfer to the crock pot. Add the tomatoes, wine, sugar, 2 tablespoons of the basil, and thyme and stir to combine. Cover and simmer on high for 2 to 2½ hours.
3. Season the sauce with salt and pepper and stir in the remaining 2 tablespoons of basil and the parsley. Cover and cook on low for 20 to 30 minutes longer. Serve the sauce hot. It will keep, refrigerated, for up to a week and frozen for 2 months.

Alfredo Sauce

Prep time: 10 minutes | Cook time: 4 to 6 hours | Serves 4

½ quart heavy (whipping) cream
¼ cup chicken stock
¼ cup butter, melted
2 garlic cloves, minced
1 cup finely shredded Parmesan cheese, plus more for garnish
2 tablespoons dry sherry
¾ teaspoon kosher salt, plus more for seasoning
½ teaspoon freshly ground black pepper, plus more for seasoning
3 tablespoons all-purpose flour
Cooking spray or 1 tablespoon extra-virgin olive oil

1. Use the cooking spray or olive oil to coat the inside (bottom and sides) of the crock pot. Add the cream, chicken stock, butter, garlic, Parmesan, sherry, salt, and pepper and whisk to combine. Cover and cook on low for 4 to 6 hours.
2. About 30 minutes before serving, whisk in the flour. Leave the lid ajar and continue cooking until the sauce begins to thicken. Season with additional salt and pepper if needed before serving.

Chapter 3 Stocks and Sauces | 17

Salsa Verde

Prep time: 15 minutes | Cook time: 4 hours | Makes 7 cups

2½ pounds (1.1 kg) tomatillos, husks removed, rinsed, and chopped
1 green bell pepper, chopped
2 onions, chopped
3 garlic cloves, minced
2 jalapeño peppers, minced
½ cup chopped fresh cilantro leaves
1 teaspoon salt
⅛ teaspoon freshly ground black pepper
1 cup Vegetable Broth or water

1. In the crock pot, combine all the ingredients and stir.
2. Cover and cook on low for 4 hours.
3. Cool and serve, refrigerate for up to 4 days, or freeze in ½-cup portions for up to 3 months.

Vegan Garlic Pasta Sauce

Prep time: 20 minutes | Cook time: 4 hours | Makes 8 cups

2 tablespoon extra-virgin olive oil
2 cloves garlic, minced
½ teaspoon red pepper flakes
1 large onion, coarsely chopped
2 portobello mushrooms, coarsely chopped
1 medium red bell pepper, deseeded and coarsely chopped
1 medium yellow bell pepper, deseeded and coarsely chopped
1 tablespoon dried oregano
2 teaspoons dried basil
Salt, to taste
2 tablespoons balsamic vinegar
2 (32-ounce / 907-g) cans crushed plum tomatoes
Freshly ground black pepper, to taste

1. Heat the oil in a large sauté pan over medium-high heat. Add the garlic and red pepper flakes, and sauté until the garlic is fragrant, about 1 minute. Add the onion and sauté until the onion begins to soften, another 2 minutes. Add the remaining vegetables, the oregano, basil, and 2 teaspoons of salt and sauté until the vegetables give off some liquid, about 5 minutes.
2. Using a slotted spoon, transfer the vegetables to a crock pot. Stir in the vinegar and tomatoes. Cover and cook on high for 4 hours or on low for 8 hours. Season with salt and pepper.
3. Serve immediately or refrigerate until ready to serve.

Nacho Cheese Sauce

Prep time: 10 minutes | Cook time: 3 hours | Serves 10

1 (2-pound / 907-g) box original Velveeta cheese, cut into chunks
8 ounces (227 g) sharp Cheddar cheese, shredded
1 pound (454 g) hot breakfast sausage, browned
1 (4-ounce / 113-g) can chopped green or red chiles
1 teaspoon kosher salt
1 teaspoon freshly ground black pepper
1 tablespoon chili powder
1½ teaspoons ground cumin
½ teaspoon onion powder
¼ teaspoon garlic powder
¼ teaspoon dried oregano
¼ teaspoon red pepper flakes

1. To the crock pot, add the Velveeta and Cheddar, browned sausage, chiles, salt, pepper, chili powder, cumin, onion powder, garlic powder, oregano, and red pepper flakes. Cover and cook on low for 3 hours.
2. Season with additional salt and pepper as needed before serving.

Italian Meat Gravy

Prep time: 15 minutes | Cook time: 8 to 10 hours | Serves 6

2 tablespoons extra-virgin olive oil
4 boneless beef short ribs
1¼ teaspoons kosher salt, plus more for seasoning
1½ pounds (680 g) hot Italian sausage
1 large onion, finely chopped
1 celery stalk, finely chopped
1 large carrot, peeled and finely chopped
3 garlic cloves, minced
2 (28-ounce / 794-g) cans crushed tomatoes
2 tablespoons tomato paste
2 teaspoons Italian seasoning
2 bay leaves
Freshly ground black pepper, to taste
Pasta (any kind), for serving
½ cup grated Parmesan cheese, for garnish

1. In a skillet over medium-high heat, heat the oil until shimmering. Season the short ribs with salt and pepper, and brown, along with the Italian sausage, about 3 minutes per side.
2. Put the ribs and sausage in the crock pot, along with the onion, celery, carrot, garlic, canned tomatoes, tomato paste, Italian seasoning, bay leaves, and salt. Stir to combine. Cover and cook on low for 8 to 10 hours.
3. Remove the lid and discard the bay leaves. Season with additional salt and pepper, if needed. Pour the sauce on pasta, toss, and serve immediately, passing the Parmesan at the table as a garnish.

Chapter 4 Desserts

Black and Blue Berry Cobbler

Prep time: 20 minutes | Cook time: 2 to 2½ hours | Serves 6

1 cup flour
¾ cup sugar
1 teaspoon baking powder
¼ teaspoon salt
¼ teaspoon ground cinnamon
¼ teaspoon ground nutmeg
2 eggs, beaten
2 tablespoons milk
2 tablespoons vegetable oil
Berry:
2 cups fresh or frozen blueberries
2 cups fresh or frozen blackberries
¾ cup water
1 teaspoon grated orange peel
¾ cup sugar

1. Combine flour, sugar, baking powder, salt, cinnamon, and nutmeg in a bowl.
2. Whisk eggs, milk, and oil in a separate bowl. Stir into dry ingredients until moistened.
3. Spread the batter evenly over bottom of a greased crock pot.
4. In a saucepan, combine berries, water, orange peel, and sugar. Bring to a boil. Remove from heat and pour over batter in the crock pot.
5. Cover and cook on high for 2 to 2½ hours, or until a toothpick inserted into batter comes out clean.
6. Turn off the crock pot. Uncover and let stand for 30 minutes before serving.

Creamy Pumpkin Pie Pudding

Prep time: 10 minutes | Cook time: 3 hours | Serves 8

1 (15-ounce / 425-g) can pumpkin
1 (12-ounce / 340-g) can evaporated skim milk
¾ cup Splenda
½ cup low-fat buttermilk baking mix
2 eggs, beaten, or 6 egg whites
2 teaspoons pumpkin pie spice
1 teaspoon lemon zest
Cooking spray

1. Combine all ingredients in a crock pot sprayed with cooking spray. Stir until lumps disappear.
2. Cover and cook on low for 3 hours.
3. Serve warm or cold.

Pineapple Tapioca

Prep time: 10 minutes | Cook time: 3 hours | Serves 4 to 6

2½ cups water
2½ cups pineapple juice
½ cup dry small pearl tapioca
¾ to 1 cup sugar
1 (15-ounce / 425-g) can crushed pineapple, undrained

1. Mix first four ingredients together in a crock pot.
2. Cover and cook on high for 3 hours.
3. Stir in crushed pineapple. Chill for several hours before serving.

Raisin Rice Pudding

Prep time: 10 minutes | Cook time: 2 hours | Serves 6

2½ cups rice, cooked
1½ cups evaporated milk or scalded milk
⅔ cup brown or white sugar
1 tablespoon butter, softened
2 teaspoons vanilla
½ to 1 teaspoon nutmeg
1 eggs, beaten
½ to 1 cup raisins

1. Mix together all ingredients in a bowl. Pour into lightly greased crock pot.
2. Cover and cook on high for 2 hours, or on low for 4 to 6 hours. Stir after first hour.
3. Serve warm or cold.

Chocolate Fondue

Prep time: 5 minutes | Cook time: 1 to 3 hours | Serves 6

1 (8 squares) package semisweet chocolate
1 (4-ounce / 113-g) package sweet cooking chocolate
¾ cup sweetened condensed milk
¼ cup sugar
2 tablespoons kirsch

1. Break both chocolates into pieces and place in a crock pot. Set crock pot to high and stir chocolate constantly until it melts.
2. Turn crock pot to low and stir in milk and sugar. Stir until thoroughly blended.
3. Stir in kirsch. Cover and cook on low until fondue comes to a very gentle simmer, about 1 to 3 hours. Serve warm.

Chocolate Chip Graham Cracker Cookies

Prep time: 10 minutes | Cook time: 1½ hours | Makes 4 dozen

1 (12-ounce / 340-g) package semi-sweet chocolate chips
2 (1-ounce / 28-g) squares unsweetened baking chocolate, shaved
2 (14-ounce / 397-g) cans sweetened condensed milk
3¾ cups crushed graham cracker crumbs, divided
1 cup finely chopped walnuts

1. Place chocolate in a crock pot.
2. Cover and cook on high for 1 hour, stirring every 15 minutes. Continue to cook on low, stirring every 15 minutes, or until chocolate is melted (about 30 minutes).
3. Stir milk into melted chocolate.
4. Add 3 cups of graham cracker crumbs, 1 cup at a time, stirring after each addition.
5. Stir in nuts. Mixture should be thick but not stiff.
6. Stir in remaining ¾ cup of graham cracker crumbs to reach consistency of cookie dough.
7. Drop by heaping teaspoonfuls onto lightly greased cookie sheets. Keep remaining mixture warm by covering and turning the crock pot to Warm.
8. Bake in oven at 325ºF (163ºC) for 7 to 9 minutes, or until tops of cookies begin to crack. Remove from oven and cool for 10 minutes before serving.

Fallen Chocolate Soufflé Cake

Prep time: 5 minutes | Cook time: 6 hours | Serves 10 to 12

1 (18¼-ounce / 517-g) package chocolate cake mix
½ cup vegetable oil
2 cups sour cream
4 eggs, beaten
1 (3-ounce / 85-g) box instant chocolate pudding mix
1 cup chocolate chips (optional)

1. Combine all ingredients in a greased crock pot.
2. Cover and cook on low for 6 hours. (Do not lift the lid until the end of the cooking time!)
3. Insert a toothpick into the center of cake to see if it comes out clean. If it does, the soufflé is finished. If it doesn't, continue cooking for another 15 minutes. Check again. Repeat until it's finished cooking.
4. Serve warm.

Fruity Cake with Walnuts

Prep time: 10 minutes | Cook time: 3 to 5 hours | Serves 10 to 12

1 or 2 (21-ounce / 595-g) cans apple, blueberry, or peach pie filling
1 (18¼-ounce / 517-g) package yellow cake mix
1 stick (½ cup) butter, melted
1⅓ cup chopped walnuts
Nonstick cooking spray

1. Spray the insert of the crock pot with nonstick cooking spray.
2. Place pie filling in a crock pot.
3. In a mixing bowl, combine dry cake mix and butter. Spoon over filling.
4. Drop walnuts over top.
5. Cover and cook on low for 3 to 5 hours, or until a toothpick inserted into the center of topping comes out clean. Serve warm.

Stewed Dried Apricots

Prep time: 5 minutes | Cook time: 3 to 4 hours | Serves 6

1 (12-ounce / 340-g) package dried apricots
1 strip lemon or orange zest

1. Put the apricots and citrus zest in the crock pot and add water to cover. Cover and cook on low until plump and tender, 3 to 4 hours.
2. Turn off the crock pot, remove the lid, and let the apricots cool. Serve.

Strawberry Rhubarb Compote

Prep time: 10 minutes | Cook time: 3 to 4 hours | Serves 6

¼ cup water or orange juice
1 cup sugar
1 pound (454 g) fresh rhubarb, trimmed of leaves and cut into 1½-inch chunks (about 4 cups)
2 teaspoons fresh lemon juice
2 pints fresh strawberries, hulled and cut in half

1. Combine the water, sugar, and rhubarb in the crock pot. Cover and cook on low until soft, 3 to 4 hours.
2. Mash the rhubarb a bit with a fork or the back of a large spoon. Add the lemon juice and strawberries and stir once to distribute.
3. Turn off the crock pot and let the fruit cool a bit. Serve warm or at room temperature. Or transfer to a storage container, refrigerate, and serve chilled, ladled into dessert bowls. The compote will keep, tightly covered, for 4 days in the refrigerator.

Fudgy Brownies

Prep time: 10 minutes | Cook time: 3 to 4 hours | Serves 6

½ cup all-purpose flour
½ teaspoon baking powder
⅛ teaspoon salt
2 ounces (57 g) unsweetened chocolate, chopped
5 tablespoons unsalted butter
2⅓ cup packed brown sugar
1 large egg plus 1 large yolk, room temperature
½ teaspoon vanilla extract
1⅓ cup toasted and chopped walnuts (optional)

1. Fill a crock pot with ½ inch water (about 2 cups) and place aluminum foil rack in bottom. Grease a springform pan and line with parchment paper.
2. Whisk flour, baking powder, and salt together in a bowl. In a large bowl, microwave chocolate and butter at 50 percent power, stirring occasionally, until melted, 1 to 2 minutes; let cool slightly. Whisk sugar, egg and yolk, and vanilla into cooled chocolate mixture until well combined. Stir in flour mixture until just incorporated.
3. Scrape batter into prepared pan, smooth top, and sprinkle with walnuts, if using. Set pan on prepared rack, cover, and cook until toothpick inserted into center comes out with few moist crumbs attached, 3 to 4 hours on high.
4. Let brownies cool completely in pan on the wire rack, 1 to 2 hours. Cut into wedges and serve.

Pecan-Crusted Blueberry Crisp

Prep time: 10 minutes | Cook time: 3 to 4 hours | Serves 8

5 tablespoons coconut oil, melted, divided
4 cups blueberries
¾ cup plus 2 tablespoons granulated erythritol
1 cup ground pecans
1 teaspoon baking soda
½ teaspoon ground cinnamon
2 tablespoons coconut milk
1 egg

1. Lightly grease the crock pot with 1 tablespoon of the coconut oil.
2. Add the blueberries and 2 tablespoons of erythritol to the crock pot.
3. In a large bowl, stir together the remaining ¾ cup of the erythritol, ground pecans, baking soda, and cinnamon until well mixed.
4. Add the coconut milk, egg, and remaining coconut oil, and stir until coarse crumbs form.
5. Top the contents in the crock pot with the pecan mixture.
6. Cover and cook on low for 3 to 4 hours.
7. Serve warm.

Chapter 4 Desserts | 21

Lemon Blueberry Cornmeal Cake

Prep time: 10 minutes | Cook time: 2 to 3 hours | Serves 6

1 cup all-purpose flour
¼ cup cornmeal
½ teaspoon baking powder
½ teaspoon baking soda
Salt, to taste
½ cup plain yogurt
1⅓ cup granulated sugar
1 large egg
2 teaspoons grated lemon zest plus 4 teaspoons juice
½ teaspoon vanilla extract
4 tablespoons unsalted butter, melted
5 ounces (142 g) blueberries
¾ cup confectioners' sugar
Cooking spray

1. Fill a crock pot with ½ inch water (about 2 cups) and place aluminum foil rack in bottom. Make foil sling for 8½ by 4½-inch loaf pan by folding 2 long sheets of foil; first sheet should be 8½ inches wide and second sheet should be 4½ inches wide. Lay sheets of foil in a pan perpendicular to each other, with extra foil hanging over edges of pan. Push foil into corners and up sides of pan, smoothing foil flush to pan. Lightly grease foil with cooking spray.
2. Whisk flour, cornmeal, baking powder, baking soda, and ½ teaspoon of salt together in a bowl. In a large bowl, whisk yogurt, granulated sugar, egg, lemon zest, and vanilla until smooth, then slowly whisk in melted butter until well combined. Stir in flour mixture until just incorporated. Gently fold in blueberries.
3. Scrape batter into prepared pan and smooth top. Gently tap pan on the counter to release air bubbles. Set pan on prepared rack, cover, and cook until toothpick inserted in center comes out clean, 2 to 3 hours on high.
4. Let cake cool in pan on wire rack for 10 minutes. Using foil overhang, lift cake out of pan and transfer to rack, discarding foil. Let cake cool completely, 1 to 2 hours.
5. Whisk confectioners' sugar, pinch salt, and lemon juice in a small bowl until smooth. Flip cake over onto a serving dish. Drizzle top and sides with glaze and let glaze set before serving, about 25 minutes.

Chocolate Snack Cake

Prep time: 10 minutes | Cook time: 1 to 2 hours | Serves 6

½ cup all-purpose flour
½ teaspoon salt
½ teaspoon baking soda
⅛ teaspoon baking powder
1½ ounces (43 g) unsweetened chocolate, chopped
3 tablespoons unsweetened cocoa powder
3 tablespoons unsalted butter, cut into 3 pieces
¼ teaspoon instant espresso powder
¼ cup boiling water
½ cup packed light brown sugar
¼ cup sour cream
1 large egg
½ teaspoon vanilla extract
Confectioners' sugar, for dusting

1. Fill a crock pot with ½ inch water (about 2 cups) and place aluminum foil rack in bottom. Grease a springform pan and line with parchment paper.
2. Whisk flour, salt, baking soda, and baking powder together in a bowl. In a large bowl, combine chocolate, cocoa, butter, and espresso powder. Pour boiling water over chocolate mixture, cover, and let sit until chocolate and butter are melted, 3 to 5 minutes. Whisk mixture until smooth and let cool slightly. Whisk brown sugar, sour cream, egg, and vanilla into cooled chocolate mixture until well combined. Stir in flour mixture until just incorporated.
3. Scrape batter into prepared pan and smooth top. Gently tap pan on the counter to release air bubbles. Set pan on prepared rack, cover, and cook until toothpick inserted in center comes out with few moist crumbs attached, 1 to 2 hours on high.
4. Let cake cool in pan on wire rack for 10 minutes. Run a small knife around edge of cake, then remove sides of pan. Remove cake from pan bottom, discarding parchment, and let cool completely on a rack, 1 to 2 hours. Transfer to a serving dish and dust with confectioners' sugar. Serve.

Carrot Cake with Cream Cheese Frosting

Prep time: 15 minutes | Cook time: 3 to 4 hours | Serves 6

Cake:
¾ cup plus 2 tablespoons all-purpose flour
½ teaspoon baking powder
½ teaspoon baking soda
½ teaspoon ground cinnamon
Pinch ground cloves
Pinch salt
½ cup packed brown sugar
1 large egg
7 tablespoons vegetable oil
¾ cup shredded carrots

Frosting:
4 ounces (113 g) cream cheese, softened
2 tablespoons unsalted butter, softened
1 teaspoon vanilla extract
Pinch salt
½ cup confectioner's sugar

1. For the cake: Fill a crock pot with ½ inch water (about 2 cups) and place aluminum foil rack in bottom. Grease a springform pan and line with parchment paper.
2. Whisk flour, baking powder, baking soda, cinnamon, cloves, and salt together in a bowl. In a large bowl, whisk sugar and egg until smooth, then slowly whisk in oil until well combined. Stir in flour mixture until just incorporated. Gently fold in carrots.
3. Scrape batter into prepared pan and smooth top. Gently tap pan on the counter to release air bubbles. Set pan on prepared rack, cover, and cook until toothpick inserted in center comes out clean, 3 to 4 hours on high.
4. Let cake cool in pan on wire rack for 10 minutes. Run a small knife around edge of cake, then remove sides of pan. Remove cake from pan bottom, discarding parchment, and let cool completely on a rack, 1 to 2 hours. Transfer cake to a serving dish.
5. For the frosting: Using a handheld mixer set at medium-high speed, beat cream cheese, butter, vanilla, and salt in a medium bowl until smooth, 1 to 2 minutes, scraping down sides of bowl as needed. Reduce speed to medium-low, gradually add sugar, and beat until smooth, 2 to 3 minutes. Increase speed to medium-high and beat until frosting is pale and fluffy, 2 to 3 minutes. Spread frosting evenly over top of cake. Serve.

Sour Cream Cheesecake

Prep time: 10 minutes | Cook time: 1½ to 2½ hours | Serves 8

6 whole graham crackers, broken into 1-inch pieces
2 tablespoons unsalted butter, melted
2⅓ cup plus 1 tablespoon sugar, divided
½ teaspoon ground cinnamon
Salt, to taste
18 ounces (510 g) cream cheese, softened
1 teaspoon vanilla extract
¼ cup sour cream
2 large eggs

1. Pulse graham crackers in a food processor to fine crumbs, about 20 pulses. Add melted butter, 1 tablespoon sugar, cinnamon, and pinch salt and pulse to combine, about 4 pulses. Sprinkle crumbs into a springform pan and press into an even layer using the bottom of the dry measuring cup. Wipe out processor bowl.
2. Process cream cheese, vanilla, ¼ teaspoon salt, and remaining 2⅓ cup sugar in the processor until combined, about 15 seconds, scraping down sides of bowl as needed. Add sour cream and eggs and process until just incorporated, about 15 seconds; do not over mix. Pour filling into prepared pan and smooth top.
3. Fill a crock pot with ½ inch water (about 2 cups) and place aluminum foil rack in bottom. Set pan on prepared rack, cover, and cook until cheesecake registers 150°F (66°C), 1½ to 2½ hours on high. Turn off crock pot and let cheesecake sit, covered, for 1 hour.
4. Transfer cheesecake to a wire rack. Run a small knife around edge of cake and gently blot away condensation using paper towels. Let cheesecake cool in pan to room temperature, about 1 hour. Cover with plastic wrap and refrigerate until well chilled, at least for 3 hours or up to 3 days.
5. About 30 minutes before serving, run a small knife around edge of cheesecake, then remove sides of pan. Invert cheesecake onto sheet of parchment paper, then turn cheesecake right side up onto a serving dish. Serve.

Pumpkin Spice Cheesecake

Prep time: 10 minutes | Cook time: 1½ to 2½ hours | Serves 8

6 whole graham crackers, broken into 1-inch pieces
2 tablespoons unsalted butter, melted
²⅓ cup plus 1 tablespoon sugar, divided
1½ teaspoons ground cinnamon, divided
Salt, to taste
1 cup canned unsweetened pumpkin purée
12 ounces (340 g) cream cheese, softened
½ teaspoon ground ginger
⅛ teaspoon ground cloves
¼ cup sour cream
2 large eggs

1. Pulse graham crackers in a food processor to fine crumbs, about 20 pulses. Add melted butter, 1 tablespoon sugar, ½ teaspoon cinnamon, and pinch salt and pulse to combine, about 4 pulses. Sprinkle crumbs into a springform pan and press into an even layer using the bottom of the dry measuring cup. Wipe out processor bowl.
2. Spread pumpkin purée over baking sheet lined with several layers of paper towels and press dry with additional towels. Transfer purée to the processor bowl (purée will separate easily from towels). Add cream cheese, ginger, cloves, ½ teaspoon salt, remaining ²⅓ cup sugar, and remaining 1 teaspoon cinnamon and process until combined, about 15 seconds, scraping down sides of bowl as needed. Add sour cream and eggs and process until just incorporated, about 15 seconds; do not over mix. Pour filling into prepared pan and smooth top.
3. Fill a crock pot with ½ inch water (about 2 cups) and place aluminum foil rack in bottom. Set pan on prepared rack, cover, and cook until cheesecake registers 150°F (66°C), 1½ to 2½ hours on high. Turn off crock pot and let cheesecake sit, covered, for 1 hour.
4. Transfer cheesecake to a wire rack. Run a small knife around edge of cake and gently blot away condensation using paper towels. Let cheesecake cool in pan to room temperature, about 1 hour. Cover with plastic wrap and refrigerate until well chilled, at least for 3 hours or up to 3 days.
5. About 30 minutes before serving, run a small knife around edge of cheesecake, then remove sides of pan. Invert cheesecake onto sheet of parchment paper, then turn cheesecake right side up onto a serving dish. Serve.

Ultimate Chocolate Cheesecake

Prep time: 5 minutes | Cook time: 1½ to 2½ hours | Serves 8

8 chocolate sandwich cookies
2 tablespoons unsalted butter, melted
4 ounces (113 g) semisweet chocolate, chopped
18 ounces (510 g) cream cheese, softened
²⅓ cup sugar
¼ teaspoon salt
¼ cup sour cream
2 large eggs
2 tablespoons unsweetened cocoa powder
1 teaspoon vanilla extract

1. Pulse cookies in a food processor to fine crumbs, about 20 pulses. Add melted butter and pulse to combine, about 4 pulses. Sprinkle crumbs into a springform pan and press into an even layer using the bottom of the dry measuring cup. Wipe out processor bowl.
2. Microwave chocolate in a bowl at 50 percent power, stirring occasionally, until melted, 1 to 2 minutes. Let cool slightly. Process cream cheese, sugar, and salt in the processor until combined, about 15 seconds, scraping down sides of bowl as needed. Add cooled chocolate, sour cream, eggs, cocoa, and vanilla and process until just incorporated, about 15 seconds; do not over mix. Pour filling into prepared pan and smooth top.
3. Fill a crock pot with ½ inch water (about 2 cups) and place aluminum foil rack in bottom. Set pan on prepared rack, cover, and cook until cheesecake registers 150°F (66°C), 1½ to 2½ hours on high. Turn off crock pot and let cheesecake sit, covered, for 1 hour.
4. Transfer cheesecake to a wire rack. Run a small knife around edge of cake and gently blot away condensation using paper towels. Let cheesecake cool in pan to room temperature, about 1 hour. Cover with plastic wrap and refrigerate until well chilled, at least for 3 hours or up to 3 days.
5. About 30 minutes before serving, run a small knife around edge of cheesecake, then remove sides of pan. Invert cheesecake onto sheet of parchment paper, then turn cheesecake right side up onto a serving dish. Serve.

Coconut Key Lime Pie

Prep time: 10 minutes | Cook time: 1 to 2 hours | Serves 8

6 whole graham crackers, broken into 1-inch pieces
2 tablespoons unsalted butter, melted
1 tablespoon sugar
Salt, to taste
1 (14-ounce / 397-g) can sweetened condensed milk
1 tablespoon grated lime zest plus ½ cup juice (4 limes)
2 ounces (57 g) cream cheese, softened
1 large egg yolk, room temperature
¼ cup sweetened shredded coconut, toasted

1. Pulse graham crackers in a food processor to fine crumbs, about 20 pulses. Add melted butter, sugar, and pinch salt and pulse to combine, about 4 pulses. Sprinkle crumbs into a springform pan and press into an even layer using the bottom of the dry measuring cup. Wipe out processor bowl.
2. Process condensed milk, lime zest and juice, and cream cheese in the processor until combined, about 15 seconds, scraping down sides of bowl as needed. Add egg yolk and process until just incorporated, about 5 seconds. Pour filling into prepared pan and smooth top.
3. Fill a crock pot with ½ inch water (about 2 cups) and place aluminum foil rack in bottom. Set pan on prepared rack, cover, and cook until pie registers 150°F (66°C), 1 to 2 hours on high. Turn crock pot off and let pie sit, covered, for 1 hour.
4. Transfer pie to a wire rack. Run a small knife around edge of pie and gently blot away condensation using paper towels. Let pie cool in pan to room temperature, about 1 hour. Cover with plastic wrap and refrigerate until well chilled, at least for 3 hours or up to 3 days.
5. About 30 minutes before serving, run a small knife around edge of pie, then remove sides of pan. Invert pie onto sheet of parchment paper, then turn pie right side up onto a serving dish. Press coconut gently against sides of pie to adhere, wiping away excess coconut. Serve.

Ginger Peach Crumble

Prep time: 15 minutes | Cook time: 3 to 4 hours | Serves 8 to 10

Filling:
4 pounds (1.8 kg) frozen sliced peaches, thawed and drained (7 cups)
¾ cup granulated sugar
3 tablespoons chopped crystallized ginger
4 teaspoons instant tapioca
1 teaspoon lemon juice
1 teaspoon vanilla extract

Topping:
1 cup all-purpose flour
¼ cup granulated sugar
¼ cup packed light brown sugar
2 teaspoons vanilla extract
¾ teaspoon ground ginger
⅛ teaspoon salt
8 tablespoons unsalted butter, cut into 6 pieces and softened
½ cup sliced almonds, divided

1. For the filling: Combine all ingredients in a crock pot. Cover and cook until peaches are tender and sauce is thickened, 3 to 4 hours on low or 2 to 3 hours on high.
2. For the topping: Preheat the oven to 350°F (180°C). Pulse flour, granulated sugar, brown sugar, vanilla, ginger, and salt in a food processor until combined, about 5 pulses. Sprinkle butter and ¼ cup almonds over top and process until mixture clumps together into large crumbly balls, about 30 seconds. Sprinkle remaining ¼ cup almonds over top and pulse to incorporate, about 2 pulses.
3. Spread topping evenly over parchment paper-lined rimmed baking sheet and pinch it between your fingers into small pea-size pieces (with some smaller loose bits). Bake until golden brown, about 18 minutes, rotating sheet halfway through baking. Let cool slightly. (Topping can be stored in an airtight container for up to 1 day.)
4. Turn off crock pot and let peach filling cool for 20 minutes. Gently stir peaches to coat with sauce. Sprinkle individual portions of filling with crumbles before serving.

Apple Crisp with Oat Topping

Prep time: 15 minutes | Cook time: 3 to 4 hours | Serves 6 to 8

Filling:
1½ pounds (680 g) Granny Smith apples, peeled, cored, and cut into ½-inch-thick wedges
1½ pounds (680 g) Golden Delicious apples, peeled, cored, and cut into ½-inch-thick wedges
½ cup apple cider
2 tablespoons packed light brown sugar
4 teaspoons instant tapioca
2 teaspoons lemon juice
¼ teaspoon ground cinnamon

Topping:
½ cup sliced almonds
½ cup all-purpose flour
¼ cup packed light brown sugar
¼ teaspoon ground cinnamon
¼ teaspoon salt
⅛ teaspoon ground nutmeg
5 tablespoons unsalted butter, melted
¾ cup old-fashioned rolled oats
2 tablespoons honey

1. For the filling: Combine all ingredients in a crock pot. Cover and cook until apples are tender and sauce is thickened, 3 to 4 hours on low or 2 to 3 hours on high.
2. For the topping: Preheat the oven to 400°F (205°C). Pulse almonds, flour, sugar, cinnamon, salt, and nutmeg in a food processor until nuts are finely chopped, about 10 pulses. Drizzle melted butter over top and pulse until mixture resembles crumbly wet sand, about 5 pulses. Add oats and honey and pulse until evenly incorporated, about 3 pulses.
3. Spread topping evenly over parchment paper-lined rimmed baking sheet and pinch it between your fingers into small pea-size pieces (with some smaller loose bits). Bake until golden brown, 8 to 12 minutes, rotating sheet halfway through baking. Let cool slightly. (Topping can be stored in airtight container for up to 1 day.)
4. Turn off crock pot and let apple filling cool for 20 minutes. Gently stir apples to coat with sauce. Sprinkle individual portions of filling with crumbles before serving.

Hearty Apricot Cheesecake

Prep time: 20 minutes | Cook time: 4 hours | Serves 2

1⅓ cup graham cracker crumbs
1 tablespoon melted butter
8 ounces (227 g) cream cheese, at room temperature
2 teaspoons cornstarch
1⅓ cup granulated sugar
Pinch salt
1 egg
¼ cup Mascarpone cheese
1 cup canned sliced apricots, drained, divided
½ cup water
2 tablespoons honey
1 tablespoon orange juice
Nonstick cooking spray

1. Spray a springform pan with the nonstick cooking spray.
2. In a small bowl, combine the graham cracker crumbs and butter and mix well. Press the mixture into the bottom of the pan.
3. In a medium bowl, beat the cream cheese until smooth.
4. Add the cornstarch, sugar, salt, and egg, and beat until smooth. Beat in the Mascarpone cheese.
5. Chop the apricots and stir 1⅓ cup into the cream cheese mixture.
6. Spoon the cream cheese mixture on top of the crust in the springform pan.
7. Place a small rack in the crock pot and add the water. Place the springform pan on the rack.
8. Cover and cook on low for 4 hours. Remove the pan from the crock pot and cool for 1 hour.
9. In a small pan over low heat, bring the remaining 1⅓ cup chopped apricots and the honey and orange juice to a simmer. Simmer for 5 minutes, until thickened. Spoon the mixture over the cheesecake, and then chill until cold, about 3 to 4 hours, and serve.

Rhubarb and Strawberry Compote

Prep time: 10 minutes | Cook time: 1 to 2 hours | Serves 6

1 pound (454 g) rhubarb, peeled and sliced 1 inch thick
¼ cup honey
2 tablespoons water
1 teaspoon vanilla extract
Pinch salt
4 cups strawberries, hulled and quartered
1 tablespoon unsalted butter
2 pints vanilla ice cream or frozen yogurt

1. Combine the rhubarb, honey, water, vanilla, and salt in the crock pot.
2. Cover and cook until the rhubarb is softened and sauce is thickened, 1 to 2 hours on high.
3. Stir strawberries and butter into the compote and let sit until heated through, about 5 minutes.
4. Portion the ice cream into individual bowls and spoon the compote over. Serve.

Cherry and Hazelnut Stuffed Apples

Prep time: 10 minutes | Cook time: 4 to 5 hours | Serves 6

7 large Granny Smith apples
8 tablespoons unsalted butter, softened
¼ cup packed brown sugar
1⅓ cup dried cherries, chopped
1⅓ cup hazelnuts, toasted, skinned, and chopped
3 tablespoons old-fashioned rolled oats
1 teaspoon grated orange zest
½ teaspoon pepper
Pinch salt
Vegetable oil spray
1⅓ cup maple syrup

1. Peel and core 1 apple and cut into ¼-inch pieces. Combine apple pieces, 5 tablespoons butter, sugar, cherries, hazelnuts, oats, orange zest, pepper, and salt in a bowl. Set aside.
2. Shave thin slice off bottom (blossom end) of remaining 6 apples to allow them to sit flat. Cut top ½ inch off stem end of apples and reserve. Peel apples and use melon baller or small measuring spoon to cut 1½-inch diameter opening from core, being careful not to cut through bottom of apple. Spoon filling inside apples, mounding excess filling over cavities. Top with reserved apple caps.
3. Lightly coat crock pot with vegetable oil spray. Arrange stuffed apples in a prepared crock pot. Drizzle with maple syrup, cover, and cook until skewer inserted into apples meets little resistance, 4 to 5 hours on low.
4. Using tongs and sturdy spatula, transfer apples to a serving dish. Whisk remaining 3 tablespoons butter into cooking liquid, 1 tablespoon at a time, until incorporated. Spoon sauce over apples and serve.

Vanilla Creme Brûlée

Prep time: 5 minutes | Cook time: 2 to 3 hours | Serves 4

2 cups heavy cream
5 large egg yolks
1⅓ cup granulated sugar
1 teaspoon vanilla extract
Pinch salt
4 teaspoons turbinado or Demerara sugar

1. Whisk cream, egg yolks, granulated sugar, vanilla, and salt in a bowl until sugar has dissolved. Strain custard through a fine-mesh strainer into a 4-cup liquid measuring cup. Divide custard evenly among four 6-ounce / 170-g ramekins. Fill a crock pot with ½ inch water (about 2 cups) and set ramekins in a crock pot. Cover and cook until centers are just barely set and register 185ºF (85ºC), 2 to 3 hours on low.
2. Using tongs and sturdy spatula, transfer ramekins to a wire rack and let cool to room temperature, about 2 hours. Cover with plastic wrap and refrigerate until well chilled, at least for 4 hours or up to 2 days.
3. To serve, gently blot away condensation using paper towels. Sprinkle each ramekin with 1 teaspoon turbinado sugar. Tilt and tap each ramekin to distribute sugar evenly, then dump out excess sugar and wipe rims of ramekins clean. Ignite torch and caramelize sugar. Refrigerate ramekins, uncovered, to re-chill custard before serving, 30 to 45 minutes.

Spiced Applesauce Cake

Prep time: 10 minutes | Cook time: 3 to 4 hours | Serves 6

1 cup all-purpose flour
½ teaspoon baking soda
¼ teaspoon ground cinnamon
¼ teaspoon salt
Pinch ground nutmeg
Pinch ground cloves
½ cup granulated sugar
½ cup unsweetened applesauce
1 large egg
½ teaspoon vanilla extract
6 tablespoons unsalted butter, melted
Confectioners' sugar, for dusting

1. Fill a crock pot with ½ inch water (about 2 cups) and place aluminum foil rack in bottom. Grease a springform pan and line with parchment paper.
2. Whisk flour, baking soda, cinnamon, salt, nutmeg, and cloves together in a bowl. In a large bowl, whisk granulated sugar, applesauce, egg, and vanilla until smooth, then slowly whisk in melted butter until well combined. Stir in flour mixture until just incorporated.
3. Scrape batter into prepared pan and smooth top. Gently tap pan on the counter to release air bubbles. Set pan on prepared rack, cover, and cook until toothpick inserted in center comes out clean, 3 to 4 hours on high.
4. Let cake cool in pan on wire rack for 10 minutes. Run a small knife around edge of cake, then remove sides of pan. Remove cake from pan bottom, discarding parchment, and let cool completely on a rack, 1 to 2 hours. Transfer to a serving dish and dust with confectioners' sugar. Serve.

Mixed Fruit Curry

Prep time: 10 minutes | Cook time: 8 to 10 hours | Serves 8 to 10

1 can pears, undrained
1 can apricots, undrained
1 can peaches, undrained
1 can black cherries, undrained
1 large can pineapple chunks, undrained
½ cup brown sugar
1 teaspoon curry powder
3 to 4 tablespoons quick-cooking tapioca

1. Combine the fruit in a large bowl. Toss to mix well. Let stand for at least 2 hours, or up to 8 hours, to allow flavors to blend. Drain. Place in the crock pot.
2. Add the remaining ingredients. Mix well.
3. Cover. Cook on low for 8 to 10 hours.
4. Serve warm.

Sweet Cherry Grunt

Prep time: 15 minutes | Cook time: 2 to 3 hours | Serves 8

2¼ pounds (1.0 kg) frozen sweet cherries, thawed
2 cups all-purpose flour, divided
1 cup plus 3 tablespoons sugar, divided
1 tablespoon lemon juice
1¼ teaspoons ground cinnamon, divided
1 teaspoon almond extract
1 tablespoon baking powder
½ teaspoon salt
½ cup plus 2 tablespoons milk
4 tablespoons unsalted butter, melted and cooled

1. Combine the cherries, ¼ cup flour, 1 cup sugar, lemon juice, 1 teaspoon cinnamon, and almond extract in a medium bowl. Microwave until cherries release their liquid, about 5 minutes, stirring halfway through microwaving. Stir cherry mixture well, transfer to the crock pot, and spread into an even layer.
2. In a large bowl, combine the remaining 1¾ cups of flour, 2 tablespoons sugar, baking powder, and salt. Stir in the milk and melted butter until just combined, then do not over-mix.
3. In a small bowl, combine the remaining 1 tablespoon sugar and remaining ¼ teaspoon cinnamon.
4. Using greased ¼ cup measure, drop 8 dumplings around the perimeter of the crock pot on top of cherries, leaving center empty. Sprinkle dumplings with cinnamon-sugar mixture.
5. Cover and cook until toothpick inserted in center of dumplings comes out clean, 3 to 4 hours on low or 2 to 3 hours on high. Turn off crock pot and let cool for 20 minutes before serving.

Apple Crumble

Prep time: 10 minutes | Cook time: 5 to 6 hours | Serves 4 to 5

4 to 5 cooking apples, peeled and sliced
²⅓ cup packed brown sugar
½ cup flour
½ cup quick-cooking dry oats
½ teaspoon cinnamon
¼-½ teaspoon nutmeg
1⅓ cup butter, softened
2 tablespoons peanut butter

1. Place the apple slices in the crock pot.
2. Combine the brown sugar, flour, oats, cinnamon, and nutmeg in a large bowl.
3. Cut in the butter and peanut butter. Sprinkle the mixture over the apples.
4. Cover and cook on low for 5 to 6 hours.
5. Serve warm or cold.

Posh Fruit Compote

Prep time: 20 minutes | Cook time: 3¼ to 4¼ hours | Makes 8 cups

5 medium apples, peeled and chopped
3 medium pears, chopped
1 medium orange, thinly sliced
½ cup dried cranberries
½ cup packed brown sugar
½ cup maple syrup
1⅓ cup butter, cubed
2 tablespoons lemon juice
2 teaspoons ground cinnamon
1 teaspoon ground ginger
5 tablespoons orange juice, divided
4 teaspoons cornstarch
Sweetened whipped cream and toasted chopped pecans, optional

1. In the crock pot, combine the first 10 ingredients. Stir in 2 tablespoons orange juice.
2. Cook, covered, on low for 3 to 4 hours or until fruit is tender.
3. In a small bowl, mix cornstarch and remaining orange juice until smooth, then gradually stir into fruit mixture.
4. Cook, covered, on high for 15 to 20 minutes longer or until sauce is thickened. If desired, top with whipped cream and pecans before serving.

Apple and Walnut Pie

Prep time: 5 minutes | Cook time: 2 to 3 hours | Serves 10 to 12

1 (21-ounce / 595-g) can cherry or apple pie filling
1 package yellow cake mix (regular size)
½ cup butter, melted
1⅓ cup chopped walnuts, optional

1. Place the pie filling in the crock pot. Combine the cake mix and butter (mixture will be crumbly) in a small bowl, then sprinkle over filling. Sprinkle with walnuts, if desired.
2. Cover and cook on low for 2 to 3 hours. Serve in bowls.

Flan

Prep time: 10 minutes | Cook time: 4 hours | Serves 6

3 tablespoons unsalted butter
¾ cup sugar
5 eggs
1 (12-ounce / 340-g) can evaporated milk
1 (14-ounce / 397-g) can dulce de leche
4 ounces (113 g) cream cheese, cut into 1-inch cubes
1 teaspoon pure vanilla extract
Vanilla sea salt, to taste

1. Grease 6 ramekins with the butter.
2. In a blender, add the sugar, eggs, evaporated milk, dulce de leche, cream cheese, and vanilla, and blend until smooth.
3. On the bottom of the crock pot, place a folded tea towel.
4. Pour the flan mixture into the ramekins and arrange the ramekins on the towel in the crock pot. Cover the ramekins tightly with foil.
5. Pour warm water into the crock pot until it reaches halfway up the sides of the ramekins. (Make sure the water reaches no more than halfway up the sides—it will ruin the flans if it splashes into the ramekins.)
6. Cook on high for 4 hours. Then remove the ramekins from the crock pot, take off the aluminum foil, and let them cool for at least an hour in the refrigerator.
7. Sprinkle with the vanilla sea salt before serving.

Baked Raisin Stuffed Apples

Prep time: 25 minutes | Cook time: 4 to 5 hours | Serves 6

6 medium tart apples
½ cup raisins
1⅓ cup packed brown sugar
1 tablespoon orange zest
1 cup water
3 tablespoons thawed orange juice concentrate
2 tablespoons butter

1. Core apples and peel top third of each if desired. Combine the raisins, brown sugar and orange zest, then spoon into apples. Place in the crock pot.
2. Pour the water around apples. Drizzle with orange juice concentrate. Dot with butter. Cover and cook on low for 4 to 5 hours or until apples are tender.
3. Serve warm.

Pumpkin Pie Custard

Prep time: 15 minutes | Cook time: 7 hours | Serves 2

1½ cups light cream
1 (15-ounce / 425-g) can solid-pack pumpkin
½ cup brown sugar
¼ cup granulated sugar
2 eggs, beaten
3 tablespoons melted butter
2 teaspoons vanilla
1⅓ cup all-purpose flour
½ teaspoon baking powder
1 teaspoon ground cinnamon
¼ teaspoon ground nutmeg
¼ teaspoon ground allspice
3 large sugar cookies
Whipped cream, for garnish
Nonstick cooking spray

1. Spritz the crock pot with the nonstick cooking spray.
2. In a large bowl, gradually add the light cream to the pumpkin, beating with a hand mixer.
3. Beat in the brown sugar, granulated sugar, eggs, butter, and vanilla.
4. Add the flour, baking powder, cinnamon, nutmeg, and allspice.
5. Pour the mixture into the crock pot. Cover and cook on low for 7 hours, or until the mixture is set.
6. Crumble the sugar cookies on top of each serving and serve with whipped cream.

Self-Frosting Chocolate Cake

Prep time: 10 minutes | Cook time: 2 to 3 hours | Serves 8 to 10

2½ cups chocolate fudge pudding cake mix
2 eggs
1 cup water, divided
3 tablespoons olive oil
1⅓ cup pecan halves
¼ cup chocolate syrup
3 tablespoons sugar

1. Combine the cake mix, eggs, ¾ cup water, and oil in a blender. Pulse to mix well.
2. Pour into buttered and floured cake pan that will fit into the crock pot.
3. Sprinkle the pecans over the mixture.
4. Blend chocolate syrup, ¼ cup water, and sugar. Spoon over batter.
5. Cover. Bake on high for 2 to 3 hours.
6. Serve warm.

Super Lemony Rice Pudding

Prep time: 10 minutes | Cook time: 6 hours | Serves 2

1 cup long-grain white rice
2⅓ cup granulated sugar
4 cups milk
1 cup water
1⅓ cup freshly squeezed lemon juice
2 teaspoons lemon zest
Pinch salt
4 tablespoons butter, melted
Nonstick cooking spray

1. Spray the crock pot with the nonstick cooking spray.
2. In the crock pot, combine all the ingredients and stir.
3. Cover and cook on low for 6 hours, or until the rice is very tender and the mixture has thickened, and serve.

Pineapple and Mango Crisp

Prep time: 5 minutes | Cook time: 2½ hours | Serves 6

4 tablespoons unsalted butter, cut into tiny pieces, plus more for greasing the crock pot
3 cups diced pineapple, drained if canned
2 cups diced mango
½ cup packed brown sugar
¼ cup orange or pineapple juice
2 tablespoons dark rum
¼ cup chopped candied ginger (optional)
2½ cups granola

1. Generously grease the crock pot with butter.
2. In the crock pot, combine all the ingredients except the granola and remaining 4 tablespoons of butter.
3. Scatter the butter pieces on top of the fruit and sprinkle the granola on top of the butter.
4. Cook on low for 5 hours or on high for 2½ hours, until the fruit is tender.
5. Serve hot.

Chocolate Brownie Cake

Prep time: 10 minutes | Cook time: 3 hours | Serves 12

½ cup plus 1 tablespoon unsalted butter, melted, divided
1½ cups almond flour
¾ cup cocoa powder
¾ cup granulated erythritol
1 teaspoon baking powder
¼ teaspoon fine salt
1 cup heavy (whipping) cream
3 eggs, beaten
2 teaspoons pure vanilla extract
1 cup whipped cream

1. Generously grease the crock pot with 1 tablespoon of the melted butter.
2. In a large bowl, stir together the almond flour, cocoa powder, erythritol, baking powder, and salt.
3. In a medium bowl, whisk together the remaining ½ cup of the melted butter, heavy cream, eggs, and vanilla until well blended.
4. Whisk the wet ingredients into the dry ingredients and spoon the batter into the crock pot.
5. Cover and cook on low for 3 hours, then let the cake sit for 1 hour.
6. Serve warm with the whipped cream.

Vanilla Chocolate Cake

Prep time: 15 minutes | Cook time: 3 hours | Serves 2

1 cup all-purpose flour
1⅓ cup granulated sugar
1⅓ cup brown sugar
1 teaspoon baking powder
½ teaspoon baking soda
Pinch salt
¼ cup cocoa powder
¼ cup semisweet chocolate chips, finely chopped
3 tablespoons butter
¼ cup boiling water
½ cup light cream
1 egg
2 teaspoons vanilla
½ cup water
Nonstick baking spray containing flour

1. Spray a loaf pan with the nonstick baking spray containing flour.
2. In a medium bowl, mix the flour, granulated sugar, brown sugar, baking powder, baking soda, and salt.
3. In a small saucepan over low heat, heat the cocoa powder, chocolate chips, butter, and boiling water, stirring frequently, until the chocolate chips melt, about 5 minutes.
4. Add the cocoa mixture to the flour mixture. Add the cream, egg, and vanilla, and beat for 1 minute.
5. Pour the mixture into the loaf pan.
6. Place the loaf pan in the crock pot and pour ½ cup of water around the pan. Place a double layer of paper towels on top of the crock pot and add the cover.
7. Cook on low for 3 hours, or until the cake springs back when lightly touched with a finger.
8. Remove the pan from the crock pot and cool for 5 minutes, then invert onto a cooling rack, cool completely, and serve.

Cherry Molton Cake

Prep time: 15 minutes | Cook time: 5 hours | Serves 2

1 cup all-purpose flour
½ cup brown sugar
½ cup granulated sugar
¼ cup cocoa powder
1½ teaspoons baking powder
Pinch salt
½ cup chocolate milk
2 tablespoons melted butter
1 teaspoon vanilla
½ cup cherry preserves
3 tablespoons honey
1 cup boiling water
Nonstick cooking spray

1. Spray the crock pot with the nonstick cooking spray.
2. In the crock pot, combine the flour, brown sugar, granulated sugar, cocoa powder, baking powder, and salt.
3. Whisk in the chocolate milk, butter, and vanilla.
4. Drop the cherry preserves by small spoonfuls over the batter.
5. Drizzle with the honey and pour the boiling water over them. Do not stir.
6. Cover and cook on low for 5 hours, or until the cake looks done (toothpick tests will not work since there is a layer of sauce on the bottom).
7. Scoop out of the crock pot to serve.

Pot De Crème

Prep time: 10 minutes | Cook time: 3 hours | Serves 6

6 egg yolks
2 cups heavy (whipping) cream
1⅓ cup cocoa powder
1 tablespoon pure vanilla extract
½ teaspoon liquid stevia

1. In a medium bowl, whisk together the yolks, heavy cream, cocoa powder, vanilla, and stevia.
2. Pour the mixture into a baking dish and place the dish in the crock pot.
3. Pour in enough water to reach halfway up the sides of the baking dish.
4. Cover and cook on low for 3 hours.
5. Remove the baking dish from the crock pot and cool to room temperature on a wire rack.
6. Chill the dessert completely in the refrigerator. Serve chilled.

Pumpkin and Mixed Berry Compote

Prep time: 10 minutes | Cook time: 3 to 4 hours | Serves 10

1 tablespoon coconut oil
2 cups diced pumpkin
1 cup cranberries
1 cup blueberries
½ cup granulated erythritol
Juice and zest of 1 orange
½ cup coconut milk
1 teaspoon ground cinnamon
½ teaspoon ground allspice
¼ teaspoon ground nutmeg
1 cup whipped cream

1. Lightly grease the crock pot with the coconut oil.
2. Place the pumpkin, cranberries, blueberries, erythritol, orange juice and zest, coconut milk, cinnamon, allspice, and nutmeg in the crock pot.
3. Cover and cook on low for 3 to 4 hours.
4. Let the compote cool for 1 hour and serve warm with a generous scoop of whipped cream.

Cinnamon Applesauce

Prep time: 5 minutes | Cook time: 6 to 8 hours | Makes 5 cups

8 to 10 large tart apples, peeled and cut into chunks
½ to 1 cup sugar
½ cup water
1 teaspoon ground cinnamon

1. Combine apples, sugar, water and cinnamon in the crock pot, then stir gently.
2. Cover and cook on low for 6 to 8 hours or until apples are tender.
3. Serve warm.

Almond Cake

Prep time: 15 minutes | Cook time: 3 hours | Serves 8

½ cup coconut oil, divided
1½ cups almond flour
½ cup coconut flour
½ cup granulated erythritol
2 teaspoons baking powder
3 eggs
½ cup coconut milk
2 teaspoons pure vanilla extract
½ teaspoon almond extract

1. Line the crock pot with aluminum foil and grease the aluminum foil with 1 tablespoon of the coconut oil.
2. In a medium bowl, mix the almond flour, coconut flour, erythritol, and baking powder.
3. In a large bowl, whisk together the remaining coconut oil, eggs, coconut milk, vanilla, and almond extract.
4. Add the dry ingredients to the wet ingredients and stir until well blended.
5. Transfer the batter to the crock pot and use a spatula to even the top.
6. Cover and cook on low for 3 hours, or until a toothpick inserted in the center comes out clean.
7. Remove the cake from the crock pot and cool completely before serving.

Gingerbread

Prep time: 10 minutes | Cook time: 3 hours | Serves 8

1 tablespoon coconut oil
2 cups almond flour
¾ cup granulated erythritol
2 tablespoons coconut flour
2 tablespoons ground ginger
2 teaspoons baking powder
2 teaspoons ground cinnamon
½ teaspoon ground nutmeg
¼ teaspoon ground cloves
Pinch salt
¾ cup heavy (whipping) cream
½ cup butter, melted
4 eggs
1 teaspoon pure vanilla extract

1. Lightly grease the crock pot with coconut oil.
2. In a large bowl, stir together the almond flour, erythritol, coconut flour, ginger, baking powder, cinnamon, nutmeg, cloves, and salt.
3. In a medium bowl, whisk together the heavy cream, butter, eggs, and vanilla.
4. Add the wet ingredients to the dry ingredients and stir to combine.
5. Spoon the batter into the crock pot.
6. Cover and cook on low for 3 hours, or until a toothpick inserted in the center comes out clean.
7. Serve warm.

Almond and Sour Cream Cheesecake

Prep time: 15 minutes | Cook time: 5 to 6 hours | Serves 10

¼ cup butter, melted, divided
1 cup ground almonds
¾ cup plus 1 tablespoon granulated erythritol, divided
¼ teaspoon ground cinnamon
12 ounces (340 g) cream cheese, at room temperature
2 eggs
2 teaspoons pure vanilla extract
1 cup sour cream

1. Lightly grease a springform pan with 1 tablespoon of the butter.
2. In a small bowl, stir together the almonds, 1 tablespoon of the erythritol, and cinnamon until blended.
3. Add the remaining 3 tablespoons of the butter and stir until coarse crumbs form.
4. Press the crust mixture into the springform pan along the bottom and about 2 inches up the sides.
5. In a large bowl, using a handheld mixer, beat together the cream cheese, eggs, vanilla, and remaining ¾ cup of the erythritol. Beat the sour cream into the cream-cheese mixture until smooth.
6. Spoon the batter into the springform pan and smooth out the top.
7. Place a wire rack in the crock pot and place the springform pan on top.
8. Cover and cook on low for 5 to 6 hours, or until the cheesecake doesn't jiggle when shaken.
9. Cool completely before removing from pan.
10. Chill the cheesecake completely before serving.

Chapter 4 Desserts | 33

Almond and Peanut Butter Cheesecake

Prep time: 15 minutes | Cook time: 5 to 6 hours | Serves 10

¼ cup butter, melted, divided
1 cup ground almonds
2 tablespoons cocoa powder
1 cup granulated erythritol, divided
12 ounces (340 g) cream cheese, room temperature
½ cup natural peanut butter
2 eggs, room temperature
1 teaspoon pure vanilla extract

1. Lightly grease a springform pan with 1 tablespoon butter.
2. In a small bowl, stir together the almonds, cocoa powder, and ¼ cup erythritol until blended. Add the remaining 3 tablespoons of the butter and stir until coarse crumbs form.
3. Press the crust mixture into the springform pan along the bottom and about 2 inches up the sides.
4. In a large bowl, using a handheld mixer, beat together the cream cheese and peanut butter until smooth. Beat in the remaining ¾ cup of the erythritol, eggs, and vanilla.
5. Spoon the batter into the springform pan and smooth out the top.
6. Place a wire rack in the crock pot and place the springform pan on the wire rack.
7. Cover and cook on low for 5 to 6 hours, or until the cheesecake doesn't jiggle when shaken.
8. Cool completely before removing from pan.
9. Chill the cheesecake completely before serving.

Pound Cake

Prep time: 10 minutes | Cook time: 5 to 6 hours | Serves 8

1 tablespoon coconut oil
2 cups almond flour
1 cup granulated erythritol
½ teaspoon cream of tartar
Pinch salt
1 cup butter, melted
5 eggs
2 teaspoons pure vanilla extract

1. Lightly grease a loaf pan with the coconut oil.
2. In a large bowl, stir together the almond flour, erythritol, cream of tartar, and salt, until well mixed.
3. In a small bowl, whisk together the butter, eggs, and vanilla.
4. Add the wet ingredients to the dry ingredients and stir to combine.
5. Transfer the batter to the loaf pan.
6. Place the loaf pan in the crock pot.
7. Cover and cook until a toothpick inserted in the center comes out clean, about 5 to 6 hours on low.
8. Serve warm.

Raspberry and Lime Custard Cake

Prep time: 15 minutes | Cook time: 3 hours | Serves 8

1 teaspoon coconut oil
6 eggs, whites and yolks separated
2 cups heavy (whipping) cream
¾ cup granulated erythritol
½ cup coconut flour
¼ teaspoon salt
Juice and zest of 2 limes
½ cup raspberries

1. Lightly grease a springform pan with the coconut oil.
2. In a large bowl, using a hand mixer, beat the egg whites until stiff peaks form, about 5 minutes.
3. In a large bowl, whisk together the yolks, heavy cream, erythritol, coconut flour, salt, and lime juice and zest.
4. Fold the egg whites into the mixture.
5. Transfer the batter to the springform pan and sprinkle the raspberries over.
6. Place a wire rack in the crock pot and place the springform pan on the wire rack.
7. Cover and cook on low for 3 hours, or until a toothpick inserted in the center comes out clean.
8. Remove the cover and allow the cake to cool to room temperature.
9. Place the springform pan in the refrigerator for at least 2 hours until the cake is firm.
10. Carefully remove the sides of the springform pan. Slice and serve.

Chapter 5 Classic Comfort Foods

Chili Mac and Cheese

Prep time: 25 minutes | Cook time: 1 to 2 hours | Serves 6 to 8

1 slice hearty white sandwich bread, torn into 1-inch pieces
2 tablespoons whole milk
Salt and pepper, to taste
1 pound (454 g) 85% lean ground beef
3 tablespoons vegetable oil
2 onions, finely chopped
3 tablespoons chili powder
6 garlic cloves, minced
4 teaspoons ground cumin
1 pound (454 g) elbow macaroni or small shells
1 (28-ounce / 794-g) can crushed tomatoes
2½ cups water, plus extra as needed
1 (15-ounce / 425-g) can tomato sauce
8 ounces (227 g) Pepper Jack cheese, shredded (2 cups)
Vegetable oil spray

1. Line crock pot with aluminum foil collar and lightly coat with vegetable oil spray. Mash bread, milk, ¼ teaspoon salt, and ¼ teaspoon pepper into paste in a large bowl using a fork. Add ground beef and knead with hands until well combined.
2. Heat oil in a Dutch oven over medium heat until shimmering. Add beef mixture and cook, breaking up meat into rough 1-inch pieces with wooden spoon, until no longer pink, about 5 minutes. Add onions, ½ teaspoon salt, and ¼ teaspoon pepper and cook until onions are softened, about 5 minutes. Stir in chili powder, garlic, and cumin and cook until fragrant, about 1 minute.
3. Reduce heat to medium-low. Add macaroni and cook, stirring occasionally, until edges are translucent, about 4 minutes. Off heat, stir in tomatoes, water, and tomato sauce, scraping up any browned bits. Stir in 1 cup pepper Jack. Transfer mixture to prepared crock pot, cover, and cook until macaroni is tender, 1 to 2 hours on high.
4. Discard foil collar. Gently stir macaroni to recombine. Adjust consistency with extra hot water as needed. Season with salt and pepper to taste. Sprinkle with remaining 1 cup pepper Jack, cover, and let sit until melted, about 20 minutes. Serve.

Mushroom Macaroni and Cheese

Prep time: 20 minutes | Cook time: 1 to 2 hours | Serves 6 to 8

1 pound (454 g) elbow macaroni or small shells
1 tablespoon extra-virgin olive oil
3 cups boiling water, plus extra as needed
2 (12-ounce / 340-g) cans evaporated milk
2 (11-ounce / 312-g) cans condensed onion soup
8 ounces (227 g) Comté cheese, shredded (2 cups)
8 ounces (227 g) Monterey Jack cheese, shredded (2 cups)
¼ cup dry white wine
¼ ounce (7 g) dried porcini mushrooms, rinsed and minced
1 teaspoon dry mustard
Salt and pepper, to taste
Vegetable oil spray

1. Line crock pot with aluminum foil collar and lightly coat with vegetable oil spray. Microwave macaroni and oil in a bowl at 50 percent power, stirring occasionally, until macaroni begin to look toasted and blistered, 5 to 8 minutes.
2. Transfer hot macaroni to prepared crock pot and immediately stir in 2¾ cups boiling water. Stir in evaporated milk, condensed soup, Comté, Monterey Jack, wine, mushrooms, mustard, 1 teaspoon pepper, and ½ teaspoon salt. Cover and cook until macaroni are tender, 1 to 2 hours on high.
3. Discard foil collar. Gently stir remaining ¼ cup boiling water into macaroni until combined. Season with salt and pepper to taste. Adjust consistency with extra boiling water as needed. Serve. (Macaroni can be held on warm or low setting for up to 30 minutes.)

Broccoli and Three-Cheese Lasagna

Prep time: 20 minutes | Cook time: 4 to 5 hours | Serves 6 to 8

12 ounces (340 g) broccoli florets, cut into 2-inch pieces
Salt and pepper, to taste
8 curly-edged lasagna noodles, broken in half
1 pound (454 g) whole-milk ricotta cheese
2½ ounces (71 g) Parmesan cheese, grated (1¼ cups)
¾ cup oil-packed sun-dried tomatoes, patted dry and quartered
1 large egg
1 teaspoon minced fresh oregano
1 teaspoon garlic powder
½ teaspoon red pepper flakes
3 cups jarred pasta sauce
1 pound (454 g) Mozzarella cheese, shredded (4 cups)
Vegetable oil spray

1. Line crock pot with aluminum foil collar, then press 2 large sheets of foil into crock pot perpendicular to one another, with extra foil hanging over edges. Lightly coat prepared crock pot with vegetable oil spray.
2. Bring 4 quarts water to boil in a large pot. Add broccoli and 1 tablespoon salt and cook until broccoli is bright green and just tender, about 3 minutes. Transfer to a paper towel-lined plate. Let broccoli cool slightly, then chop coarsely.
3. Return water to boil, add noodles, and cook, stirring often, until al dente. Drain noodles, rinse under cold water, then spread out in a single layer over clean dish towels and let dry. (Do not use paper towels; they will stick to noodles.)
4. Combine ricotta, 1 cup Parmesan, tomatoes, egg, oregano, garlic powder, pepper flakes, ½ teaspoon salt, and ½ teaspoon pepper in bowl. Spread ½ cup pasta sauce into prepared crock pot.
5. Arrange 4 noodle pieces in a crock pot (they may overlap), then dollop 10 rounded tablespoons of ricotta mixture over noodles. Scatter one-third of broccoli over ricotta. Sprinkle with 1 cup Mozzarella, then spoon ½ cup sauce over top. Repeat layering of noodles, ricotta mixture, broccoli, Mozzarella, and sauce twice more.
6. For the final layer, arrange remaining 4 noodles in a crock pot, then top with remaining 1 cup sauce and sprinkle with remaining 1 cup Mozzarella and remaining ¼ cup Parmesan. Cover and cook until lasagna is heated through, 4 to 5 hours on low.
7. Let lasagna cool for 20 minutes. (If desired, use sling to transfer lasagna to serving dish. Press edges of foil flat; discard any juices.) Serve.

Baked Ziti with Sausage

Prep time: 15 minutes | Cook time: 2¹⁄₃ to 3¹⁄₃ hours | Serves 6 to 8

2 tablespoons extra-virgin olive oil
1 pound (454 g) hot or sweet Italian sausage, casings removed
1 onion, finely chopped
Salt and pepper, to taste
3 garlic cloves, minced
2 teaspoons minced fresh oregano or ½ teaspoon dried
8 ounces (227 g) ziti
1 (28-ounce / 794-g) can crushed tomatoes
1 (15-ounce / 425-g) can tomato sauce
8 ounces (227 g) whole-milk ricotta cheese
4 ounces (113 g) Mozzarella cheese, shredded (1 cup)
2 tablespoons shredded fresh basil
Vegetable oil spray

1. Line crock pot with aluminum foil collar and lightly coat with vegetable oil spray. Heat oil in a Dutch oven over medium-high heat until just smoking. Cook sausage, breaking up pieces with wooden spoon, until well browned, 6 to 8 minutes. Stir in onion, ½ teaspoon salt, and ½ teaspoon pepper and cook until onion is softened and lightly browned, 5 to 7 minutes. Stir in garlic and oregano and cook until fragrant, about 1 minute.
2. Reduce heat to medium-low. Add ziti and cook, stirring constantly, until edges of pasta become translucent, about 4 minutes. Off heat, stir in tomatoes and tomato sauce, scraping up any browned bits. Transfer mixture to prepared crock pot. Cover and cook until pasta is tender, 2 to 3 hours on high.
3. Discard foil collar. Dollop ricotta over ziti and sprinkle with Mozzarella. Cover and let sit until cheese is melted, about 20 minutes. Sprinkle with basil and serve.

Ham and Potato Casserole

Prep time: 15 minutes | Cook time: 4 to 5 hours | Serves 4

1 (10¾-ounce / 305-g) can condensed cream of mushroom soup, undiluted
½ cup 2% milk
1 tablespoon dried parsley flakes
6 medium potatoes, peeled and thinly sliced
1 small onion, chopped
1½ cups cubed fully cooked ham
6 slices process American cheese

1. In a small bowl, combine the soup, milk and parsley. In a crock pot, layer half of the potatoes, onion, ham, cheese, and soup mixture. Repeat layers. Cover and cook on low for 4 to 5 hours or until potatoes are tender. Serve warm.

Italian Meatball Stew

Prep time: 20 minutes | Cook time: 8½ to 10½ hours | Serves 8

2 (12-ounce / 340-g) packages frozen fully cooked Italian meatballs
5 medium potatoes, peeled and cubed
1 pound (454 g) fresh baby carrots
1 medium onion, halved and sliced
1 (4½-ounce / 128-g) jar sliced mushrooms, drained
2 (8-ounce / 227-g) cans tomato sauce
1 (10½-ounce / 298-g) can condensed beef broth, undiluted
¾ cup water
¾ cup dry red wine or beef broth
½ teaspoon garlic powder
¼ teaspoon pepper
2 tablespoons all-purpose flour
½ cup cold water

1. Place the meatballs, potatoes, carrots, onion, and mushrooms in a crock pot. In a large bowl, combine the tomato sauce, broth, water, wine, garlic powder and pepper; pour over top. Cover and cook on low for 8 to 10 hours or until vegetables are tender.
2. Combine flour and water until smooth, then gradually stir into stew. Cover and cook on high for 30 minutes or until thickened. Serve.

Grape-Nuts Custard Pudding

Prep time: 10 minutes | Cook time: 2 hours | Serves 8

1½ cups grape-nuts cereal (nuggets, not flakes)
6 large eggs
4 cups milk
1¹¹⁄₃ cups sugar
1 tablespoon vanilla bean paste
1 teaspoon ground cinnamon
2½ cups heavy cream
Nonstick cooking spray

1. Spray the crock pot with nonstick cooking spray. Pour the cereal in the crock pot.
2. Whisk together the eggs, milk, sugar, vanilla bean paste, and cinnamon in a large mixing bowl. Gently pour over the cereal.
3. Cover and cook on high for 2 hours, until the custard is just set. It may seem a little jiggly in the center, but will firm while the custard cools. Allow the pudding to cool to room temperature. Cover with plastic wrap and chill.
4. Whip the cream in a mixing bowl until it forms stiff peaks.
5. Scoop the pudding into bowls and top each serving with a dollop of the cream.

Chicken and Red Potato Stew

Prep time: 15 minutes | Cook time: 7 to 9 hours | Serves 4

1 pound (454 g) small red potatoes, halved
1 large onion, finely chopped
¾ cup shredded carrots
3 tablespoons all-purpose flour
6 garlic cloves, minced
2 teaspoons lemon zest
2 teaspoons dried thyme
½ teaspoon salt
¼ teaspoon pepper
1½ pounds (680 g) boneless skinless chicken thighs, halved
2 cups chicken broth
2 bay leaves
2 tablespoons minced fresh parsley

1. Place the potatoes, onion and carrots in the crock pot. Sprinkle with flour, garlic, lemon zest, thyme, salt and pepper, then toss to coat. Place the chicken over. Add broth and bay leaves.
2. Cook, covered, on low for 7 to 9 hours or until chicken and vegetables are tender. Remove the bay leaves. Sprinkle with parsley and serve.

Caramelized Onion Pot Roast

Prep time: 15 minutes | Cook time: 8 to 10 hours | Serves 4

1 cup water
1 cup beer or beef broth
½ cup beef broth
¼ cup packed brown sugar
3 tablespoons Dijon mustard
2 tablespoons cider vinegar
1 boneless beef chuck roast (4 pounds / 1.8 kg), trimmed
1 teaspoon onion salt
1 teaspoon coarsely ground pepper
1 tablespoon olive oil
3 large sweet onions, halved and sliced
2 tablespoons cornstarch
2 tablespoons cold water

1. In a large bowl, combine the first six ingredients; set aside. Sprinkle roast with onion salt and pepper. In a large skillet, brown meat in oil on all sides. Place onions and roast in a crock pot; pour beer mixture over top. Cover and cook on low for 8 to 10 hours or until meat is tender.
2. Remove roast and onions and keep warm. Skim fat from cooking juices; transfer 2 cups to a small saucepan. Bring liquid to a boil. Combine cornstarch and water until smooth, then gradually stir into the pan. Bring to a boil, cook and stir for 2 minutes or until thickened. Serve the gravy with the roast and onions.

Smothered Pork

Prep time: 20 minutes | Cook time: 4 to 6 hours | Serves 6

1 tablespoon extra-virgin olive oil
6 (1-inch-thick) sirloin pork chops
½ teaspoon kosher salt, plus more for seasoning
½ teaspoon freshly ground black pepper, plus more for seasoning
1 onion, finely chopped
4 garlic cloves, minced
½ cup dry white wine
2 cups chicken stock
1⅓ cup all-purpose flour
½ teaspoon garlic powder
2 bay leaves
1 tablespoon browning sauce

1. In a saucepan over medium-high heat, heat the oil until shimmering. Season the chops with salt and pepper, and brown, about 3 minutes per side. Remove and set aside.
2. In the same saucepan, add the onion and garlic. Sauté until tender, about 5 minutes. Add the wine and bring to a boil. Simmer for a minute before adding the chicken stock. Whisk in the flour, stirring until no lumps remain.
3. Place the pork chops and the sauce mixture in the crock pot. Add the garlic powder, salt, pepper, bay leaves, and browning sauce. Stir to combine. Cover and cook on low for 4 to 6 hours.
4. Discard the bay leaves. Season with additional salt and pepper, as needed. Serve, spooning the sauce on top of the chops.

Thai Red Curry Chicken with Vegetables

Prep time: 15 minutes | Cook time: 6 to 8 hours | Serves 4

¼ cup creamy peanut butter
2 tablespoons red curry paste
2 tablespoons packed brown sugar
2 tablespoons fish sauce
½ teaspoon kosher salt, plus more for seasoning
2 tablespoons freshly squeezed lime juice
1 (14-ounce / 397-g) can coconut milk
½ cup chicken stock
1 pound (454 g) boneless, skinless chicken thighs
3 garlic cloves, minced
3 cups mixed vegetables, such as sliced red pepper, sliced red onion, and snap peas
¼ cup finely chopped fresh cilantro, for garnish

1. In a medium bowl, whisk together the peanut butter, curry paste, brown sugar, fish sauce, salt, lime juice, coconut milk, and chicken stock until thoroughly combined.
2. Put the chicken and garlic in the crock pot, then spoon the sauce on top. Cover and cook on low for 6 to 8 hours.
3. During the last hour of cooking, add the vegetables. Cover and continue cooking until the vegetables are crisp-tender. Season with additional salt, as needed. Garnish with the cilantro before serving.

Chicken and Wild Rice Soup

Prep time: 20 minutes | Cook time: 4 to 5 hours | Serves 6 to 8

4 tablespoons (½ stick) unsalted butter

1 medium onion, finely chopped

4 medium carrots, finely chopped

4 medium stalks celery with leaves, finely chopped

1 pound (454 g) cremini mushrooms, cut into ½-inch slices

1 teaspoon dried thyme

1 teaspoon dried sage, crushed

1½ teaspoons salt

1 teaspoon freshly ground black pepper

8 cups chicken broth

3 cups bite-size pieces cooked chicken or turkey, either shredded or diced

2 cups wild rice, rinsed several times with cold water

1 cup heavy cream

1. Heat the butter in a large skillet over medium-high heat.
2. Add the onion, carrots, and celery and sauté until the vegetables are softened, about 3 minutes.
3. Add the mushrooms, thyme, and sage to the pan and season with the salt and pepper.
4. Transfer the contents of the skillet to the crock pot. Stir in the chicken broth, chicken, and wild rice.
5. Cover the crock pot and cook on low for 4 to 5 hours, until the wild rice is tender and the soup is thickened.
6. Stir in the cream, turn the crock pot to warm, and serve the soup.

Cheesy Sausage Lasagna

Prep time: 15 minutes | Cook time: 4 to 5 hours | Serves 6 to 8

8 curly-edged lasagna noodles, broken in half
Salt and ground black pepper, to taste
1 pound (454 g) whole-milk ricotta cheese
1¼ cups Parmesan cheese, grated, divided
½ cup chopped fresh basil
1 large egg
3 cups jarred pasta sauce, divided
1 pound (454 g) hot or sweet Italian sausage, casings removed, divided
4 cups Mozzarella cheese, shredded, divided
Cooking spray

1. Line crock pot with aluminum foil, then press 2 large sheets of foil into crock pot perpendicular to one another, with extra foil hanging over edges. Lightly spritz the prepared crock pot with cooking spray.
2. Bring 4 quarts water to boil in a large pot. Add noodles and 1 tablespoon salt and cook, stirring often, until al dente. Drain noodles, rinse under cold water, then spread out in a single layer over clean dish towels and let dry. (Do not use paper towels, then they will stick to noodles.)
3. Combine ricotta, 1 cup Parmesan, basil, egg, ½ teaspoon salt, and ½ teaspoon pepper in a bowl. Spread ½ cup pasta sauce into the prepared crock pot.
4. Arrange 4 noodle pieces in the crock pot (they may overlap), then dollop 10 rounded tablespoons of ricotta mixture over noodles. Pinch off one-third of sausage into tablespoon-size pieces and scatter over ricotta. Sprinkle with 1 cup Mozzarella, then spoon ½ cup sauce over. Repeat layering of noodles, ricotta mixture, sausage, Mozzarella, and sauce twice more.
5. For the final layer, arrange remaining 4 noodles in the crock pot, then top with remaining 1 cup sauce and sprinkle with remaining 1 cup Mozzarella and remaining ¼ cup Parmesan. Cover and cook until lasagna is heated through, 4 to 5 hours on low.
6. Let lasagna cool for 20 minutes. Serve warm.

Super Bean Soup

Prep time: 20 minutes | Cook time: 7 hours | Serves 8 to 10

¼ cup dried red beans
¼ cup dried small white beans
¼ cup dried pinto beans
¼ cup dried kidney beans
¼ cup dried cranberry beans
¼ cup dried baby lima beans
¼ cup dried black-eyed peas
¼ cup dried yellow split peas
¼ cup dried green split peas
¼ cup dried brown lentils
¼ cup dried red lentils
1 (15-ounce / 425-g) can chopped plum tomatoes, with their juice
1 smoked ham hock or ham bone
3 medium carrots, chopped
3 stalks celery, finely chopped
1 large onion, finely chopped
8 cups chicken or vegetable broth
2 teaspoons dried thyme
1 bay leaf
Salt and freshly ground black pepper, to taste

1. Soak the red, white, pinto, kidney, cranberry, lima beans, and black-eyed peas overnight in water to cover. Drain and rinse thoroughly.
2. Add the soaked beans, split peas, and lentils to the crock pot. Add the remaining ingredients and stir to combine.
3. Cook on low for 8 to 10 hours, until the beans are tender and the ham is falling off the bone.
4. Remove the ham hock or bone from the soup, chop any meat, removing the fat, and return the meat to the crock pot.
5. Season with salt and pepper. Remove the bay leaf before serving.

Chicken and Carrot Fricassee

Prep time: 15 minutes | Cook time: 6 to 8 hours | Serves 6

3½ pounds (1.6 kg) chicken drumsticks and thighs, skinned
4 medium carrots, cut into matchsticks (about 2 cups)
1 small onion, diced
2 garlic cloves, minced
1½ cups chicken stock
½ cup dry white wine
¼ cup heavy (whipping) cream
1 teaspoon poultry seasoning
½ teaspoon kosher salt, plus more for seasoning
½ teaspoon freshly ground black pepper
2 tablespoons all-purpose flour
2 tablespoons freshly squeezed lemon juice
3 tablespoons chopped fresh tarragon leaves, for garnish

1. Put the chicken in the crock pot, along with the carrots, onion, garlic, chicken stock, wine, heavy cream, poultry seasoning, salt, and pepper. Stir to combine. Cover and cook on low for 6 to 8 hours.
2. About 30 minutes before serving, spoon out ¼ cup of cooking liquid from the crock pot and whisk it in a small bowl with the flour.
3. Pour the mixture back into the crock pot, add the lemon juice, and whisk to combine. Cover and continue cooking until the sauce is slightly thickened.
4. Season with additional salt, as needed. Serve garnished with the tarragon.

Chapter 6 Soups, Stews, and Chilies

Cream of Zucchini Soup

Prep time: 10 minutes | Cook time: 6 to 7 hours | Serves 4

6 tablespoons (¾ stick) unsalted butter, cut into 3 or 4 pieces
1 large yellow onion, chopped
½ teaspoon curry powder
1½ pounds (680 g) zucchini, ends trimmed, and cut into chunks
2 heaping tablespoons white basmati rice or long-grain white rice
1 tablespoon chopped fresh basil
3 cups chicken or vegetable broth
Salt and freshly ground black pepper, to taste
1 cup half-and-half
Croutons, for serving (optional)

1. Put the butter, onion, curry powder, and zucchini in the crock pot, cover, and cook on high to sweat the vegetables for 30 minutes.
2. Add the rice, basil, and broth, cover, and cook on low for 5 to 6 hours.
3. Purée with a handheld immersion blender or transfer to a food processor or blender and purée in batches. Season with salt and pepper. Stir in the half-and-half, cover, and continue to cook on low until heated through, 20 minutes; do not boil.
4. Ladle the hot soup into bowls and garnish with croutons, if desired.

Nutmeg Carrot Soup

Prep time: 15 minutes | Cook time: 6 to 8 hours | Serves 8

¼ cup olive oil
2 medium-size yellow onions, chopped
2 large russet potatoes, peeled and chopped
3 pounds (1.4 kg) carrots (about 15 medium-size), scrubbed, tops cut off, and chopped
1 or 2 small cloves garlic, pressed
½ teaspoon each dried thyme and marjoram
4 to 6 cups water or chicken broth, plus more as needed
2 heaping tablespoons honey
½ to 1 teaspoon freshly grated nutmeg, to your taste
Sea salt and freshly ground black pepper, to taste

1. Heat the oil in a large skillet over medium heat. Add the onions and cook until softened, 6 to 8 minutes, stirring often to cook evenly.
2. Put the potatoes, carrots, garlic, and herbs in the crock pot; add the onions and oil, scraping them out of the pan. Add enough of the water to cover everything. Cover and cook on high for 1 hour.
3. Turn the crock pot to low and cook until the vegetables are soft, 5 to 7 hours. Purée in batches in a food processor or right in the crock pot with a handheld immersion blender; the soup will be nice and thick. Stir in the honey and grate the nutmeg right over the crock. Season with salt and pepper. Keep warm on low without letting it come to a boil until serving. Ladle the hot soup into bowls and enjoy.

Beef Alphabet Soup

Prep time: 10 minutes | Cook time: 6½ to 8½ hours | Serves 5 to 6

½ pound (227 g) beef stewing meat or round steak, cubed
1 (14½-ounce / 411-g) can stewed tomatoes
1 (8-ounce / 227-g) can tomato sauce
1 cup water
1 envelope dry onion soup mix
1 (10-ounce / 283-g) package frozen vegetables, partially thawed
½ cup alphabet noodles, uncooked

1. Combine meat, tomatoes, tomato sauce, water, and soup mix in a crock pot.
2. Cover. Cook on low 6 to 8 hours. Turn to high.
3. Stir in vegetables and noodles. Add more water if mixture is too dry and thick.
4. Cover. Cook on high 30 minutes, or until vegetables are tender.

Ham and Vegetable Soup

Prep time: 10 minutes | Cook time: 9 to 10 hours | Serves 12

4 medium carrots, thinly sliced
2 celery ribs, chopped
1 medium onion, chopped
2 cups fully cooked ham cubes, trimmed of fat
1½ cups dried navy beans
1 (68-ounce / 1.9-kg) package dry vegetable soup mix
1 envelope dry onion soup mix
1 bay leaf
½ teaspoon black pepper
8 cups water
1 teaspoon salt (optional)

1. Combine all the ingredients in a crock pot.
2. Cover. Cook on low for 9 to 10 hours.
3. Discard the bay leaf before serving.

Mushroom and Bacon Soup

Prep time: 10 minutes | Cook time: 3 hours | Serves 8

8 strips bacon, cut into ½-inch dice
1 large onion, finely chopped
1 teaspoon dried sage leaves, crushed
1 pound (454 g) cremini mushrooms, sliced
1 pound (454 g) shiitake mushrooms, stems removed, and caps sliced
1 ounce (28 g) dried porcini mushrooms
¼ cup soy sauce
3 cups chicken broth
1 cup heavy cream
½ cup snipped fresh chives, for garnish

1. Sauté the bacon in a large skillet over medium heat until crisp and remove it from the pan to drain.
2. Add the onion and sage to the pan and sauté until the onion is softened. Add the cremini and shiitake mushrooms and toss until the mixture is combined.
3. Transfer the contents of the skillet to the insert of a crock pot. Add the porcini mushrooms, soy sauce, broth, and bacon.
4. Cover and cook on high for 3 hours or on low for 5 to 6 hours. At the end of the cooking time, add the cream and stir to combine.
5. Serve the soup garnished with the chives.

Italian Beef Minestrone

Prep time: 15 minutes | Cook time: 6 hours | Serves 12

1 pound (454 g) extra-lean ground beef
1 large onion, chopped
1 clove garlic, minced
2 (15½-ounce / 439-g) cans low-sodium stewed tomatoes
1 (15-ounce / 425-g) can kidney beans, drained
1 (10-ounce / 283-g) package frozen corn
2 ribs celery, sliced
2 small zucchini, sliced
1 cup macaroni, uncooked
2½ cups hot water
2 beef bouillon cubes
½ teaspoon salt
2 teaspoons Italian seasoning

1. Brown ground beef in nonstick skillet.
2. Combine browned ground beef, onion, garlic, stewed tomatoes, kidney beans, corn, celery, zucchini, and macaroni in a crock pot.
3. Dissolve bouillon cubes in hot water. Combine with salt and Italian seasoning. Add to a crock pot.
4. Cover. Cook on low 6 hours.

Ground Beef Macaroni Soup

Prep time: 10 minutes | Cook time: 6¼ to 8¼ hours | Serves 6

1 pound (454 g) extra-lean ground beef
¼ teaspoon black pepper
¼ teaspoon dried oregano
¼ teaspoon seasoned salt
1 envelope dry onion soup mix
3 cups hot water
1 (8-ounce / 227-g) can tomato sauce
1 tablespoon low-sodium soy sauce
1 cup carrots, sliced
1 cup celery, sliced
1 cup macaroni, cooked
¼ cup grated Parmesan cheese

1. Combine all ingredients except macaroni and Parmesan cheese in a crock pot.
2. Cook on low 6 to 8 hours.
3. Turn to high. Add macaroni and Parmesan cheese.
4. Cook for another 15 to 20 minutes.

Thyme Onion Soup

Prep time: 10 minutes | Cook time: 7½ to 8½ hours | Serves 8

½ cup (1 stick) unsalted butter
2 tablespoons olive oil
5 large sweet onions, such as Vidalia, thinly sliced
2 tablespoons sugar
1 tablespoons dried thyme
1 teaspoon salt
½ teaspoon freshly ground black pepper
1 bay leaf
½ cup white wine
5 cups beef stock
1½ cups finely shredded Gruyère cheese, for garnish

1. Turn a crock pot on high, add the butter and oil to the insert, cover until the butter is melted.
2. Remove the cover and add the onions, sugar, thyme, salt, pepper, and bay leaf. Stir the onions until they are coated with the butter and seasonings.
3. Cover and cook on high for 7 to 8 hours, until they are caramelized to a deep golden brown.
4. Remove the cover and add the wine and beef stock. Cover and cook the soup on high for an additional 30 minutes or on low for an additional 1 hour.
5. Remove the bay leaf before serving and garnish each serving with a sprinkling of Gruyère cheese.

Butternut Squash Soup with Thyme

Prep time: 10 minutes | Cook time: 3 hours | Serves 8

4 tablespoons (½ stick) unsalted butter
1 cup finely chopped sweet onion
½ cup finely chopped carrot
½ cup finely chopped celery
2 teaspoons dried thyme
8 cups 1-inch pieces peeled and deseeded butternut squash
4 cups chicken or vegetable broth
Salt and freshly ground black pepper, to taste

1. Melt the butter in a large skillet over medium-high heat. Add the onion, carrot, celery, and thyme and sauté until the vegetables are softened, 3 to 4 minutes.
2. Transfer the contents of the skillet to the insert of a crock pot. Add the squash and broth, and season with salt and pepper.
3. Cover the crock pot and cook on high for 3 hours or on low for 6 hours. At the end of the cooking time, stir the soup and season with salt and pepper. If you would like to purée the soup, use an immersion blender, or cool the soup and purée it in a blender.
4. Serve warm from the crock pot.

Creamy Cheddar Potato Soup

Prep time: 15 minutes | Cook time: 3 hours | Serves 8 to 10

4 tablespoons (½ stick) unsalted butter
2 medium leeks, finely chopped, using the white and some of the tender green parts
4 large russet potatoes, peeled and cut into ½-inch dice
4 cups chicken broth
1 cup whole milk
2 cups finely shredded sharp Cheddar cheese
6 green onions, finely chopped, using the white and some of the tender green parts
8 strips bacon, cooked crisp, drained, and crumbled
Salt and freshly ground black pepper, to taste
1 cup sour cream, for garnish

1. Heat the butter in a large skillet over medium-high heat. Add the leeks and sauté until softened, 2 to 3 minutes. Transfer the leeks to the insert of a crock pot and add the potatoes and broth. Cover the crock pot and cook on high for 3 hours or on low for 5 to 6 hours, until the potatoes are tender. Using an immersion blender, purée the soup, or cool the soup and purée it in a blender.
2. Reduce the heat to low and add the milk, cheese, green onions, and bacon. Cover the crock pot and cook for an additional 1 hour. Season with salt and pepper.
3. Serve the soup garnished with a dollop of sour cream.

Garbanzo Bean Soup

Prep time: 15 minutes | Cook time: 6 hours | Serves 8

3 tablespoons olive oil
1 large sweet onion, such as Vidalia, finely chopped
3 stalks celery, finely chopped
2 carrots, finely chopped
3 cloves garlic, finely chopped
2 tablespoons finely chopped fresh rosemary
1 (14- to 15-ounce / 397- to 425-g) can crushed tomatoes, with their juice
4 cups vegetable broth
2 (14- to 15-ounce / 397- to 425-g) cans garbanzo beans, drained and rinsed
2 cups cooked small pasta, such as ditalini or tubetti
½ cup freshly grated Pecorino-Romano cheese, for garnish

1. Heat the oil in a skillet over medium-high heat. Add the onion, celery, carrots, garlic, and rosemary and sauté until the vegetables begin to soften and are fragrant, 3 to 4 minutes.
2. Add the tomatoes and sauté for another minute to incorporate. Transfer the contents of the skillet to the insert of a crock pot and add the broth and garbanzo beans.
3. Cover and cook on low for 6 hours or on high for 3 hours. Remove the cover, stir in the pasta, and cook for an additional 20 minutes on low or 10 minutes on high.
4. Serve the soup garnished with the cheese.

Rosemary White Bean Soup

Prep time: 15 minutes | Cook time: 8 to 9 hours | Serves 8

3 tablespoons extra-virgin olive oil
4 ounces (113 g) spicy Italian ham or Capicola, cut into ½-inch dice
1 medium onion, finely chopped
2 cloves garlic, minced
3 stalks celery with leaves, finely chopped
3 medium carrots, finely chopped
2 teaspoons finely minced fresh rosemary
1 (14- to 15-ounce / 397- to 425-g) can plum tomatoes, crushed and drained
2 cups dried beans, picked over for stones, soaked, or 2 (14- to 15-ounce / 397- to 425-g) cans small white beans, drained and rinsed
6 cups chicken or vegetable broth
Salt and freshly ground black pepper, to taste

1. Heat the oil in a skillet over medium-high heat.
2. Add the ham and sauté until it begins to get crisp, about 3 minutes. Add the onion, garlic, celery, carrots, and rosemary and sauté until the vegetables begin to soften, about 3 minutes. Add the tomatoes and stir to combine.
3. Transfer the contents of the skillet to the insert of a crock pot. Stir in the beans and the broth.
4. Cover the crock pot and cook on low for 8 to 9 hours, until the beans are tender. Season with salt and pepper before serving.

Pork Veggie Soup

Prep time: 20 minutes | Cook time: 7 to 8 hours | Serves 6

1 pork tenderloin (1 pound / 454 g), cut into 1-inch pieces
1 teaspoon garlic powder
2 teaspoons canola oil
1 (28-ounce / 794-g) can diced tomatoes
4 medium carrots, cut into ½-inch pieces
2 medium potatoes, cubed
1 (12-ounce / 340-g) can light or nonalcoholic beer
¼ cup quick-cooking tapioca
2 bay leaves
1 tablespoon Worcestershire sauce
1 tablespoon honey
1 teaspoon dried thyme
¼ teaspoon salt
¼ teaspoon pepper
⅛ teaspoon ground nutmeg

1. Sprinkle the pork with the garlic powder. In a large skillet, brown the pork in the oil for 4 minutes. Drain.
2. Transfer to a crock pot. Add the remaining ingredients. Cover and cook on low for 7 to 8 hours or until meat is tender.
3. Discard the bay leaves. Serve warm.

Red Pear and Pumpkin Soup

Prep time: 10 minutes | Cook time: 3 hours | Serves 8

4 tablespoons (½ stick) unsalted butter
½ cup finely chopped sweet onion
½ cup finely chopped celery
½ cup finely chopped carrot
2 medium red pears, peeled, cored, and finely chopped
½ teaspoon ground ginger
2 (15-ounce / 425-g) cans pumpkin purée
3 cups chicken broth
Salt and freshly ground black pepper, to taste
1 cup heavy cream

1. Melt the butter in a medium skillet over medium-high heat. Add the onion, celery, carrot, pears, and ginger and sauté until the vegetables begin to soften, about 3 minutes. Transfer the contents of the skillet to the insert of a crock pot.
2. Stir in the pumpkin and broth. Cover and cook on high for 3 hours or on low for 5 to 6 hours.
3. Season with salt and pepper. Stir in the cream, cover, and leave on warm for 30 minutes before serving.

Creamy Carrot and Broccoli Soup

Prep time: 15 minutes | Cook time: 2½ to 3 hours | Serves 6 to 8

2 tablespoons unsalted butter
1 medium onion, finely chopped
3 medium carrots, cut into ½-inch dice
2 bunches broccoli (about 1½ pounds / 680 g), stems trimmed and cut into florets
1 teaspoon baking soda
3 cups chicken or vegetable broth
Salt and freshly ground black pepper, to taste
1 cup heavy cream

1. Turn a crock pot on high, add the butter to the insert, and cover until the butter is melted. Add the onion, carrots, and broccoli and toss the vegetables in the butter. Dissolve the baking soda in the broth and add to the vegetables.
2. Cook on high for 2½ to 3 hours or on low for 5 to 6 hours.
3. Season with salt and pepper and stir in the cream. Turn off the crock pot and let the soup rest for 15 minutes to come to serving temperature.

Sausage Cabbage Soup

Prep time: 10 minutes | Cook time: 5¼ to 6¼ hours | Serves 8

4 cups low-fat, low-sodium chicken broth
1 medium head of cabbage, chopped
2 medium onions, chopped
½ pound (227 g) fully cooked smoked turkey sausage, halved lengthwise and sliced
½ cup all-purpose flour
¼ teaspoon black pepper
1 cup skim milk

1. Combine the chicken broth, cabbage, onions, and sausage in a crock pot.
2. Cover. Cook on high for 5 to 6 hours, or until the cabbage is tender.
3. Mix the flour and black pepper in a bowl. Gradually add the milk, stirring until smooth.
4. Gradually stir the milk mixture into the hot soup.
5. Cook, stirring occasionally for about 15 minutes, until soup is thickened. Serve.

Leek and Potato Soup

Prep time: 10 minutes | Cook time: 3 hours | Serves 8 to 10

4 tablespoons (½ stick) unsalted butter
4 leeks, finely chopped, using the white and a bit of the tender green parts
4 large russet potatoes, peeled and cut into 1-inch chunks
3 cups chicken broth
Salt and freshly ground black pepper, to taste
1 cup heavy cream
½ cup snipped fresh chives, for garnish

1. Turn a crock pot on high, add the butter to the insert, and cover until the butter is melted. Add the leeks and toss with the butter. Add the potatoes and broth. Cover the crock pot and cook the soup on high for 3 hours or on low for 5 to 6 hours, until the potatoes are tender.
2. Purée the soup with an immersion blender, or mash with a potato masher. Season with salt and pepper. Stir in the cream and turn off the crock pot. Cool the soup, then refrigerate until chilled.
3. Serve the soup in chilled bowls and garnish with the chives.

Classic Gyro Soup

Prep time: 10 minutes | Cook time: 6 to 8 hours | Serves 6

2 pounds (907 g) ground lamb
2 tablespoons extra-virgin olive oil
5 cups water
1 (14½-ounce / 411-g) can diced tomatoes, undrained
1 medium onion, chopped
¼ cup red wine
3 tablespoons minced fresh mint or 1 tablespoon dried mint
6 garlic cloves, minced
1 tablespoon dried marjoram
1 tablespoon crushed dried rosemary
2 teaspoons salt
½ teaspoon pepper
Optional Toppings:
Plain Greek yogurt
Crumbled feta cheese

1. In a large skillet, cook the lamb in the oil for 4 minutes, or until no longer pink. Drain. Transfer to a crock pot. Add the water, tomatoes, onion, wine, mint, garlic, marjoram, rosemary, salt and pepper. Cover and cook on low for 6 to 8 hours or until flavors are blended.
2. Serve with the yogurt and feta cheese, if desired.

Mushroom Tofu Soup

Prep time: 10 minutes | Cook time: 2½ to 3 hours | Serves 6 to 8

2 tablespoons vegetable oil
1 clove garlic, minced
1 teaspoon freshly grated ginger
8 ounces (227 g) shiitake mushrooms, stems removed, caps sliced
4 small baby bok choy, stem ends removed and chopped into ½-inch pieces
¼ cup light miso paste
6 cups vegetable or chicken broth
2 teaspoons soy sauce
6 green onions, white and tender green parts only, finely chopped
1 pound (454 g) firm tofu, drained and cut into ½-inch cubes

1. Heat the oil in a medium skillet over medium-high heat.
2. Add the garlic and ginger and sauté for about 1 minute until fragrant. Add the mushrooms and toss to combine.
3. Transfer the contents of the skillet to the insert of a crock pot and add the bok choy. Stir in the miso paste, broth, and soy sauce.
4. Cover the crock pot and cook on high for 2½ to 3 hours.
5. Remove the cover and stir in the green onions and tofu.
6. Serve the soup from the crock pot.

Vegetable Beef Soup

Prep time: 15 minutes | Cook time: 5¾ to 6¾ hours | Serves 6 to 8

1½ pounds (680 g) beef sirloin, cut into ½-inch pieces
1½ teaspoons salt
½ teaspoon freshly ground black pepper
2 tablespoons vegetable oil
1 medium onion, finely chopped
3 medium carrots, finely chopped
1 (15-ounce / 425-g) can tomato sauce
3 cups beef broth
2 cups chicken broth
4 ounces (113 g) green beans, ends snipped, cut into 1-inch lengths
2 cups frozen petite peas, thawed
2 cups frozen corn, thawed
2 cups cooked alphabet noodles or other small pasta shapes

1. Sprinkle the beef with the salt and pepper. Heat the oil in a large skillet over high heat. Add the beef a few pieces at a time and brown on all sides for 4 minutes.
2. Transfer the browned beef to the insert of a crock pot. Add the onion and carrots to the same skillet and sauté until the onion is softened, for about 3 minutes.
3. Transfer the contents of the skillet to the crock pot insert and add the tomato sauce, beef broth, chicken broth, and green beans. Cover and cook on low for 5 to 6 hours. Remove the cover and add the peas, corn, and noodles.
4. Cover and cook for an additional 45 minutes before serving.

Spanish Beef and Rice Soup

Prep time: 10 minutes | Cook time: 4 to 5 hours | Serves 8

1 pound (454 g) lean ground beef (90% lean)
1 medium onion, chopped
3 cups water
1 (16-ounce / 454-g) jar salsa
1 (14½-ounce / 411-g) can diced tomatoes, undrained
1 (7-ounce / 198-g) jar roasted sweet red peppers, drained and chopped
1 (4-ounce / 113-g) can chopped green chilies
1 envelope taco seasoning
1 tablespoon dried cilantro flakes
½ cup uncooked converted rice

1. In a large skillet, cook the beef and onion over medium heat for 4 minutes, or until meat is no longer pink. Drain.
2. Transfer to a crock pot. Add the water, salsa, tomatoes, red peppers, chilies, taco seasoning and cilantro. Stir in the rice. Cover and cook on low for 4 to 5 hours or until rice is tender.
3. Serve warm.

Beef and Parsnip Soup

Prep time: 15 minutes | Cook time: 4 to 5 hours | Serves 8

2 tablespoons olive oil
¼ cup all-purpose flour
Salt and freshly ground black pepper, to taste
2 pounds (907 g) beef chuck or short ribs, fat trimmed and cut into 1-inch pieces
2 medium onions, coarsely chopped
3 cloves garlic, sliced
1 teaspoon dried thyme
1 (12-ounce / 340-g) bottle dark ale
3 cups beef broth
4 cups baby carrots
4 medium parsnips, cut into 1-inch lengths
2 cups red, Yukon gold, or new white potatoes

1. Heat the oil in a large skillet over high heat. Combine the flour, 1½ teaspoons salt and ½ teaspoon pepper in a zipper top plastic bag. Toss the meat in the flour, a few pieces at a time.
2. Add the meat, a few pieces at a time, to the oil and brown on all sides for 4 minutes. Transfer the browned meat to the insert of a crock pot.
3. When all the beef is browned, add the onions, garlic, and thyme to the same skillet over medium-high heat and sauté for 3 minutes, or until the onions begin to soften and become translucent. Add the ale to the pan and scrape up any browned bits from the bottom of the pan.
4. Transfer the contents of the skillet to the crock pot insert and add the broth, carrots, parsnips, and potatoes. Cover the crock pot and cook on high for 4 to 5 hours or on low for 8 to 10 hours, until the vegetables are tender and the beef is fork tender.
5. Season with salt and pepper before serving.

Red Pepper and Lentil Soup

Prep time: 10 minutes | Cook time: 7 to 9 hours | Serves 4 to 6

2 tablespoons extra-virgin olive oil, divided
1 small onion, finely chopped
4 to 6 cloves garlic, finely chopped
1 teaspoon sweet paprika or smoked paprika
1 large or 2 medium-size red bell peppers, deseeded and finely chopped
1 cup dried brown lentils, picked over and rinsed
5 cups water
2 teaspoons salt
½ teaspoon freshly ground black pepper
1 to 2 tablespoons sherry vinegar or red or white wine vinegar

1. In a medium-size skillet, heat 1 tablespoon of the oil over medium heat. Add the onion and garlic and cook, stirring a few times, until they begin to soften, for about 3 minutes. Reduce the heat if they begin to brown.
2. Stir in the paprika and allow it to cook for about a minute more. Add the bell pepper and cook for 2 to 3 minutes, stirring a few times, until it just begins to soften. Use a heat-resistant rubber spatula to scrape the vegetables and oil into a crock pot. Add the lentils and water and stir to combine. Cover and cook on low until the lentils are completely soft, for 7 to 9 hours.
3. Season the soup with the salt and pepper and the remaining 1 tablespoon of olive oil. Stir in 1 tablespoon of the vinegar, adding more if needed. Serve hot ladled into soup bowls.

Chapter 6 Soups, Stews, and Chilies | 47

Kale and White Bean Soup

Prep time: 20 minutes | Cook time: 5½ to 7½ hours | Serves 4 to 6

3 (14-ounce / 397-g) cans vegetable broth
1 (15-ounce / 425-g) can tomato purée
1 (15-ounce / 425-g) can white, cannellini, or great northern beans, rinsed and drained
½ cup converted rice
1 medium-size yellow onion, chopped
2 cloves garlic, minced
2 teaspoons dried basil
Salt and freshly ground black pepper, to taste
1 pound (454 g) kale, stems removed and leaves coarsely cut on the diagonal into wide ribbons and coarsely chopped
1 pound (454 g) sweet Italian sausage, cooked, cooled, and thickly sliced (optional)
For Serving:
Finely shredded Parmesan cheese
Extra-virgin olive oil

1. Combine the broth, tomato purée, beans, rice, onion, garlic, and basil in a crock pot. Season with salt and pepper, and stir to blend. Cover and cook on low for 5 to 7 hours.
2. Stir in the kale and sausage (if using), cover, and continue to cook on low for another 20 to 30 minutes, or until the kale is limp and tender.
3. Ladle the soup into bowls and serve hot with the Parmesan cheese and a drizzle of olive oil.

Authentic Zuppa Bastarda

Prep time: 10 minutes | Cook time: 7 to 9 hours | Serves 8

1 pound (454 g) dried borlotti beans, picked over, soaked overnight in cold water to cover, and drained
1 large white onion, coarsely chopped
3 cloves garlic, minced
2 tablespoons finely chopped fresh sage, plus a few whole leaves
Salt and freshly ground black pepper, to taste
8 thin slices stale or toasted chewy whole grain country bread
For Serving:
Extra-virgin olive oil
Shredded or shaved Parmesan or Asiago cheese

1. Put the drained beans in a crock pot and add the water to cover by 4 inches. Add the onion and garlic. Cover and cook on low for 5 to 7 hours.
2. Stir in the sage, cover, and continue to cook on low for another 2 hours, until the beans are tender.
3. Season with salt and pepper. The soup will be very thick. Place a toasted slice of bread in each of 8 shallow soup bowls and drizzle liberally with the olive oil. Ladle the soup over the bread, sprinkle with the Parmesan cheese. Serve hot.

Beef and Pumpkin Stew

Prep time: 25 minutes | Cook time: 6½ to 8½ hours | Serves 6

1 tablespoon canola oil
1 beef top round steak (1½ pounds / 680 g), cut into 1-inch cubes
1½ cups cubed peeled pie pumpkin or sweet potatoes
3 small red potatoes, peeled and cubed
1 cup cubed acorn squash
1 medium onion, chopped
2 (14½-ounce / 411-g) cans reduced-sodium beef broth
1 (14½-ounce / 411-g) can diced tomatoes, undrained
2 bay leaves
2 garlic cloves, minced
2 teaspoons reduced-sodium beef bouillon granules
½ teaspoon chili powder
½ teaspoon pepper
¼ teaspoon ground allspice
¼ teaspoon ground cloves
¼ cup water
3 tablespoons all-purpose flour

1. In a large skillet, heat oil over medium-high heat. Brown beef in batches; remove with a slotted spoon to a crock pot. Add the pumpkin, potatoes, squash and onion. Stir in the broth, tomatoes and seasonings. Cover and cook on low for 6 to 8 hours or until meat is tender.
2. Remove bay leaves. In a small bowl, mix water and flour until smooth; gradually stir into stew. Cover and cook on high for 30 minutes or until liquid is thickened.

Sausage and Kale Soup

Prep time: 10 minutes | Cook time: 5 to 6 hours | Serves 8

2 tablespoons olive oil
1 pound (454 g) smoked linguiça, chorizo, or andouille sausage, cut into ½-inch rounds
2 medium onions, finely chopped
4 medium carrots, finely chopped
1 pound (454 g) kale, chopped into 1-inch pieces
5 medium red potatoes, peeled (or unpeeled) and cut into ½-inch pieces
6 cups chicken broth
2 bay leaves
¼ cup finely chopped fresh cilantro

1. Heat the oil in a large skillet over high heat. Add the sausage, onions, and carrots and sauté for 4 minutes, or until the onions are translucent.
2. Transfer the contents of the skillet to the insert of a crock pot. Add the kale, potatoes, broth, and bay leaves to the crock pot and stir to combine. Cover and cook on low for 5 to 6 hours, until the potatoes are tender.
3. Remove the bay leaves and stir in the cilantro before serving.

Leek and Potato Soup

Prep time: 10 minutes | Cook time: 5 to 7 hours | Serves 6

4 medium-size leeks (white part only), washed well and thinly sliced
4 medium-size to large russet potatoes, peeled and diced
4 to 6 cups water or vegetable or chicken broth
Salt, to taste
2 tablespoons unsalted butter
French bread, for serving

1. Put the leeks and potatoes in a crock pot. Add enough of the water or broth to just cover them. Cover and cook on low, until the potatoes are tender, for 5 to 7 hours.
2. Purée the soup with a handheld immersion blender or transfer to a food processor or blender and purée in batches. Add the salt and butter, swirling until it is melted. Ladle the hot soup into bowls and serve immediately with French bread.

Onion and Tomato Soup

Prep time: 10 minutes | Cook time: 5 to 6 hours | Serves 4

½ cup unsalted butter
1 large or 2 medium-size yellow onions, chopped
1 (28-ounce / 794-g) can imported Italian whole or chopped plum tomatoes, with their juice
½ cup dry vermouth or dry white wine
1 tablespoon sugar
1 heaping teaspoon dried tarragon
Sea salt, to taste
Cold sour cream, for serving

1. In a large skillet over medium heat, melt the butter. Add the onion and cook until golden, for about 15 minutes, stirring often to cook evenly.
2. Combine the tomatoes, vermouth, sugar, and tarragon in a crock pot. Add the onion and butter, scraping out the pan. Cover and cook on low for 5 to 6 hours.
3. Purée in batches in a food processor or with a handheld immersion blender. Season with salt. Ladle the hot soup into bowls and top with a spoonful of cold sour cream.

Tangy Carrot Bisque

Prep time: 10 minutes | Cook time: 8 hours | Serves 2

½ cup diced onion
¼ cup diced celery
1 tablespoon minced ginger
2 cups low-sodium chicken broth
2 cups diced carrots
1 white potato, peeled and diced
1 teaspoon curry powder
⅛ teaspoon sea salt
1 tablespoon freshly squeezed lime juice
2 tablespoons heavy cream (optional)
¼ cup roughly chopped fresh cilantro

1. Put the onion, celery, ginger, broth, carrots, potato, curry powder, and salt in a crock pot and stir to combine. Cover and cook on low for 8 hours.
2. Add the lime juice to the crock pot and purée the bisque with an immersion blender.
3. Swirl in the heavy cream (if using) just before serving. Garnish each bowl with the cilantro and serve.

Pork and Butternut Squash Stew

Prep time: 20 minutes | Cook time: 8½ to 10½ hours | Serves 6

1⅓ cup plus 1 tablespoon all-purpose flour, divided
1 tablespoon paprika
1 teaspoon salt
1 teaspoon ground coriander
1½ pounds (680 g) boneless pork shoulder butt roast, cut into 1-inch cubes
1 tablespoon canola oil
2¾ cups cubed peeled butternut squash
1 (14½-ounce / 411-g) can diced tomatoes, undrained
1 cup frozen corn, thawed
1 medium onion, chopped
2 tablespoons cider vinegar
1 bay leaf
2½ cups reduced-sodium chicken broth
1²⁄₃ cups frozen shelled edamame, thawed

1. In a large resealable plastic bag, combine 1⅓ cup flour, paprika, salt and coriander. Add pork, a few pieces at a time, and shake to coat.
2. In a large skillet, brown pork in oil in batches; drain. Transfer to a crock pot. Add squash, tomatoes, corn, onion, vinegar and bay leaf. In a small bowl, combine broth and the remaining flour until smooth; stir into crock pot.
3. Cover and cook on low for 8 t0 10 hours or until pork and vegetables are tender. Stir in edamame; cover and cook 30 minutes longer. Discard the bay leaf.

Vegetable and Black-Eyed Pea Chili

Prep time: 20 minutes | Cook time: 6 to 8 hours | Serves 4 to 6

1 cup finely chopped onions
1 cup finely chopped carrots
1 cup finely chopped red or green pepper, or mixture of two
1 garlic clove, minced
4 teaspoons chili powder
1 teaspoon ground cumin
2 tablespoons chopped cilantro
1 (14½-ounce / 411-g) can diced tomatoes
3 cups black-eyed peas, cooked or 2 (15-ounce / 425-g) cans black-eyed peas, drained
1 (4-ounce / 113-g) can chopped green chilies
¾ cup orange juice
¾ cup water or broth
1 tablespoon cornstarch
2 tablespoons water
½ cup shredded Cheddar cheese
2 tablespoons chopped cilantro

1. Combine all ingredients except cornstarch, 2 tablespoons water, cheese, and cilantro.
2. Cover. Cook on low 6 to 8 hours, or high 4 hours.
3. Dissolve cornstarch in water. Stir into soup mixture 30 minutes before serving.
4. Garnish individual servings with cheese and cilantro.

Corn and Beef Chili

Prep time: 15 minutes | Cook time: 5 to 6 hours | Serves 4 to 6

1 pound (454 g) ground beef
½ cup chopped onions
½ cup chopped green peppers
½ teaspoon salt
⅛ teaspoon pepper
¼ teaspoon dried thyme
1 (14½-ounce / 411-g) can diced tomatoes with Italian herbs
1 (6-ounce / 170-g) can tomato paste, diluted with 1 can water
2 cups frozen whole-kernel corn
1 (16-ounce / 454-g) can kidney beans
1 tablespoon chili powder
Sour cream, for serving
Shredded cheese, for serving

1. Sauté ground beef, onions, and green peppers in a deep saucepan. Drain and season with salt, pepper, and thyme.
2. Stir in tomatoes, tomato paste, and corn.
3. Heat until corn is thawed. Add kidney beans and chili powder. Pour into a crock pot. Cover. Cook on low 5 to 6 hours.
4. Top individual servings with dollops of sour cream, or sprinkle with shredded cheese.

Creamy Butternut Squash Soup

Prep time: 10 minutes | Cook time: 8 hours | Serves 2

2 cups peeled, diced butternut squash
1 cup peeled, diced parsnip
1 Granny Smith apple, cored, peeled, and diced
½ cup diced onion
⅛ teaspoon sea salt
2 cups low-sodium vegetable broth
1 sprig fresh thyme
1 tablespoon heavy cream

1. Put the butternut squash, parsnip, apple, onion, salt, vegetable broth, and thyme into a crock pot and stir to combine.
2. Cover and cook on low for 8 hours. Remove the thyme sprig and stir in the heavy cream.
3. Use an immersion blender to purée the soup until smooth.

Curried Vegetable Soup

Prep time: 10 minutes | Cook time: 6 to 8 hours | Serves 2

1 small eggplant, cut into 1-inch cubes
1 teaspoon sea salt
1 cup quartered button mushrooms
1 onion, halved and sliced into thick half-circles
1 red bell pepper, cut into long strips
1 cup coconut milk
2 cups low-sodium chicken broth
1 tablespoon Thai red curry paste
1 tablespoon freshly squeezed lime juice
¼ cup fresh cilantro, for garnish

1. Put the eggplant in a colander over the sink. Sprinkle it with the salt and allow it to rest for 10 minutes, or up to 30 minutes.
2. Put the mushrooms, onion, red bell pepper, coconut milk, broth, and red curry paste into a crock pot.
3. Rinse the eggplant in the colander and gently press to squeeze out any excess moisture from each cube. Add the eggplant to the crock pot. Stir the ingredients to combine.
4. Cover and cook on low for 6 to 8 hours.
5. Just before serving, stir in the lime juice and garnish each serving with the cilantro.

Beef and Barley Soup

Prep time: 10 minutes | Cook time: 8 hours | Serves 2

8 ounces (227 g) beef stew meat, trimmed of fat and cut into 1-inch cubes
¼ cup pearl barley
1 cup diced onion
1 cup diced carrot
1 teaspoon fresh thyme
½ teaspoon dried oregano
2 cups low-sodium beef stock
⅛ teaspoon sea salt

1. Put all the ingredients in a crock pot and stir to combine.
2. Cover and cook on low for 8 hours. The meat should be tender and the barley soft.
3. Serve hot.

Black Bean and Turkey Sausage Stew

Prep time: 20 minutes | Cook time: 5½ to 7½ hours | Serves 6

3 (15-ounce / 425-g) cans black beans, drained and rinsed
1 (14½-ounce / 411-g) can fat-free, reduced-sodium chicken broth
1 cup celery, sliced
2 (4-ounce / 113-g) cans green chilies, chopped
3 cloves garlic, minced
1½ teaspoons dried oregano
¾ teaspoon ground coriander
½ teaspoon ground cumin
¼ teaspoon ground red pepper (not cayenne)
1 pound (454 g) link turkey sausage, thinly sliced and cooked

1. Combine all ingredients in a crock pot except sausage.
2. Cover. Cook on low 5 to 7 hours.
3. Remove 1½ cups of the bean mixture and purée in blender. Return to crock pot.
4. Add sliced sausage.
5. Cover. Cook on low 30 minutes.

Turkey Sausage and Navy Bean Stew

Prep time: 20 minutes | Cook time: 8 to 9 hours | Serves 6

½ pound (227 g) turkey sausage, removed from casing
1 large onion, chopped
2 garlic cloves, minced
¾ cup chopped carrots
1 fennel bulb, chopped
½ cup chopped celery
1 (10¾-ounce / 305-g) can fat-free, reduced-sodium chicken broth
3 medium tomatoes, peeled, deseeded, and chopped
1 teaspoon dried basil
1 teaspoon dried oregano
¼ teaspoon salt
1 cup shell pasta, uncooked
1 (15-ounce / 425-g) can navy beans, drained and rinsed
½ cup low-fat Parmesan cheese

1. In the nonstick skillet, brown turkey sausage, onion, and garlic. Drain well.
2. Combine all ingredients except cheese in a crock pot.
3. Cook on low 8 to 9 hours.
4. Sprinkle with cheese to serve.

Macaroni Bean Stew

Prep time: 10 minutes | Cook time: 5 to 6 hours | Serves 6

1 cup chopped tomatoes
¾ cup macaroni shells, uncooked
¼ cup chopped onions
¼ cup chopped green bell peppers
1 teaspoon dried basil leaves
1 teaspoon Worcestershire sauce
1 clove garlic, chopped
1 (15-ounce / 425-g) can kidney beans, drained
1 (8-ounce / 227-g) can garbanzo beans, drained
1 (14½-ounce / 411-g) can fat-free chicken broth

1. Combine all ingredients in a crock pot.
2. Cook on low 5 to 6 hours.

Veggie and Brown Rice Stew

Prep time: 15 minutes | Cook time: 9 to 11 hours | Serves 10

5 to 6 potatoes, cubed
3 carrots, cubed
1 onion, chopped
½ cup chopped celery
2 cups canned diced or stewed tomatoes
3 chicken bouillon cubes, dissolved in 3 cups water
1½ teaspoons dried thyme
½ teaspoon dried parsley
½ cup brown rice, uncooked
1 pound (454 g) frozen green beans
1 pound (454 g) frozen corn
1 (15-ounce / 425-g) can butter beans
1 (46-ounce / 1.3-kg) can V8 juice

1. Combine potatoes, carrots, onion, celery, tomatoes, chicken stock, thyme, parsley, and rice in a crock pot.
2. Cover. Cook on high 2 hours. purée one cup of mixture and add back to the crock pot to thicken the soup.
3. Stir in beans, corn, butter beans, and juice.
4. Cover. Cook on high 1 more hour, then reduce to low and cook 6 to 8 more hours.

Fennel and Leek Soup

Prep time: 10 minutes | Cook time: 8 hours | Serves 2

1 teaspoon freshly ground fennel seed
1 fennel bulb, cored and chopped
1 leek, white and pale green parts only, sliced thin
1 white potato, peeled and diced
⅛ teaspoon sea salt
2 cups low-sodium chicken broth
1 teaspoon white wine vinegar or lemon juice
2 tablespoons heavy cream
1 sprig fresh tarragon, roughly chopped (optional)

1. Put the fennel seed, fennel bulb, leek, potato, salt, and broth in a crock pot and stir to combine. Cover and cook on low for 8 hours.
2. Just before serving, add the vinegar to the crock and then purée the soup with an immersion blender. Stir in the heavy cream.
3. Serve garnished with fresh tarragon (if using).

Vegetable and Rice Stew

Prep time: 20 minutes | Cook time: 8 to 9 hours | Serves 12

1 pound (454 g) dry beans, assorted
2 cups fat-free vegetable broth
½ cup white wine
1⅓ cup soy sauce
1⅓ cup unsweetened apple or pineapple juice
Vegetable stock or water
½ cup diced celery
½ cup diced parsnips
½ cup diced carrots
½ cup sliced mushrooms
1 onion, sliced
1 teaspoon dried basil
1 teaspoon parsley flakes
1 bay leaf
3 cloves garlic, minced
1 teaspoon black pepper
1 cup rice or pasta, cooked

1. Sort and rinse beans and soak overnight in water. Drain. Place in a crock pot.
2. Add vegetable juice, wine, soy sauce, and apple or pineapple juice.
3. Cover with vegetable stock or water.
4. Cover. Cook on high 2 hours.
5. Add vegetables, herbs, and spices.
6. Cover crock pot. Cook on low 5 to 6 hours, or until carrots and parsnips are tender.
7. Add cooked rice or pasta.
8. Cover. Cook 1 hour more.

Beef and Kidney Bean Stew

Prep time: 15 minutes | Cook time: 6 hours | Serves 4 to 6

¾ cup sliced onion
1 pound (454 g) ground beef
¼ cup long-grain rice, uncooked
3 cups diced raw potatoes
1 cup diced celery
2 cups canned kidney beans, drained
1 teaspoon salt
⅛ teaspoon pepper
¼ teaspoon chili powder
¼ teaspoon Worcestershire sauce
1 cup tomato sauce
½ cup water

1. Brown onions and ground beef in a skillet. Drain.
2. Layer ingredients in a crock pot in order given.
3. Cover. Cook on low 6 hours, or until potatoes and rice are cooked.

Southern Brunswick Stew

Prep time: 10 minutes | Cook time: 6½ to 8½ hours | Serves 10 to 12

2 to 3 pounds (0.9 to 1.4 kg) pork butt
1 (17-ounce / 482-g) can white corn
1 (14-ounce / 397-g) bottle ketchup
2 cups diced potatoes, cooked
1 (10-ounce / 284-g) package frozen peas, thawed
2 (10¾-ounce / 305-g) cans tomato soup
Hot sauce, as needed
Salt and pepper, to taste

1. Place the pork in a crock pot.
2. Cover. Cook on low for 6 to 8 hours. Remove the meat from bone and shred.
3. Combine all the ingredients in the crock pot.
4. Cover. Bring to a boil on high. Reduce heat to low and simmer for 30 minutes.
5. Serve hot.

Chickpea and Lentil Stew

Prep time: 10 minutes | Cook time: 6 to 8 hours | Serves 2

½ cup canned chickpeas, drained and rinsed
½ cup canned white beans, drained and rinsed
½ cup lentils, rinsed and sorted
½ cup white rice
½ cup diced carrots
½ cup diced red bell pepper
¼ cup parsley
1 ounce (28 g) pancetta, diced
2 cups low-sodium vegetable broth
⅛ teaspoon sea salt

1. Put all the ingredients into a crock pot and stir to mix thoroughly.
2. Cover and cook on low for 6 to 8 hours.
3. Serve hot.

Beef and Pearl Barley Stew

Prep time: 10 minutes | Cook time: 8 hours | Serves 2

¼ cup pearl barley
½ cup water
½ teaspoon ground cinnamon
½ teaspoon ground coriander
Freshly ground black pepper, to taste
⅛ teaspoon sea salt
1 tablespoon tomato paste
¼ cup red wine vinegar
1 cup dry red wine
12 ounces (340 g) beef brisket, cut into 1-inch cubes
½ cup minced onions
¼ cup minced celery
2 garlic cloves, minced
2 tablespoons minced fresh flat-leaf parsley

1. Put the pearl barley and water in a crock pot and give it a stir to make sure all the barley is submerged.
2. In a large bowl, combine the cinnamon, coriander, black pepper, salt, tomato paste, vinegar, and red wine. Add the beef, onions, celery, garlic, and parsley to the bowl and stir together. Gently pour this mixture over the barley. Do not stir.
3. Cover and cook on low for 8 hours.
4. Serve hot.

Brown Sugar Beef Chili

Prep time: 15 minutes | Cook time: 2 hours | Serves 8

1 pound (454 g) extra-lean ground beef
½ cup brown sugar
2 tablespoons prepared mustard
1 medium onion, chopped
2 (14-ounce / 397-g) cans kidney beans, drained
1 pint low-sodium tomato juice
½ teaspoon salt
¼ teaspoon black pepper
1 teaspoon chili powder

1. Brown lean ground beef and onion in a nonstick skillet over medium heat. Stir brown sugar and mustard into meat.
2. Combine all ingredients in a crock pot.
3. Cover. Cook on high 2 hours. If it's convenient, stir several times during cooking.

Brown Rice and Black Bean Chili

Prep time: 10 minutes | Cook time: 6 to 8 hours | Serves 4

2 (15-ounce / 425-g) cans black beans
1 (14½- to 16-ounce / 411- to 454-g) can crushed or chopped tomatoes, with their liquid
½ cup brown rice
1 teaspoon onion powder
⅛ teaspoon garlic powder
¼ teaspoon ground cumin
½ teaspoon dried oregano
½ to 1 whole canned chipotle chile, cut into small pieces
Plain yogurt or warm flour tortillas, for serving

1. Pour the beans with their liquid and the tomatoes with their liquid into a crock pot. Add the brown rice, onion powder, garlic powder, cumin, oregano, and chipotle. Stir to combine. Cover and cook on low for 6 to 8 hours.
2. Serve the chili in bowls, topped with a spoonful of yogurt, or wrap some in a warm tortilla.

Sweet Potato and Sirloin Stew

Prep time: 20 minutes | Cook time: 7 to 9 hours | Serves 8

2 pounds (907 g) sirloin tip, cut into 2-inch pieces
2 onions, chopped
3 garlic cloves, minced
2 large sweet potatoes, peeled and cubed
2⅓ cup chopped dried apricots
2⅓ cup golden raisins
5 large tomatoes, deseeded and chopped
9 cups beef stock
2 teaspoons curry powder
1 cup cooked whole-wheat couscous

1. In a crock pot, mix the sirloin, onions, garlic, sweet potatoes, apricots, raisins, tomatoes, beef stock, and curry powder. Cover and cook on low for 7 to 9 hours, or until the sweet potatoes are tender.
2. Stir in the couscous. Cover and let stand for 5 to 10 minutes, or until the couscous has softened.
3. Stir the stew and serve.

Beef Chili

Prep time: 15 minutes | Cook time: 4 to 6 hours | Serves 4

1 pound (454 g) ground beef
1 onion, chopped
1 (15-ounce / 425-g) can chili, with or without beans
1 (14½-ounce / 411-g) can diced tomatoes with green chilies, or with basil, garlic, and oregano
1 cup tomato juice
Chopped onion, for serving
Shredded Cheddar cheese, for serving

1. Brown ground beef and onion in the skillet. Drain and put in a crock pot.
2. Add chili, diced tomatoes, and tomato juice.
3. Cover. Cook on low 4 to 6 hours.
4. Serve with onion and cheese on top of each individual serving.

Veggie and Cashew Chili

Prep time: 20 minutes | Cook time: 8½ hours | Serves 8 to 10

2 tablespoons oil
2 cups minced celery
1½ cups chopped green pepper
1 cup minced onions
4 garlic cloves, minced
5½ cups stewed tomatoes
2 (1-pound / 454-g) cans kidney beans, undrained
1½ to 2 cups raisins
¼ cup wine vinegar
1 tablespoon chopped parsley
2 teaspoons salt
1½ teaspoons dried oregano
1½ teaspoons cumin
¼ teaspoon pepper
¼ teaspoon Tabasco sauce
1 bay leaf
¾ cup cashews
1 cup shredded cheese (optional)

1. Combine all ingredients except cashews and cheese in a crock pot.
2. Cover. Simmer on low for 8 hours. Add cashews and simmer 30 minutes.
3. Garnish individual servings with shredded cheese.

Hamburger Chili with Beans

Prep time: 15 minutes | Cook time: 8 to 10 hours | Serves 12

½ pound (227 g) lean hamburger or ground turkey
½ pound (227 g) sausage
1 onion, chopped
1 (15-ounce / 425-g) can kidney beans or chili beans, undrained
1 (15-ounce / 425-g) can ranch-style beans, undrained
1 (15-ounce / 425-g) can pinto beans, undrained
1 (14½-ounce / 411-g) can stewed tomatoes, undrained
1 (15-ounce / 425-g) can tomato sauce
1 envelope dry chili seasoning mix
3 tablespoons brown sugar
3 tablespoons chili powder

1. Brown hamburger, sausage, and onion together in a nonstick skillet.
2. Combine all ingredients in a large crock pot. Mix well.
3. Cook on low 8 to 10 hours.

Potato and Beef Chili

Prep time: 20 minutes | Cook time: 4 hours | Serves 8

1 pound (454 g) ground beef
½ cup chopped onions, or 2 tablespoons dried minced onions
½ cup chopped green peppers
1 tablespoon poppy seeds (optional)
1 teaspoon salt
½ teaspoon chili powder
1 package au gratin or scalloped potato mix
1 cup hot water
1 (15-ounce / 425-g) can kidney beans, undrained
1 (16-ounce / 454-g) can stewed tomatoes
1 (4-ounce / 113-g) can mushroom pieces, undrained

1. Brown ground beef in skillet. Remove meat and place in a crock pot. Sauté onions and green peppers in drippings until softened.
2. Combine all ingredients in a crock pot.
3. Cover. Cook on high 4 hours, or until liquid is absorbed and potatoes are tender.

Chapter 6 Soups, Stews, and Chilies | 55

Bacon and Beef Chili

Prep time: 20 minutes | Cook time: 9 to 10 hours | Serves 15

8 bacon strips, diced
2½ pounds (1.1 kg) beef stewing meat, cubed
1 (28-ounce / 794-g) can stewed tomatoes
1 (14½-ounce / 411-g) can stewed tomatoes
2 (8-ounce / 227-g) cans tomato sauce
1 (16-ounce / 454-g) can kidney beans, rinsed and drained
2 cups sliced carrots
1 medium onion, chopped
1 cup chopped celery
½ cup chopped green pepper
¼ cup minced fresh parsley
1 tablespoon chili powder
1 teaspoon salt
½ teaspoon ground cumin
¼ teaspoon pepper

1. Cook bacon in the skillet until crisp. Drain on paper towel.
2. Brown beef in bacon drippings in the skillet.
3. Combine all ingredients in a crock pot.
4. Cover. Cook on low 9 to 10 hours, or until meat is tender. Stir occasionally.

Indian-Style Chili

Prep time: 10 minutes | Cook time: 5½ to 6½ hours | Serves 4 to 6

2 tablespoons olive oil
2 medium-size red onions, chopped
3 cloves garlic, minced
2 tablespoons grated fresh ginger
1 to 2 canned jalapeños en escabeche, to your taste, chopped
2 teaspoons ground coriander
1¼ teaspoons ground cumin
½ teaspoon cayenne pepper
¼ teaspoon ground turmeric
1 (14½-ounce / 411-g) can diced tomatoes, with their juice
3 tablespoons tomato paste
1 cup water
3 (15-ounce / 425-g) cans red kidney beans, rinsed and drained
½ teaspoon salt, or more to taste
½ cup evaporated milk or heavy cream
For Serving:
Chopped red onion
Chopped fresh cilantro
Plain yogurt
Warm chapatis

1. Heat the olive oil in a large skillet over medium-high heat, then cook the onions, stirring, until softened, about 5 minutes. Add the garlic, ginger, jalapeños, and spices, and cook, stirring, until the onions are browned. Transfer to the crock pot, add the tomatoes with their juice, tomato paste, water, and kidney beans, and stir to combine. Cover and cook on low for 5 to 6 hours.
2. Stir in the salt and evaporated milk, cover, and continue to cook on low for another 30 minutes.
3. Serve the chili in bowls with the toppings and warm chapatis, if you can find them.

Brown Lentil Chili

Prep time: 20 minutes | Cook time: 6 to 8 hours | Serves 4 to 6

1 medium-size yellow onion, diced
1 medium-size red bell pepper, deseeded and chopped
1 jalapeño, deseeded and finely chopped
2 ribs celery, chopped
1 medium-size carrot, chopped
3 cloves garlic, minced
2 tablespoons light or dark brown sugar
2 tablespoons chili powder
1 tablespoon ground cumin
½ teaspoon cayenne pepper or 1 teaspoon pure New Mexico chile powder
2 teaspoons dried oregano
1 teaspoon dried thyme
1 teaspoon dry mustard
2½ cups dried brown lentils, rinsed and picked over
8 cups chicken broth
3 tablespoons olive oil
Salt, to taste
For Serving:
Sour cream or crema Mexicana
Chopped fresh tomatoes
Chopped green onions, white part and some of the green
Chopped fresh cilantro

1. Combine all the ingredients in a crock pot, except for the olive oil and salt. Cover and cook on low for 6 to 8 hours, stirring occasionally, until the lentils are soft. During the last hour, add the olive oil and season with salt. Continue cooking.
2. Serve the chili in bowls with the toppings.

Beef Chili with Cilantro Cream

Prep time: 15 minutes | Cook time: 7 to 8 hours | Serves 4

1 pound (454 g) boneless beef chuck, tri tip (a triangular sirloin cut), or round steak, trimmed of excess fat and cut into bite-size pieces
1 large yellow onion, chopped
2 cloves garlic, finely chopped
1 tablespoon chili powder
2 teaspoons ground cumin
2 (16-ounce / 454-g) jars thick-and-chunky salsa, mild or hot
1 (14½-ounce / 411-g) can diced tomatoes, with their juice
1 medium-size red or green bell pepper, deseeded and chopped
1 (15-ounce / 425-g) can pinto beans, rinsed and drained
Salt, to taste
Warm cornbread, for serving
Cilantro Cream:
2⅓ cup sour cream
¼ cup minced fresh cilantro
2 tablespoons fresh lime juice

1. Put the meat, onion, garlic, chili powder, cumin, salsa, and tomatoes in a crock pot and stir to combine. Cover and cook on low for 5 to 6 hours.
2. Add the bell pepper and pinto beans, season with salt, and continue to cook on low for another 2 hours.
3. Combine all the ingredients for the cilantro cream in a small bowl, and stir until well combined. Cover and chill until serving. Serve the chili in bowls with a dollop of the cilantro cream and cornbread.

Hominy and Turkey Thigh Chili

Prep time: 20 minutes | Cook time: 6 to 8 hours | Serves 6

1 medium-size yellow onion, chopped
1 medium-size red bell pepper, deseeded and chopped
1 jalapeño, deseeded and minced
2 ribs celery, chopped
3 cloves garlic, minced
1 cup chicken broth
1 tablespoon chili powder
1½ teaspoons ground cumin
½ teaspoon pure ancho chile powder
1½ teaspoons dried oregano
3 pounds (1.4 kg) turkey thighs (about 3), skin and excess fat removed and rinsed
1 (15-ounce / 425-g) can golden or white hominy, rinsed and drained
2 (15-ounce / 425-g) cans chopped golden tomatoes, drained; or 1 (28-ounce / 794-g) can chopped plum tomatoes, drained
Salt, to taste
For Serving:
Shredded Monterey Jack cheese
Sliced ripe California black olives
Minced red onion
Chopped fresh cilantro

1. Combine the onion, bell pepper, jalapeño, celery, garlic, broth, chili powder, cumin, ancho powder, and oregano in a crock pot. Arrange the turkey thighs on top and pour the hominy and tomatoes over them. Cover and cook on low until the turkey meat pulls away easily from the bone, for 6 to 7 hours.
2. Remove the turkey from the crock pot and shred the meat, discarding the bones. Return the meat to the chili. Season with salt. Serve the chili in shallow bowls with the toppings.

Veggie Bulgur Wheat Chili

Prep time: 25 minutes | Cook time: 5 to 7 hours | Serves 4

1⅓ cup bulgur wheat
2⅓ cup boiling water
2 tablespoons olive oil
2 medium-size yellow onions, chopped
1 medium-size green, yellow, or red bell pepper, deseeded and chopped
2 to 3 cloves garlic, minced
1 (28-ounce / 794-g) can diced tomatoes, drained
1 (15-ounce / 425-g) can tomato purée
2 (15-ounce / 425-g) cans red kidney or pinto beans, rinsed and drained
2 tablespoons chopped canned jalapeño
2 tablespoons chili powder or pure New Mexican chile powder
1½ tablespoons ground cumin
2 tablespoons light or dark brown sugar
2 teaspoons dried oregano or marjoram
½ teaspoon ground coriander
¼ teaspoon ground cloves
Pinch of ground allspice
Salt, to taste

For Serving:
Shredded Monterey Jack cheese
Sliced ripe California black olives
Sliced avocado
Extra-firm tofu, rinsed, blotted dry, and cut into cubes
Chopped fresh cilantro

1. Put the bulgur in a crock pot and add the boiling water. Let stand for 15 minutes.
2. Heat the olive oil in a large skillet over medium-high heat and cook the onions, bell pepper, and garlic, stirring, until softened, for 5 to 10 minutes. Transfer the mixture to the crock pot. Add the drained tomatoes, tomato purée, beans, jalapeño, chili powder, cumin, brown sugar, oregano, coriander, cloves, and allspice, and stir to combine. Cover and cook on high for 1 hour.
3. Turn the crock pot to low and cook for 4 to 6 hours. During the last hour, season with salt.
4. Serve the chili in bowls topped with the cheese, olives, avocado slices, tofu, and lots of cilantro.

Chapter 7 Side Dishes

Cider Butternut Squash Purée

Prep time: 15 minutes | Cook time: 5 to 6 hours | Serves 6 to 8

3 pounds (1.4 kg) butternut squash, peeled, deseeded, and cut into 1-inch pieces (8 cups)
½ cup apple cider, plus extra as needed
Salt and pepper, to taste
4 tablespoons unsalted butter, melted
2 tablespoons heavy cream, warmed
2 tablespoons packed brown sugar, plus extra for seasoning

1. Combine squash, cider, and ½ teaspoon salt in a crock pot. Press 16 by 12-inch sheet of parchment paper firmly onto squash, folding down edges as needed. Cover and cook until squash is tender, 5 to 6 hours on low or 3 to 4 hours on high.
2. Discard parchment. Mash squash with potato masher until smooth. Stir in melted butter, cream, and sugar. Season with salt, pepper, and extra sugar to taste. Serve. (Squash can be held on warm or low setting for up to 2 hours; adjust consistency with extra hot cider as needed before serving.)

Braised Butternut Squash with Pecans

Prep time: 15 minutes | Cook time: 4 to 5 hours | Serves 4 to 6

1 cup vegetable or chicken broth
2 garlic cloves, peeled and smashed
2 sprigs fresh thyme
Salt and pepper, to taste
2 pounds (907 g) butternut squash, peeled, halved lengthwise, deseeded, and sliced 1 inch thick
2 tablespoons extra-virgin olive oil
1 teaspoon grated lemon zest plus 2 teaspoons juice
¼ cup toasted and chopped pecans
¼ cup dried cranberries
1 tablespoon minced fresh parsley

1. Combine broth, garlic, thyme sprigs, and ¼ teaspoon salt in a crock pot. Nestle squash into a crock pot. Cover and cook until squash is tender, 4 to 5 hours on low or 3 to 4 hours on high.
2. Using a slotted spoon, transfer squash to a serving dish, brushing away any garlic cloves or thyme sprigs that stick to squash. Whisk oil and lemon zest and juice together in the bowl. Season with salt and pepper to taste. Drizzle squash with dressing and sprinkle with pecans, cranberries, and parsley. Serve.

Acorn Squash with Maple Orange Glaze

Prep time: 15 minutes | Cook time: 3 to 4 hours | Serves 4 to 6

2 teaspoons grated orange zest plus ½ cup juice
5 whole cloves
1 cinnamon stick
2 small acorn squashes (1 pound / 454 g each), quartered pole to pole and seeded
Salt and pepper, to taste
¼ cup maple syrup
⅛ teaspoon ground coriander
Pinch cayenne pepper
¼ cup hazelnuts, toasted, skinned, and chopped
1 tablespoon chopped fresh parsley

1. Combine 1 cup water, orange juice, cloves, and cinnamon stick in a crock pot. Season squashes with salt and pepper and shingle cut side down in a crock pot. Cover and cook until squashes are tender, 3 to 4 hours on low or 2 to 3 hours on high.
2. Using tongs, transfer squashes to the serving dish, brushing away any cloves that stick to squashes. Microwave maple syrup, coriander, cayenne, and orange zest in bowl until heated through, about 1 minute. Season with salt and pepper to taste. Drizzle glaze over squashes and sprinkle with hazelnuts and parsley. Serve.

Sake-Cooked Asparagus

Prep time: 10 minutes | Cook time: 1¼ to 1½ hours | Serves 4 to 5

1¼ to 1½ pounds (567 to 680 g) asparagus
1 tablespoon olive oil
1 tablespoon sake
1 teaspoon soy sauce
Pinch of brown sugar
Pinch of salt
1 to 2 teaspoons toasted sesame seeds, for garnish (optional)

1. Wash and drain the asparagus. One by one, hold each spear in both of your hands. Bend the spear at the stem end until the end snaps off. Discard the stem end. Put the asparagus in the crock pot. Drizzle in the olive oil, sake, and soy sauce. Sprinkle with the brown sugar and salt. With your hands, gently toss the asparagus to coat them lightly with the seasonings. Cover and cook on high until tender when pierced with a sharp knife, 1¼ to 1½ hours.
2. Use a pair of tongs to place the asparagus on a serving platter. Pour the liquid from the crock over the asparagus. Sprinkle with the toasted sesame seeds just before serving.

Garlic Mushrooms with Crème Fraîche

Prep time: 15 minutes | Cook time: 2 to 3 hours | Serves 6 to 10

1½ pounds (680 g) cremini or white mushrooms, stems trimmed
1 cup vegetable broth
2 tablespoons dry white or red wine
3 cloves garlic, chopped
1⅓ bunch green onions (white and a few inches of green parts), chopped
1¼ teaspoons dried Italian herbs or herbes de Provence
1⅓ cup crème fraîche (optional)
2 tablespoons unsalted butter
Sea salt and freshly ground black pepper, to taste

1. Combine the mushrooms, broth, wine, garlic, green onions, and herbs in the crock pot; stir to mix well.
2. Cover and cook on high for 2 to 3 hours, or on low for 4 to 6 hours, until the mushrooms are tender. Check at the halfway point. Stir in the crème fraîche (if using) and butter. Season to taste and serve hot, or set aside to cool and then refrigerate, covered, in the poaching liquid. The mushrooms will keep in the refrigerator for up to 4 days.

Braised Peas with Lettuce and Onions

Prep time: 20 minutes | Cook time: 2½ to 3½ hours | Serves 8

1 medium-size head Boston lettuce
1 sprig fresh thyme, savory, or mint
8 white boiling onions (16 if they are really tiny), peeled
½ cup (1 stick) unsalted butter, softened
½ teaspoon sugar
½ teaspoon salt
½ teaspoon ground white pepper
3½ to 4 pounds (1.6 to 1.8 kg) fresh peas in the pod (5 to 6 cups shelled peas of a uniform size), or 2 (12-ounce / 340-g) bags frozen garden peas (not petites), thawed
¼ cup water

1. Coat the crock pot with nonstick cooking spray or butter; line the bottom and sides with the outer lettuce leaves. Reserve some leaves for the top. Open the lettuce heart, place the single herb sprig inside, and tie with kitchen twine. Put it in the crock pot and add the onions.
2. In a small bowl, mash together the butter, sugar, salt, and pepper. Add to the bowl of shelled peas and, with your hands, gently squeeze the butter into the mass of peas to coat them; it is okay if some peas are bruised, but try not to crush any. Pack the peas around the heart of lettuce in the crock pot and top with more lettuce leaves. Add the water. Cover and cook on high for 30 minutes to get the pot heated up.
3. Reduce the heat setting to low and cook until the peas are tender, 2 to 3 hours. At 2 hours, lift the cover to check their progress. Remove the lettuce leaves and the lettuce heart, and serve the hot peas from the crock.

Thyme Garlic Tomatoes

Prep time: 15 minutes | Cook time: 5 to 6 hours | Serves 4 to 6

6 ripe tomatoes, cored and halved crosswise
½ cup extra-virgin olive oil
6 garlic cloves, peeled and smashed
2 teaspoons minced fresh thyme or ¾ teaspoon dried
Salt and pepper, to taste

1. Combine tomatoes, oil, garlic, thyme, ¾ teaspoon salt, and ¼ teaspoon pepper in a crock pot. Cover and cook until tomatoes are tender and slightly shriveled around edges, 5 to 6 hours on low or 3 to 4 hours on high.
2. Let tomatoes cool in oil for at least 15 minutes or up to 4 hours. Season with salt and pepper to taste. Serve.

Garlic Collard Greens and Kale

Prep time: 15 minutes | Cook time: 4 to 5 hours | Serves 4 to 6

1 bunch collards (1½ pounds / 680 g)
1 bunch kale (1½ pounds / 680 g)
3 tablespoons olive oil
4 cloves garlic or 2 small shallots, chopped
1 cup chicken, beef, or vegetable broth
1 canned chipotle pepper in adobo sauce or small dried hot pepper (optional)
Salt and freshly ground black pepper, to taste
Juice of 1 lemon
1 tablespoon cider vinegar

For Serving:
Unsalted butter
Cornbread

1. Rinse the greens well in the sink. Drain and trim off the tough stems. Cut the leaves crosswise into ½-inch-wide strips; you will have about 12 to 14 cups.
2. In a deep saucepan, heat the olive oil over medium heat. Add the garlic and cook, stirring, just 30 seconds to 1 minute. Add the greens in handfuls and toss to coat with the oil. With each addition, cover for a minute until wilted, then add some more. Transfer to the crock pot once they've all been wilted and add the broth. If using the chipotle pepper, nestle it down in the center of the greens. Cover and cook on low until tender, 4 to 5 hours.
3. Season with salt and pepper and stir in the lemon juice and vinegar. Serve nice and hot with a pat of butter and some cornbread.

Buttered Parsley Red Potatoes

Prep time: 10 minutes | Cook time: 2½ to 3 hours | Serves 6

1½ pounds (680 g) medium red potatoes
¼ cup water
¼ cup butter, melted
3 tablespoons minced fresh parsley
1 tablespoon lemon juice
1 tablespoon minced chives
Salt and pepper, to taste

1. Cut a strip of peel from around the middle of each potato. Place potatoes and water in a crock pot. Cover and cook on high for 2½ to 3 hours or until tender (do not overcook); drain.
2. In a small bowl, combine the butter, parsley, lemon juice and chives. Pour over the potatoes and toss to coat. Season with salt and pepper.

Shoepeg Corn Casserole

Prep time: 20 minutes | Cook time: 3 to 4 hours | Serves 8

1 (14½-ounce / 411-g) can French-style green beans, drained
2 (7-ounce / 198-g) cans white or shoepeg corn
1 (10¾-ounce / 305-g) can condensed cream of mushroom soup, undiluted
1 (4½-ounce / 128-g) jar sliced mushrooms, drained
½ cup slivered almonds
½ cup shredded Cheddar cheese
½ cup sour cream
¾ cup French-fried onions

1. In a crock pot, combine the first seven ingredients. Cover and cook on low for 3 to 4 hours or until vegetables are tender, stirring occasionally. Sprinkle with onions during the last 15 minutes of cooking.

Black-Eyed Peas with Ham

Prep time: 20 minutes | Cook time: 6 to 8 hours | Serves 12

1 (16-ounce / 454-g) package dried black-eyed peas, rinsed and sorted
½ pound (227 g) fully cooked boneless ham, finely chopped
1 medium onion, finely chopped
1 medium sweet red pepper, finely chopped
5 bacon strips, cooked and crumbled
1 large jalapeño pepper, deseeded and finely chopped
2 garlic cloves, minced
1½ teaspoons ground cumin
1 teaspoon reduced-sodium chicken bouillon granules
½ teaspoon salt
½ teaspoon cayenne pepper
¼ teaspoon pepper
6 cups water
Minced fresh cilantro (optional)
Hot cooked rice, for serving

1. In a crock pot, combine the first 13 ingredients. Cover and cook on low for 6 to 8 hours or until peas are tender. Sprinkle with cilantro if desired. Serve with rice.

Balsamic Fresh Shell Beans with Herbs

Prep time: 10 minutes | Cook time: 1½ to 4 hours | Serves 6

3 tablespoons olive oil
2 shallots, minced
3 pounds (1.4 kg) fresh shell beans, shelled
1 cup water, vegetable broth, or chicken broth
Salt and freshly ground black pepper, to taste
2 to 3 teaspoons fresh chopped herbs, such as thyme, parsley, marjoram, or basil
2 to 3 teaspoons dark or white balsamic vinegar

1. In a small skillet over medium heat, warm the olive oil and cook the shallots, stirring, until softened. Put in the crock pot along with the beans and water. Cover and cook on high for 1½ to 4 hours, depending on the size of the bean.
2. Season with salt and pepper and stir in the herbs and vinegar. Serve immediately, or refrigerate and eat cold.

Cowboy Calico Beans with Ground Beef

Prep time: 30 minutes | Cook time: 4 to 5 hours | Serves 8

1 pound (454 g) 90% lean ground beef
1 large sweet onion, chopped
½ cup packed brown sugar
¼ cup ketchup
3 tablespoons cider vinegar
2 tablespoons yellow mustard
1 (16-ounce / 454-g) can butter beans, drained
1 (16-ounce / 454-g) can kidney beans, rinsed and drained
1 (15-ounce / 425-g) can pork and beans
1 (15¼-ounce / 432-g) can lima beans, rinsed and drained

1. In a large skillet, cook beef and onion over medium heat until meat is no longer pink; drain.
2. Transfer to a crock pot. Combine the brown sugar, ketchup, vinegar and mustard; add to meat mixture. Stir in the beans. Cover and cook on low for 4 to 5 hours or until heated through.

Spanish Hominy

Prep time: 20 minutes | Cook time: 6 to 8 hours | Serves 12

4 (15½-ounce / 439-g) cans hominy, rinsed and drained
1 (14½-ounce / 411-g) can diced tomatoes, undrained
1 (10-ounce / 283-g) can diced tomatoes and green chilies, undrained
1 (8-ounce / 227-g) can tomato sauce
¾ pound (340 g) sliced bacon, diced
1 large onion, chopped
1 medium green pepper, chopped

1. In a crock pot, combine the hominy, tomatoes and tomato sauce.
2. In a large skillet, cook bacon until crisp; remove with a slotted spoon to paper towels. Drain, reserving 1 tablespoon drippings.
3. In the same skillet, sauté onion and green pepper in drippings until tender. Stir onion mixture and bacon into hominy mixture. Cover and cook on low for 6 to 8 hours or until heated through.

Green Beans and Potatoes with Bacon

Prep time: 20 minutes | Cook time: 6 to 8 hours | Serves 10

8 bacon strips, chopped
1½ pounds (680 g) fresh green beans, trimmed and cut into 2-inch pieces (about 4 cups)
4 medium potatoes, peeled and cubed (½-inch)
1 small onion, halved and sliced
¼ cup reduced-sodium chicken broth
½ teaspoon salt
¼ teaspoon pepper

1. In a large skillet, cook bacon over medium heat until crisp, stirring occasionally. Remove to paper towels with a slotted spoon; drain, reserving 1 tablespoon drippings. Cover and refrigerate bacon until serving.
2. In a crock pot, combine the remaining ingredients; stir in reserved drippings. Cover and cook on low for 6 to 8 hours or until potatoes are tender. Stir in bacon; heat through.

Zucchini Stuffed Sweet Onions

Prep time: 20 minutes | Cook time: 4 to 5 hours | Serves 4

4 medium sweet onions
2 small zucchini, shredded
1 large garlic clove, minced
1 tablespoon olive oil
1 teaspoon dried basil
1 teaspoon dried thyme
¼ teaspoon salt
¼ teaspoon pepper
½ cup dry bread crumbs
4 thick-sliced bacon strips, cooked and crumbled
¼ cup grated Parmesan cheese
¼ cup reduced-sodium chicken broth

1. Peel onions and cut a ¼-inch slice from the top and bottom. Carefully cut and remove the center of each onion, leaving a ½-in. shell; chop removed onion.
2. In a large skillet, sauté the zucchini, garlic and chopped onions in oil until tender and juices are reduced. Stir in the basil, thyme, salt and pepper. Remove from the heat. Stir in the bread crumbs, bacon and Parmesan cheese. Fill onion shells with the zucchini mixture.
3. Place in a greased crock pot. Add broth to the crock pot. Cover and cook on low for 4 to 5 hours or until onions are tender.

Maple Baked Beans with Bacon

Prep time: 15 minutes | Cook time: 6 to 8 hours | Serves 8

3 (15-ounce / 425-g) cans pork and beans
½ cup finely chopped onion
½ cup chopped green pepper
½ cup ketchup
½ cup maple syrup
2 tablespoons finely chopped, deseeded jalapeño pepper
½ cup crumbled cooked bacon

1. In a crock pot, combine the first six ingredients. Cover and cook on low for 6 to 8 hours or until vegetables are tender. Just before serving, stir in bacon.

Root Vegetable Medley

Prep time: 20 minutes | Cook time: 5 to 6 hours | Serves 8

4 large carrots, cut into 1½-inch pieces
3 fresh beets, peeled and cut into 1½-inch pieces
2 medium sweet potatoes, peeled and cut into 1½-inch pieces
2 medium onions, peeled and quartered
½ cup water
2 teaspoons salt
½ teaspoon pepper
¼ teaspoon dried thyme
1 tablespoon olive oil
Fresh parsley or dried parsley flakes (optional)

1. Place the carrots, beets, sweet potatoes, onions and water in a greased crock pot. Sprinkle with salt, pepper and thyme. Drizzle with olive oil. Cover and cook on low for 5 to 6 hours or until tender.
2. Stir vegetables and sprinkle with parsley if desired.

Coconut Curried Butternut Squash

Prep time: 20 minutes | Cook time: 4 to 5 hours | Serves 9

1 cup chopped carrots
1 small onion, chopped
1 tablespoon olive oil
1½ teaspoons brown sugar
1½ teaspoons curry powder
1 garlic clove, minced
½ teaspoon ground cinnamon
¼ teaspoon ground ginger
⅛ teaspoon salt
1 medium butternut squash (about 2½ pounds / 1.1 kg), cut into 1-inch cubes
2½ cups vegetable broth
¾ cup coconut milk
½ cup uncooked basmati or jasmine rice

1. In a large skillet, sauté carrots and onion in oil until onion is tender. Add the brown sugar, curry, garlic, cinnamon, ginger and salt. Cook and stir 2 minutes longer.
2. In a crock pot, combine the butternut squash, broth, coconut milk, rice and carrot mixture. Cover and cook on low for 4 to 5 hours or until rice is tender.

Cheesy Red Potatoes

Prep time: 15 minutes | Cook time: 5 to 6 hours | Serves 8

7 cups cubed uncooked red potatoes
1 cup (8 ounces / 227 g) 4% cottage cheese
½ cup sour cream
½ cup cubed process cheese (Velveeta)
1 tablespoon dried minced onion
2 garlic cloves, minced
½ teaspoon salt
Paprika and minced chives (optional)

1. Place the potatoes in a crock pot. In a blender, purée cottage cheese and sour cream until smooth. Transfer to a large bowl; stir in the process cheese, onion, garlic and salt. Pour over potatoes and mix well.
2. Cover and cook on low for 5 to 6 hours or until potatoes are tender. Stir well before serving. Garnish with paprika and chives if desired.

Zucchini Tomato Casserole

Prep time: 20 minutes | Cook time: 3½ to 4½ hours | Serves 6

3 medium zucchini, cut into ¼-inch slices
1 teaspoon salt, divided
½ teaspoon pepper, divided
1 medium onion, thinly sliced
1 medium green pepper, thinly sliced
3 medium tomatoes, sliced
⅔ cup condensed tomato soup, undiluted
1 teaspoon dried basil
1 cup shredded Cheddar cheese

1. Place zucchini in greased crock pot. Sprinkle with ½ teaspoon salt and ¼ teaspoon pepper. Layer with onion, green pepper and tomatoes. In a small bowl, combine the soup, basil and remaining salt and pepper; spread over tomatoes.
2. Cover and cook on low for 3 to 4 hours or until vegetables are tender. Sprinkle with cheese. Cover and cook 30 minutes longer or until cheese is melted.

Creamed Broccoli

Prep time: 10 minutes | Cook time: 2½ to 3 hours | Serves 8 to 10

6 cups frozen chopped broccoli, partially thawed
1 (10¾-ounce / 305-g) can condensed cream of celery soup, undiluted
1½ cups (6 ounces / 170 g) shredded sharp Cheddar cheese, divided
¼ cup chopped onion
½ teaspoon Worcestershire sauce
¼ teaspoon pepper
1 cup crushed butter-flavored crackers
2 tablespoons butter

1. In a large bowl, combine the broccoli, cream of celery soup, 1 cup cheese, onion, Worcestershire sauce and pepper. Pour into a greased crock pot. Sprinkle the crushed butter-flavored crackers on top; dot with butter.
2. Cover and cook on high for 2½ to 3 hours. Sprinkle with the remaining cheese. Cook 10 minutes longer or until the cheese is melted.

Jalapeño Creamed Corn

Prep time: 15 minutes | Cook time: 4 to 5 hours | Serves 8

2 (16-ounce / 454-g) packages frozen corn
1 (8-ounce / 227-g) package cream cheese, softened and cubed
4 jalapeño peppers, deseeded and finely chopped
¼ cup butter, cubed
2 tablespoons water
½ teaspoon salt
¼ teaspoon pepper

1. In a crock pot, combine all ingredients. Cover and cook on low for 4 to 5 hours or until corn is tender, stirring occasionally.

Warm Fruit Salad

Prep time: 15 minutes | Cook time: 2 hours | Serves 14 to 18

2 (29-ounce / 822-g) cans sliced peaches, drained
2 (29-ounce / 822-g) cans pear halves, drained and sliced
1 (20-ounce / 567-g) can pineapple chunks, drained
1 (15¼-ounce / 432-g) can apricot halves, drained and sliced
1 (21-ounce / 595-g) can cherry pie filling

1. In a crock pot, combine the peaches, pears, pineapple and apricots. Top with pie filling. Cover and cook on high for 2 hours or until heated through. Serve with a slotted spoon.

Cinnamon Glazed Acorn Squash

Prep time: 15 minutes | Cook time: 3½ to 4 hours | Serves 4

¾ cup packed brown sugar
1 teaspoon ground cinnamon
1 teaspoon ground nutmeg
2 small acorn squash, halved and seeded
¾ cup raisins
4 tablespoons butter
½ cup water

1. In a small bowl, mix brown sugar, cinnamon and nutmeg; spoon into squash halves. Sprinkle with raisins. Top each with 1 tablespoon butter. Wrap each half individually in heavy-duty foil, sealing tightly.
2. Pour water into a crock pot. Place squash in a crock pot, cut side up (packets may be stacked). Cook, covered, on high 3½ to 4 hours or until squash is tender. Open foil carefully to allow steam to escape.

Spinach and Cheese Casserole

Prep time: 10 minutes | Cook time: 2½ hours | Serves 8

2 (10-ounce / 283-g) packages frozen chopped spinach, thawed and well drained
2 cups 4% cottage cheese
1 cup cubed process cheese (Velveeta)
¾ cup egg substitute
2 tablespoons butter, cubed
¼ cup all-purpose flour
½ teaspoon salt

1. In a crock pot, combine all ingredients. Cover and cook on low for 2½ hours or until cheese is melted.

Bacon Hash Brown Casserole

Prep time: 15 minutes | Cook time: 4 to 5 hours | Serves 14

1 (2-pound / 907-g) package frozen cubed hash brown potatoes
2 cups cubed process cheese (Velveeta)
2 cups sour cream
1 (10¾-ounce / 305-g) can condensed cream of celery soup, undiluted
1 (10¾-ounce / 305-g) can condensed cream of chicken soup, undiluted
1 pound (454 g) sliced bacon, cooked and crumbled
1 large onion, chopped
¼ cup butter, melted
¼ teaspoon pepper

1. Place the cubed hash brown potatoes in a crock pot. In a large bowl, combine the remaining ingredients. Pour over potatoes and mix well. Cover and cook on low for 4 to 5 hours or until potatoes are tender and heated through.

Garlicky Braised Kale with Chorizo

Prep time: 10 minutes | Cook time: 7 to 8 hours | Serves 4 to 6

8 ounces (227 g) Spanish-style chorizo sausage, halved lengthwise and sliced ½ inch thick
2 garlic cloves, minced
1 tablespoon extra-virgin olive oil
1½ cups chicken broth
Salt and pepper, to taste
2 pounds (907 g) kale, stemmed and cut into 1-inch pieces
Vegetable oil spray

1. Lightly coat the insert of a crock pot with vegetable oil spray. Microwave the chorizo, garlic, and oil in a bowl, stirring occasionally, until fragrant, for about 1 minute. Transfer to the prepared crock pot. Stir in the broth and ¼ teaspoon salt.
2. Microwave half of the kale in a covered bowl until slightly wilted, for about 5 minutes. Transfer to the crock pot. Stir in the remaining kale, cover, and cook until kale is tender, for 7 to 8 hours on low for or 4 to 5 hours on high. Season with salt and pepper. Serve.

Leeks Braised in Cream

Prep time: 10 minutes | Cook time: 3 to 4 hours | Serves 4 to 6

3 pounds (1.4 kg) leeks, white and light green parts only, halved lengthwise, sliced thin, and washed and dried thoroughly
1 tablespoon vegetable oil
2 garlic cloves, minced
2 teaspoons minced fresh thyme or ½ teaspoon dried
Salt and pepper, to taste
1 cup heavy cream
½ cup dry white wine
¼ cup grated Pecorino Romano cheese

1. Microwave the leeks, oil, garlic, thyme, 1 teaspoon salt, and ¼ teaspoon pepper in a bowl, stirring occasionally, until leeks are softened, for 8 to 10 minutes. Transfer to a crock pot. Stir in the cream and wine, cover, and cook until leeks are tender but not mushy, for 3 to 4 hours on low or 2 to 3 hours on high.
2. Stir the Pecorino into the leek mixture and season with salt and pepper. Let sit for 5 minutes until slightly thickened. Serve.

Thyme Root Veggies

Prep time: 20 minutes | Cook time: 6 to 8 hours | Serves 8

6 carrots, cut into 1-inch chunks
2 yellow onions, each cut into 8 wedges
2 sweet potatoes, peeled and cut into chunks
6 Yukon Gold potatoes, cut into chunks
8 whole garlic cloves, peeled
4 parsnips, peeled and cut into chunks
3 tablespoons olive oil
1 teaspoon dried thyme leaves
½ teaspoon salt
⅛ teaspoon freshly ground black pepper

1. In a crock pot, mix all the ingredients. Cover and cook on low for 6 to 8 hours, or until the vegetables are tender.
2. Serve warm.

Root Veggie Gratin with Barley

Prep time: 10 minutes | Cook time: 7 to 9 hours | Serves 8

2 cups hulled barley
2 onions, chopped
5 garlic cloves, minced
3 large carrots, peeled and sliced
2 sweet potatoes, peeled and cubed
4 Yukon Gold potatoes, cubed
7 cups vegetable broth
1 teaspoon dried tarragon leaves
½ cup grated Parmesan cheese

1. In a crock pot, mix the barley, onions, garlic, carrots, sweet potatoes, and Yukon Gold potatoes. Add the vegetable broth and tarragon leaves.
2. Cover and cook on low for 7 to 9 hours, or until the barley and vegetables are tender.
3. Stir in the cheese and serve.

Mashed Squash with Garlic

Prep time: 20 minutes | Cook time: 6 to 7 hours | Serves 8

1 (3-pound / 1.4-kg) butternut squash, peeled, deseeded, and cut into 1-inch pieces
3 (1-pound / 454-g) acorn squash, peeled, deseeded, and cut into 1-inch pieces
2 onions, chopped
3 garlic cloves, minced
2 tablespoons olive oil
1 teaspoon dried marjoram leaves
½ teaspoon salt
⅛ teaspoon freshly ground black pepper

1. In a crock pot, mix all the ingredients. Cover and cook on low for 6 to 7 hours, or until the squash is tender when pierced with a fork.
2. Use a potato masher to mash the squash right in the crock pot. Serve.

Leafy Greens with Onions

Prep time: 20 minutes | Cook time: 3 to 4 hours | Serves 8

2 bunches Swiss chard, washed and cut into large pieces
2 bunches collard greens, washed and cut into large pieces
2 bunches kale, washed and cut into large pieces
3 onions, chopped
1½ cups vegetable broth
¼ cup honey
2 tablespoons lemon juice
1 teaspoon dried marjoram
1 teaspoon dried basil
¼ teaspoon salt

1. In a crock pot, mix the Swiss chard, collard greens, kale, and onions.
2. In a medium bowl, mix the vegetable broth, honey, lemon juice, marjoram, basil, and salt. Pour into the crock pot.
3. Cover and cook on low for 3 to 4 hours, or until the greens are very tender.
4. Serve warm.

Garlicky Balsamic Glazed Onions

Prep time: 20 minutes | Cook time: 8 to 10 hours | Serves 12

10 large yellow onions, peeled and sliced
20 garlic cloves, peeled
¼ cup olive oil
¼ teaspoon salt
2 tablespoons balsamic vinegar
1 teaspoon dried thyme leaves

1. In a crock pot, mix all the ingredients. Cover and cook on low for 8 to 10 hours, stirring once or twice.
2. serve warm.

Green Bean and Mushroom Casserole

Prep time: 10 minutes | Cook time: 6 hours | Serves 6

¼ cup butter, divided
½ sweet onion, chopped
1 cup sliced button mushrooms
1 teaspoon minced garlic
2 pounds (907 g) green beans, cut into 2-inch pieces
1 cup vegetable broth
8 ounces (227 g) cream cheese
¼ cup grated Parmesan cheese

1. Lightly grease the insert of the crock pot with 1 tablespoon of the butter.
2. In a large skillet over medium-high heat, melt the remaining butter. Add the onion, mushrooms, and garlic and sauté until the vegetables are softened, for about 5 minutes.
3. Stir the green beans into the skillet and transfer the mixture to the insert.
4. In a small bowl, whisk the broth and cream cheese together until smooth.
5. Add the cheese mixture to the vegetables and stir. Top the combined mixture with the Parmesan.
6. Cover and cook on low for 6 hours.
7. Serve warm.

Cauliflower-Bacon Casserole with Pecans

Prep time: 15 minutes | Cook time: 6 hours | Serves 6

1 tablespoon extra-virgin olive oil
2 pounds (907 g) cauliflower florets
10 bacon slices, cooked and chopped
1 cup chopped pecans
4 garlic cloves, sliced
½ teaspoon salt
½ teaspoon freshly ground black pepper
2 tablespoons freshly squeezed lemon juice
4 hard-boiled eggs, shredded, for garnish
1 scallion, white and green parts, chopped, for garnish

1. Lightly grease the insert of a crock pot with the olive oil.
2. In a medium bowl, toss together the cauliflower, bacon, pecans, garlic, salt, and pepper.
3. Transfer the mixture to the insert and drizzle the lemon juice over the top.
4. Cover and cook on low for 6 hours.
5. Garnish with the hard-boiled eggs and scallion and serve.

Citrus Carrots with Leek

Prep time: 15 minutes | Cook time: 7 to 8 hours | Serves 9

1½ pounds (680 g) whole small carrots
1 leek, white part only, sliced
3 garlic cloves, minced
¼ cup vegetable broth
2 tablespoons freshly squeezed lemon juice
2 tablespoons orange juice
2 tablespoons honey
½ teaspoon lemon zest
½ teaspoon orange zest
½ teaspoon salt
⅛ teaspoon freshly ground black pepper

1. Peel the carrots and cut off the roots. Trim off the tops, if the carrots have them. Put the carrots in the crock pot.
2. Add the leek and garlic, and stir. Then add all the remaining ingredients and stir.
3. Cover and cook on low for 7 to 8 hours, or until the carrots are tender.

Orange Cauliflower with Herbs

Prep time: 10 minutes | Cook time: 4 hours | Serves 8

2 heads cauliflower, rinsed and cut into florets
2 onions, chopped
½ cup orange juice
1 teaspoon grated orange zest
1 teaspoon dried thyme leaves
½ teaspoon dried basil leaves
½ teaspoon salt

1. In a crock pot, mix the cauliflower and onions. Top with the orange juice and orange zest, and sprinkle with the thyme, basil, and salt.
2. Cover and cook on low for 4 hours, or until the cauliflower is tender when pierced with a fork.
3. Serve warm.

Honey Parsnips and Carrots

Prep time: 15 minutes | Cook time: 5 to 7 hours | Serves 8

6 large carrots, peeled and cut into 2-inch pieces
5 large parsnips, peeled and cut into 2-inch pieces
2 red onions, chopped
4 garlic cloves, minced
2 tablespoons olive oil
1 tablespoon honey
½ teaspoon salt

1. In a crock pot, mix all the ingredients and stir gently. Cover and cook on low for 5 to 7 hours, or until the vegetables are tender.
2. Serve warm.

Carrot Cheese Casserole

Prep time: 5 minutes | Cook time: 4 to 5 hours | Serves 4 to 5

4 cups sliced carrots
1 medium onion, chopped
1 (10¾-ounce / 305-g) can cream of celery soup
½ cup Velveeta cheese, cubed
¼ to ½ teaspoon salt

1. Mix all the ingredients in a crock pot.
2. Cover and cook on low for 4 to 5 hours, or until carrots are tender but not mushy.
3. Serve hot.

Mexican Corn with Pimentos

Prep time: 10 minutes | Cook time: 2¾ to 4¾ hours | Serves 8 to 10

2 (10-ounce / 284-g) packages frozen corn, partially thawed
1 (4-ounce / 113-g) jar chopped pimentos
1⅓ cup chopped green peppers
1⅓ cup water
1 teaspoon salt
¼ teaspoon pepper
½ teaspoon paprika
½ teaspoon chili powder

1. Combine all the ingredients in a crock pot.
2. Cover. Cook on high for 45 minutes, then on low for 2 to 4 hours. Stir occasionally.
3. Serve warm.

Barbecue Collard Greens with Tofu

Prep time: 10 minutes | Cook time: 4 hours | Serves 6 to 8

¼ cup canola or safflower oil, divided
¾ cup finely chopped sweet onion
4 ounces (113 g) smoked or regular firm tofu, cut into 1-inch pieces
2 bunches collard greens (about 1 pound / 454 g each), tough stems and ribs removed, leaves cut into ½-inch ribbons
¾ cup barbecue sauce
¼ cup apple cider vinegar
Coarse salt and freshly ground pepper, to taste
3 cups boiling water

1. Heat 2 tablespoons of the oil in a large skillet over high heat. Add the onion and tofu, and cook until lightly browned, for about 8 minutes. Transfer to a crock pot.
2. In the same skillet, heat 1 tablespoon of the oil over high heat. In two batches, cook the collards for about 4 minutes, or until wilted, adding the remaining 1 tablespoon of the oil between batches.
3. Transfer the collards to the crock pot. Stir in the barbecue sauce and vinegar, and season with salt and pepper. Add the boiling water, cover, and cook on high for 4 hours or on low for 8 hours, or until very tender. Season with salt and pepper, and serve.

Spicy Corn-Ham Pudding

Prep time: 10 minutes | Cook time: 2 hours | Serves 6 to 8

4 cups fresh corn kernels, divided
1 teaspoon coarse salt
3 scallions, white and pale green parts only, thinly sliced, plus more for serving
1 (4-ounce / 113-g) can diced green chiles
¾ cup diced Black Forest ham
3 tablespoons all-purpose flour
2 cups grated manchego cheese or extra-sharp white Cheddar
5 large eggs, at room temperature
2⅓ cup heavy cream

1. Butter the insert of a crock pot.
2. Purée 3 cups of the corn in a blender or food processor. Transfer to a large bowl and stir in the remaining 1 cup of the corn, salt, scallions, chiles, ham, flour, and 1 cup of the cheese.
3. In another bowl, whisk together the eggs and cream just until combined. Stir into the corn mixture. Pour the batter into the crock pot and top with the remaining 1 cup of the cheese. Cover and cook on low for until pudding is set, for 2 hours, uncovering for last 15 minutes.
4. Let cool for 30 minutes before serving, topped with the sliced scallions.

Garlic Squash Curry

Prep time: 15 minutes | Cook time: 6 to 7 hours | Serves 8

1 large butternut squash, peeled, deseeded, and cut into 1-inch pieces
3 acorn squash, peeled, deseeded, and cut into 1-inch pieces
2 onions, finely chopped
5 garlic cloves, minced
1 tablespoon curry powder
1⅓ cup freshly squeezed orange juice
½ teaspoon salt

1. In a crock pot, mix all the ingredients. Cover and cook on low for 6 to 7 hours, or until the squash is tender when pierced with a fork.
2. Serve warm.

Pumpkin-Carrot Pudding

Prep time: 15 minutes | Cook time: 6 hours | Serves 6

1 tablespoon extra-virgin olive oil
2 cups finely shredded carrots
2 cups puréed pumpkin
½ sweet onion, finely chopped
1 cup heavy cream
½ cup cream cheese, softened
2 eggs
1 tablespoon granulated erythritol
1 teaspoon ground nutmeg
½ teaspoon salt
¼ cup pumpkin seeds, for garnish

1. Lightly grease the insert of the crock pot with the olive oil.
2. In a large bowl, whisk together the carrots, pumpkin, onion, heavy cream, cream cheese, eggs, erythritol, nutmeg, and salt.
3. Cover and cook on low for 6 hours.
4. Serve warm, topped with the pumpkin seeds.

Pecan-Stuffed Acorn Squash

Prep time: 5 minutes | Cook time: 5 to 6 hours | Serves 4

1 acorn squash
1 tablespoon honey
1 tablespoon olive oil
¼ cup chopped pecans or walnuts
¼ cup chopped dried cranberries
Sea salt, to taste

1. Cut the squash in half. Remove the seeds and pulp from the middle. Cut the halves in half again so you have quarters.
2. Place the squash quarters, cut-side up, in the crock pot.
3. Combine the honey, olive oil, pecans, and cranberries in a small bowl.
4. Spoon the pecan mixture into the center of each squash quarter. Season the squash with salt. Cook on low for 5 to 6 hours, or until the squash is tender.
5. Serve hot.

Greek Yogurt Mashed Pumpkin

Prep time: 10 minutes | Cook time: 7 to 8 hours | Serves 6

3 tablespoons extra-virgin olive oil, divided
1 pound (454 g) pumpkin, cut into 1-inch chunks
½ cup coconut milk
1 tablespoon apple cider vinegar
½ teaspoon chopped thyme
1 teaspoon chopped oregano
¼ teaspoon salt
1 cup Greek yogurt

1. Lightly grease the insert of the crock pot with 1 tablespoon of the olive oil.
2. Add the remaining 2 tablespoons of the olive oil with the pumpkin, coconut milk, apple cider vinegar, thyme, oregano, and salt to the insert.
3. Cover and cook on low for 7 to 8 hours.
4. Mash the pumpkin with the yogurt using a potato masher until smooth.
5. Serve warm.

Acorn Squash with Shallots and Dates

Prep time: 15 minutes | Cook time: 3 hours | Serves 4 to 6

2 small acorn squash (about 2 pounds / 907 g), halved, deseeded, and cut into wedges
6 shallots, quartered
10 dates, pitted and thinly sliced
6 thyme sprigs
¼ cup plus 2 tablespoons extra-virgin olive oil
¼ cup pure maple syrup
1 teaspoon coarse salt
⅛ teaspoon freshly ground black pepper
⅛ teaspoon red pepper flakes

1. Combine the squash, shallots, dates, and thyme in a large bowl. Drizzle with the oil and maple syrup, and sprinkle with salt, black pepper, and red pepper flakes. Toss well with and transfer to the crock pot.
2. Cover and cook on high for about 3 hours or on low for 6 hours, turning the squash once or twice during cooking, until squash is tender. Transfer to a large bowl and serve.

Garlic Button Mushrooms

Prep time: 10 minutes | Cook time: 6 hours | Serves 8

3 tablespoons extra-virgin olive oil
1 pound (454 g) button mushrooms, wiped clean and halved
2 teaspoons minced garlic
¼ teaspoon salt
⅛ teaspoon freshly ground black pepper
2 tablespoons chopped fresh parsley

1. Place the olive oil, mushrooms, garlic, salt, and pepper in the insert of the crock pot and toss to coat.
2. Cover and cook on low for 6 hours.
3. Serve topped with the parsley.

Thai-Flavored Green Vegetables

Prep time: 10 minutes | Cook time: 3 to 3½ hours | Serves 10

1½ pounds (680 g) green beans
3 cups fresh soybeans
3 bulbs fennel, cored and chopped
1 jalapeño pepper, minced
1 lemongrass stalk
½ cup canned coconut milk
2 tablespoons lime juice
½ teaspoon salt
1⅓ cup chopped fresh cilantro

1. In a crock pot, mix the green beans, soybeans, fennel, jalapeño pepper, lemongrass, coconut milk, lime juice, and salt. Cover and cook on low for 3 to 3½ hours, or until the vegetables are tender.
2. Remove and discard the lemongrass. Sprinkle the vegetables with the cilantro and serve.

Lemon-Rosemary Beets

Prep time: 10 minutes | Cook time: 8 hours | Serves 7

2 pounds (907 g) beets, peeled and cut into wedges
2 tablespoons fresh lemon juice
2 tablespoons extra-virgin olive oil
2 tablespoons honey
1 tablespoon apple cider vinegar
¾ teaspoon sea salt
½ teaspoon black pepper
2 sprigs fresh rosemary
½ teaspoon lemon zest

1. Place the beets in the crock pot.
2. Whisk the lemon juice, extra-virgin olive oil, honey, apple cider vinegar, salt, and pepper together in a small bowl. Pour over the beets.
3. Add the sprigs of rosemary to the crock pot.
4. Cover and cook on low for 8 hours, or until the beets are tender.
5. Remove and discard the rosemary sprigs. Stir in the lemon zest. Serve hot.

Peppery Broccoli with Sesame Seeds

Prep time: 15 minutes | Cook time: 6 hours | Serves 8

2 pounds (907 g) fresh broccoli, trimmed and chopped into bite-size pieces
1 clove garlic, minced
1 green or red bell pepper, cut into thin slices
1 onion, cut into slices
4 tablespoons light soy sauce
½ teaspoon salt
Dash of black pepper
1 tablespoon sesame seeds, for garnish (optional)

1. Combine all the ingredients, except for the sesame seeds, in a crock pot.
2. Cover and cook on low for 6 hours. Top with the sesame seeds.
3. Serve warm.

Basil Potato and Corn

Prep time: 15 minutes | Cook time: 5 to 6 hours | Serves 8

4 cups potatoes, diced and peeled
1½ cups frozen whole-kernel corn, thawed
4 medium tomatoes, deseeded and diced
1 cup sliced carrots
½ cup chopped onions
¾ teaspoon salt
½ teaspoon sugar
¾ teaspoon dill weed
¼ teaspoon black pepper
½ teaspoon dried basil
¼ teaspoon dried rosemary

1. Combine all the ingredients in a crock pot.
2. Cover. Cook on low for 5 to 6 hours, or until vegetables are tender.
3. Serve warm.

Chapter 8 Vegetarian Mains

Black Bean Spinach Enchiladas

Prep time: 10 minutes | Cook time: 6 to 8 hours | Serves 2

1 (15-ounce / 425-g) can black beans, drained and rinsed
¼ cup low-fat cream cheese
¼ cup low-fat Cheddar cheese
½ cup minced onion
1 teaspoon minced garlic
1 teaspoon ground cumin
1 teaspoon smoked paprika
2 cups shredded fresh spinach
1 teaspoon extra-virgin olive oil
1 cup enchilada sauce, divided
4 corn tortillas
¼ cup fresh cilantro, for garnish

1. In a large bowl, mix together the beans, cream cheese, Cheddar cheese, onion, garlic, cumin, paprika, and spinach.
2. Grease the inside of the crock pot with the olive oil.
3. Pour ¼ cup of enchilada sauce into the crock, spreading it across the bottom. Place one corn tortilla on top of the sauce. Top the tortilla with one-third of the black bean and spinach mixture. Top this with a second corn tortilla and then slather it with ¼ cup of enchilada sauce. Repeat this layering, finishing with a corn tortilla and the last ¼ cup of enchilada sauce.
4. Cover and cook on low for 6 to 8 hours. Garnish with the cilantro just before serving.

Spinach Mushroom Cheese Quiche

Prep time: 10 minutes | Cook time: 8 hours | Serves 2

1 teaspoon butter, at room temperature, or extra-virgin olive oil
4 eggs
1 teaspoon fresh thyme
⅛ teaspoon sea salt
Freshly ground black pepper, to taste
2 slices whole-grain bread, crusts removed and cut into 1-inch cubes
½ cup diced button mushrooms
2 tablespoons minced onion
1 cup shredded spinach
½ cup shredded Swiss cheese

1. Grease the inside of the crock pot with the butter.
2. In a small bowl, whisk together the eggs, thyme, salt, and a few grinds of the black pepper.
3. Put the bread, mushrooms, onions, spinach, and cheese in the crock pot. Pour the egg mixture over the top and stir gently to combine.
4. Cover and cook on low for 8 hours or overnight.

Seitan Tikka Masala with Green Beans

Prep time: 10 minutes | Cook time: 6 hours | Serves 2

8 ounces (227 g) seitan, cut into bite-size pieces
1 cup chopped green beans
1 cup diced onion
1 cup fire-roasted tomatoes, drained
1 teaspoon ground coriander
1 teaspoon ground cumin
1 teaspoon smoked paprika
⅛ teaspoon red pepper flakes
1 teaspoon minced fresh ginger
1 cup low-sodium vegetable broth
2 tablespoons coconut cream
¼ cup minced fresh cilantro, for garnish

1. Put the seitan, green beans, onion, tomatoes, coriander, cumin, paprika, red pepper flakes, ginger, and vegetable broth in the crock pot. Gently stir the ingredients together to combine.
2. Cover and cook on low for 6 hours.
3. Allow to the dish to rest, uncovered, for 10 minutes, then stir in the coconut cream and garnish the dish with the cilantro.

Tempeh and Vegetable Shepherd's Pie

Prep time: 10 minutes | Cook time: 8 hours | Serves 2

1 cup frozen peas, thawed
1 cup diced carrots
½ cup minced onions
8 ounces (227 g) tempeh
⅛ teaspoon sea salt
Freshly ground black pepper, to taste
1½ cups prepared mashed potatoes
2 tablespoons shredded sharp Cheddar cheese

1. Put the peas, carrots, onions, and tempeh in the crock pot and gently stir to combine. Season the mixture with the salt and black pepper.
2. Spread the prepared mashed potatoes over the tempeh and vegetable mixture.
3. Cover and cook on low for 8 hours.
4. Sprinkle with the cheese just before serving.

Tempeh and Corn Stuffed Bell Peppers

Prep time: 10 minutes | Cook time: 6 to 8 hours | Serves 2

1 teaspoon extra-virgin olive oil
8 ounces (227 g) tempeh, crumbled
1 cup frozen corn kernels, thawed
¼ cup minced onions
1 teaspoon minced garlic
1 teaspoon ground cumin
1 teaspoon smoked paprika
2 tablespoons Pepper Jack cheese
⅛ teaspoon sea salt
4 narrow red bell peppers

1. Grease the inside of the crock pot with the olive oil.
2. In a medium bowl, combine the tempeh, corn, onions, garlic, cumin, paprika, cheese, and salt.
3. Cut the tops off each of the peppers and set the tops aside. Scoop out and discard the seeds and membranes from inside each pepper. Divide the tempeh filling among the peppers. Return the tops to each of the peppers.
4. Nestle the peppers into the crock pot.
5. Cover and cook on low for 6 to 8 hours, until the peppers are very tender.

Potato Stuffed Peppers

Prep time: 15 minutes | Cook time: 4 hours | Serves 4

4 medium Yukon Gold potatoes
2 red bell peppers
2 green bell peppers
1 teaspoon rapeseed oil
1 teaspoon cumin seeds
1 cup frozen peas
1 teaspoon salt
1 fresh green chile, finely chopped
1 teaspoon garam masala
1 tablespoon fenugreek leaves
1-inch piece fresh ginger, grated
1 tablespoon finely chopped fresh coriander leaves

1. Boil the potatoes with the skin on until they're soft (about 15 minutes), then leave to cool. (I always boil potatoes with the skin on, as it stops them taking on too much water and becoming mushy.) Peel off their skins and dice the potatoes.
2. Preheat the crock pot on high and make sure the 4 peppers will fit into the crock pot side by side.
3. Heat the oil in a small frying pan, and then toast the cumin seeds until fragrant, about 1 minute. Add the peas to soften.
4. Put the toasted cumin and peas in a large bowl. Then add the cooked potatoes with the salt, chile, garam masala, fenugreek leaves, ginger, and fresh coriander leaves, and mix together. Taste the filling and adjust the seasoning.
5. Slice the tops off the peppers, keeping the stalks intact. Remove the seeds and discard. Divide the potato mixture into 4 portions and stuff each of the peppers.
6. If you have a tray for the inside of your crock pot, place this inside. If not, crumple up some foil to make a little tray for the peppers to sit on.
7. Place the stuffed peppers on the tray inside the crock pot. Replace the top of each of the peppers. Pour about ¼ to 1⅓ cup of water into the crock pot outside of the tray (so the peppers are not sitting in the water).
8. Cook on low for 4 hours, or for 2 hours on high.

Veggie Tofu Stir-Fry

Prep time: 15 minutes | Cook time: 4 to 6 hours | Serves 2

1 teaspoon extra-virgin olive oil
½ cup brown rice
1 cup water
Pinch sea salt
1 (16-ounce / 454-g) block tofu, drained and cut into 1-inch pieces
1 green bell pepper, cored and cut into long strips
½ onion, halved and thinly sliced
1 cup chopped green beans, cut into 1-inch pieces
2 carrots, cut into ½-inch dice
2 tablespoons low-sodium soy sauce
1 tablespoon hoisin sauce
1 tablespoon freshly squeezed lime juice
1 teaspoon minced garlic
Pinch red pepper flakes

1. Grease the inside of the crock pot with the olive oil.
2. Put the brown rice, water, and salt in the crock pot and gently stir so all the rice grains are submerged.
3. Put the tofu, bell pepper, onion, green beans, and carrots over the rice.
4. In a measuring cup or glass jar, whisk together the soy sauce, hoisin sauce, lime juice, garlic, and red pepper flakes. Pour this mixture over the tofu and vegetables.
5. Cover and cook on low for 4 to 6 hours, until the rice has soaked up all the liquid and the vegetables are tender.

Indian Spiced Potatoes and Cauliflower

Prep time: 15 minutes | Cook time: 3 hours | Serves 6

1 large cauliflower, cored and cut into florets
2 tablespoons mustard oil
2 teaspoons mustard seeds
2 teaspoons cumin seeds
1 onion, finely chopped
3 garlic cloves, finely chopped
2 red potatoes, peeled and cut into 1½-inch cubes
7 to 8 ounces (198 to 227 g) canned tomatoes
1 tablespoon freshly grated ginger
1 teaspoon salt
1 teaspoon turmeric
1 teaspoon chili powder
1 or 2 fresh green chiles, finely chopped
1 teaspoon dried fenugreek leaves
1 teaspoon garam masala
Handful fresh coriander leaves, chopped

1. Prepare your cauliflower and make sure it's thoroughly dry before cooking.
2. Heat the oil in a frying pan (or in the crock pot if you have a sear setting). Add the mustard seeds, and as they sizzle, add the cumin seeds.
3. Add the onions and garlic, and cook for 1 minute before adding the potatoes and cauliflower to the crock pot along with the tomatoes, ginger, salt, turmeric, chili powder, chopped chiles, and dried fenugreek leaves.
4. Turn the crock pot to low and cook for 3 hours, or for 2 hours on high. Give the dish a stir in the first hour, and it will release enough liquid to cook.
5. Before serving, sprinkle with garam masala and fresh coriander leaves.

Vegetarian Bean Cassoulet

Prep time: 10 minutes | Cook time: 6 to 8 hours | Serves 2

1 teaspoon extra-virgin olive oil
2 (15-ounce / 425-g) cans navy beans, drained and rinsed
16 ounces (454 g) vegan sausage, cut into 1-inch pieces
1 cup minced onion
¼ cup minced celery
1 tablespoon minced garlic
1 teaspoon minced fresh sage
1 cup low-sodium vegetable broth

1. Grease the inside of the crock pot with the olive oil.
2. Put the beans, sausage, onion, celery, garlic, and sage in the crock pot. Stir to mix thoroughly. Pour in the vegetable broth.
3. Cover and cook on low for 6 to 8 hours, until the beans are very tender but not falling apart.

Beans and Couscous Stuffed Peppers

Prep time: 15 minutes | Cook time: 4 hours | Serves 4

4 large bell peppers, any color
1 (15-ounce / 425-g) can cannellini beans, rinsed and drained
1 cup crumbled feta cheese
½ cup uncooked couscous
4 green onions, white and green parts separated, thinly sliced
1 garlic clove, minced
1 teaspoon oregano
Coarse sea salt and freshly ground black pepper, to taste
1 lemon cut into 4 wedges, for serving

1. Slice a very thin layer from the base of each bell pepper so they sit upright. Slice off the tops just below stem and discard the stem only. Chop the remaining top portions and place in a medium bowl. With a spoon, scoop out the ribs and seeds from the peppers.
2. Add the beans, feta, couscous, white parts of the green onions, garlic, and oregano to a medium bowl. Season with salt and pepper and toss to combine.
3. Stuff the peppers with bean mixture, and place them upright in the crock pot. Cover and cook on high for 4 hours, or until the peppers are tender and the couscous is cooked.
4. To serve, sprinkle the peppers with the green parts of the green onions and plate with 1 lemon wedge alongside each pepper.

Curried Coconut Quinoa

Prep time: 15 minutes | Cook time: 3 to 4 hours | Serves 6

2 cups coconut milk
1 cup uncooked quinoa
1⅓ cup hot water
1 (14-ounce / 397-g) can chickpeas, drained and rinsed
1 tablespoon tomato purée
1 tablespoon freshly grated ginger
1 teaspoon turmeric
1 teaspoon chili powder
1 teaspoon sea salt
2 garlic cloves, minced
1 sweet potato, peeled and chopped
1 large broccoli crown, cut into florets
1 tomato, diced
1 fresh green chile, chopped
½ white onion, finely diced (about 1 cup)
Shredded fresh coconut, for garnish
Handful fresh coriander leaves, chopped

1. Wash the quinoa in a few changes of water to rid it of its external coating, which can be bitter.
2. Add all ingredients except the shredded coconut, and the coriander leaves to the crock pot, and stir until everything is mixed.
3. Cover and cook on high for 3 to 4 hours, or for 6 hours on low, until the sweet potato is cooked through. Stir halfway through cooking, if you can.
4. Top with coconut shreds and coriander leaves, and serve hot.

Eggplant and Potato Curry

Prep time: 10 minutes | Cook time: 2 hours | Serves 6

2 tablespoons mustard oil
2 teaspoons mustard seeds
2 teaspoons cumin seeds
1 onion, finely sliced
7 to 8 ounces (198 to 227 g) canned tomatoes
1 teaspoon turmeric
1 fresh green chile, finely chopped
1 tablespoon freshly grated ginger
2 eggplants, about 1 pound (454 g) total, cut into 1-inch lengths
2 red potatoes, peeled and cut into 1-inch lengths
1 teaspoon sea salt
1 teaspoon garam masala
Handful fresh coriander leaves, chopped

1. Heat the oil in a frying pan (or in the crock pot if you have a sear setting). Add the mustard seeds, and as they are sizzling add the cumin seeds until they become fragrant.
2. Turn the crock pot to high and add the spices with the sliced onion, tomatoes, turmeric, chopped chile, and grated ginger.
3. Stir in the eggplant and potatoes. Cover and cook on high for 2 hours, or for 3 to 4 hours on low.
4. When you are ready to serve, add the salt, garam masala, and fresh coriander leaves.

Spice Stuffed Baby Eggplants

Prep time: 15 minutes | Cook time: 4 hours | Serves 6

12 baby eggplants
4 dried red chiles
2 tablespoons coriander seeds
1 teaspoon mustard seeds
1 teaspoon cumin seeds
½ teaspoon fenugreek seeds
1 teaspoon fennel seeds
1 tablespoon nigella seeds
¼ teaspoon carom seeds
½ teaspoon turmeric
1 teaspoon mango powder
Sea salt, to taste
3 tablespoons mustard oil
2 onions, sliced
Handful fresh coriander leaves, chopped

1. Preheat the crock pot on high.
2. Wash the eggplants and cut lengthwise, but leave the top intact.
3. Heat a dry frying pan on medium-high and add the red chiles, coriander seeds, mustard seeds, cumin seeds, fenugreek seeds, fennel seeds, nigella seeds, and carom seeds to the pan. Toast until fragrant, about 1 minute. Remove and put into a coffee grinder and blend to a fine powder.
4. Empty into a medium bowl and mix in the turmeric, mango powder, and salt. Add some water to make a thick paste.
5. Rub about 1 teaspoon of the paste into each of the eggplants with your fingers so the flesh is covered inside and out.
6. Heat the mustard oil in the same frying pan (or in the crock pot if you have a sear setting). Add the sliced onions and cook for 5 minutes. Add any remaining spice paste. Mix for a minute or two and add a splash of water if needed. Then pour the onion mixture into the crock pot.
7. Place the stuffed eggplants into the crock pot and cover. Cook on low for 4 hours, or on high for 2 to 3 hours.
8. Turn the eggplants a few times during cooking, if possible.
9. Check the seasoning and sprinkle in the coriander leaves.

Roasted Cauliflower with Tomato Cashew Sauce

Prep time: 15 minutes | Cook time: 4 to 5 hours | Serves 6

1 red onion, sliced
1-inch piece fresh ginger, cut into strips
4 garlic cloves, sliced
2 tomatoes, roughly chopped
1 fresh green chile, chopped
5 tablespoons raw cashews, soaked in water for 2 hours and drained
1 large head cauliflower, outer leaves trimmed
2 tablespoons ghee or rapeseed oil
1 teaspoon cumin seeds
1 teaspoon coriander seeds
1 teaspoon salt
1 teaspoon Kashmiri chili powder
1 teaspoon turmeric
1 teaspoon garam masala
$2\frac{1}{3}$ cup hot water
1 tablespoon dried fenugreek leaves
Handful fresh coriander leaves, chopped

1. Preheat the crock pot on high for 15 minutes, or use the sauté setting if you have one. Add the onions, ginger, garlic, tomatoes, and green chile. Stir and cook for 10 minutes.
2. Add the drained cashews and place the head of cauliflower on top of everything.
3. Heat the ghee or rapeseed oil, if using, in a frying pan and toast the cumin and coriander seeds until they are fragrant. Pour them over the cauliflower head and sprinkle in the salt, chili powder, turmeric, and garam masala.
4. Add the water. Cover and cook on low for 4 to 5 hours, or on high for 2 to 3 hours.
5. When it's cooked (you can check by sticking a sharp knife through the middle), transfer the cauliflower head to a shallow oven-proof dish. Using an immersion or regular blender, blend the cooking liquid that's left in the crock pot to make a smooth sauce. It should be like a thick batter; if it's too thick, you can add a little hot water.
6. Check and adjust the salt, if required. Add the dried fenugreek leaves and then pour the sauce over the cauliflower head. Place in the oven at 400°F (205°C) for 5 to 10 minutes to crisp up.
7. Sprinkle on some fresh coriander leaves and serve in chunky wedges.

Chapter 8 Vegetarian Mains

Almond Vegetable Korma

Prep time: 20 minutes | Cook time: 2 to 3 hours | Serves 6

1 tablespoon vegetable oil
3 cloves
3 green cardamom pods
1-inch piece cassia bark
1 to 3 dried red chiles
2 onions, minced
2 garlic cloves, minced
1 tablespoon freshly grated ginger
1 teaspoon turmeric
1 tablespoon ground coriander seeds
Sea salt, to taste
1⅓ cup hot water
1⅓ cup creamed coconut
2 heaped tablespoons ground almonds
1 teaspoon ground white poppy seeds
1 cup cauliflower florets
1 carrot, peeled and chopped
1 red bell pepper, deseeded and diced
1 cup peeled, deseeded, and chopped winter squash (such as butternut or pumpkin)
½ cup frozen peas, thawed
½ cup green beans
1 teaspoon garam masala
Handful fresh coriander leaves, finely chopped
3 tablespoons slivered almonds
1 lemon, quartered

1. Heat the oil in a frying pan (or in the crock pot if you have a sear setting). Add the cloves, cardamom pods, cassia bark, and dried red chiles. Cook for a few minutes until fragrant. Add the minced onions and sauté gently over medium heat for about 5 to 10 minutes.
2. Set the crock pot on high and pour the mixture inside. Add the garlic and ginger and cook for a few minutes. Then stir in the turmeric, ground coriander seeds, and salt. Pour in the hot water, creamed coconut, ground almonds, and poppy seeds, and then stir.
3. Add the cauliflower, carrot, pepper, and squash. Cover and cook on high for 2 to 3 hours, or on low for 4 to 5 hours.
4. Add the peas and green beans and cook on high for another hour.
5. When the dish is cooked, add the garam masala and stir through. Top with fresh coriander leaves, slivered almonds, and a squeeze of lemon juice for added freshness.

Red Tofu Curry and Green Beans

Prep time: 15 minutes | Cook time: 6 hours | Serves 2

1 teaspoon extra-virgin olive oil
16 ounces (454 g) firm tofu, drained and cut into 1-inch pieces
2 cups chopped green beans
½ red onion, halved and thinly sliced
1 plum tomato, diced
1 teaspoon minced fresh ginger
1 teaspoon minced garlic
2 teaspoons Thai red curry paste
1 cup coconut milk
1 cup low-sodium vegetable broth

1. Grease the inside of the crock pot with the olive oil.
2. Put all the ingredients into the crock pot and stir gently.
3. Cover and cook on low for 6 hours.

North African Pumpkin and Cauliflower Stew

Prep time: 15 minutes | Cook time: 7 to 8 hours | Serves 6

1 tablespoon extra-virgin olive oil
2 cups diced pumpkin
2 cups chopped cauliflower
1 red bell pepper, diced
½ sweet onion, diced
2 teaspoons minced garlic
2 cups coconut milk
2 tablespoons natural peanut butter
1 tablespoon ground cumin
1 teaspoon ground coriander
¼ cup chopped cilantro, for garnish

1. Lightly grease the crock pot with the olive oil.
2. Add the pumpkin, cauliflower, bell pepper, onion, and garlic to the crock pot.
3. In a small bowl, whisk together the coconut milk, peanut butter, cumin, and coriander until smooth.
4. Pour the coconut milk mixture over the vegetables in the crock pot.
5. Cover and cook on low for 7 to 8 hours.
6. Serve topped with the cilantro.

Chapter 8 Vegetarian Mains | 77

Cauliflower and Zucchini Vindaloo

Prep time: 15 minutes | Cook time: 6 hours | Serves 6

1 tablespoon extra-virgin olive oil
4 cups cauliflower florets
1 carrot, diced
1 zucchini, diced
1 red bell pepper, diced
2 cups coconut milk
½ sweet onion, chopped
1 dried chipotle pepper, chopped
1 tablespoon grated fresh ginger
2 teaspoons minced garlic
2 teaspoons ground cumin
1 teaspoon ground coriander
½ teaspoon turmeric
¼ teaspoon cayenne pepper
¼ teaspoon cardamom
1 cup Greek yogurt, for garnish
2 tablespoons chopped cilantro, for garnish

1. Lightly grease the crock pot with the olive oil.
2. Place the cauliflower, carrot, zucchini, and bell pepper in the crock pot.
3. In a small bowl, whisk together the coconut milk, onion, chipotle pepper, ginger, garlic, cumin, coriander, turmeric, cayenne pepper, and cardamom until well blended.
4. Pour the coconut milk mixture into the crock pot and stir to combine.
5. Cover and cook on low for 6 hours.
6. Serve each portion topped with the yogurt and cilantro.

Braised Eggplant and Lentils

Prep time: 20 minutes | Cook time: 2 to 3 hours | Serves 4 to 6

2 pounds (907 g) eggplant, cut into 1-inch pieces
1 onion, chopped fine
3 tablespoons extra-virgin olive oil, divided
1 tablespoon tomato paste
2 garlic cloves, minced
2 teaspoons minced fresh thyme or ½ teaspoon dried
Salt and ground black pepper, to taste
2 cups vegetable broth
1 cup French green lentils, picked over and rinsed
2 tablespoons red wine vinegar, divided
10 ounces (283 g) cherry tomatoes, halved
½ cup feta cheese, crumbled
¼ cup minced fresh parsley

1. Adjust oven rack 6 inches from broiler element and heat broiler. Line rimmed baking sheet with aluminum foil.
2. Toss eggplant and onion with 1 tablespoon oil, tomato paste, garlic, thyme, and ½ teaspoon salt in a bowl.
3. Spread eggplant mixture evenly over the prepared baking sheet. Broil until eggplant is softened and beginning to brown, 10 to 12 minutes, rotating sheet halfway through broiling.
4. Combine broth, lentils, and 1 tablespoon vinegar in the crock pot. Spread eggplant mixture and tomatoes evenly on top of lentils.
5. Cover and cook until lentils are tender, 3 to 4 hours on low or 2 to 3 hours on high. Stir in remaining 2 tablespoons oil and remaining 1 tablespoon vinegar. Season with salt and pepper to taste. Sprinkle with feta and parsley and serve.

Summer Vegetable Mélange

Prep time: 15 minutes | Cook time: 6 hours | Serves 6

½ cup extra-virgin olive oil
¼ cup balsamic vinegar
1 tablespoon dried basil
1 teaspoon dried thyme
¼ teaspoon salt
2 cups cauliflower florets
2 zucchini, diced into 1-inch pieces
1 yellow bell pepper, cut into strips
1 cup halved button mushrooms

1. In a large bowl, whisk together the oil, vinegar, basil, thyme, and salt, until blended.
2. Add the cauliflower, zucchini, bell pepper, and mushrooms, and toss to coat.
3. Transfer the vegetables to the crock pot.
4. Cover and cook on low for 6 hours.
5. Serve warm.

Caponata

Prep time: 15 minutes | Cook time: 5½ hours | Serves 6

1 pound (454 g) plum tomatoes, chopped
1 eggplant, not peeled, cut into ½-inch pieces
2 medium zucchini, cut into ½-inch pieces
1 large yellow onion, finely chopped
3 stalks celery, sliced
½ cup chopped fresh parsley
2 tablespoons red wine vinegar
1 tablespoon brown sugar
¼ cup raisins
¼ cup tomato paste
1 teaspoon sea salt
¼ teaspoon black pepper
¼ cup pine nuts
2 tablespoons capers, drained

1. Combine the tomatoes, eggplant, zucchini, onion, celery, and parsley in the crock pot. Add the vinegar, brown sugar, raisins, and tomato paste. Sprinkle with the salt and pepper.
2. Cover and cook on low for 5½ hours, or until thoroughly cooked.
3. Stir in the pine nuts and capers. Serve hot.

Barley-Stuffed Cabbage Rolls

Prep time: 15 minutes | Cook time: 3½ hours | Serves 4

1 large head green cabbage, cored
1 tablespoon olive oil
1 large yellow onion, chopped
3 cups cooked pearl barley
3 ounces (85 g) feta cheese, crumbled
½ cup dried currants
2 tablespoons pine nuts, toasted
2 tablespoons chopped fresh flat-leaf parsley
½ teaspoon sea salt, divided
½ teaspoon black pepper, divided
½ cup apple juice
1 tablespoon apple cider vinegar
1 (15-ounce / 425-g) can crushed tomatoes, with the juice

1. Steam the cabbage head in a large pot over boiling water for 8 minutes. Remove to a cutting board and let cool slightly.
2. Remove 16 leaves from the cabbage head (reserve the rest of the cabbage for another use). Cut off the raised portion of the center vein of each cabbage leaf (do not cut out the vein).
3. Heat the oil in a large nonstick lidded skillet over medium heat. Add the onion, cover, and cook 6 minutes, or until tender. Remove to a large bowl.
4. Stir the barley, feta cheese, currants, pine nuts, and parsley into the onion mixture. Season with ¼ teaspoon of the salt and ¼ teaspoon of the pepper.
5. Place cabbage leaves on a work surface. On 1 cabbage leaf, spoon about 1⅓ cup of the barley mixture into the center. Fold in the edges of the leaf over the barley mixture and roll the cabbage leaf up as if you were making a burrito. Repeat for the remaining 15 cabbage leaves and filling.
6. Arrange the cabbage rolls in the crock pot.
7. Combine the remaining ¼ teaspoon salt, ¼ teaspoon pepper, the apple juice, apple cider vinegar, and tomatoes. Pour the apple juice mixture evenly over the cabbage rolls.
8. Cover and cook on high for 2 hours or on low for 6 to 8 hours. Serve hot.

Tofu with Greens

Prep time: 20 minutes | Cook time: 6 hours | Serves 6

1 pound (454 g) firm tofu, drained and crumbled
½ cup onion, chopped
½ cup celery, chopped
2 cups bok choy, chopped
2 cups napa cabbage, chopped
½ cup pea pods, cut in half

1. Combine all the ingredients in the crock pot. Gently stir to mix well.
2. Cook on low for 6 hours.
3. Serve warm.

Sumptuous Chinese Vegetable Mix

Prep time: 10 minutes | Cook time: 3 to 6 hours | Serves 6

1 (12-ounce /340-g) package chop-suey vegetables
1 (1-pound / 454-g) can bean sprouts, drained
2 (4-ounce / 113-g) cans sliced mushrooms, drained
1 (8-ounce / 227-g) can water chestnuts, drained
1 bunch celery, sliced on the diagonal
1 large onion, sliced
3 tablespoons soy sauce
1 tablespoon sugar
¼ teaspoon black pepper, or to taste
¾ cup water
Cooking spray

1. Spritz the crock pot with cooking spray.
2. Combine all ingredients in the crock pot.
3. Cover. Cook on low for 3 to 6 hours, depending upon how soft or crunchy you like the vegetables.
4. Serve warm.

Chapter 9 Poultry

Chicken Parmesan

Prep time: 10 minutes | Cook time: 4 to 4½ hours | Serves 8

8 boneless, skinless chicken breast halves (about 2 pounds / 907 g)
½ cup water
1 cup fat-free mayonnaise
½ cup grated fat-free Parmesan cheese
2 teaspoons dried oregano
¼ teaspoon black pepper
¼ teaspoon paprika

1. Place chicken and water in a crock pot.
2. Cover. Cook on high 2 hours.
3. Mix remaining ingredients. Spread over chicken.
4. Cover. Cook on high 2 to 2½ hours.

Hawaiian Huli Huli Chicken

Prep time: 5 minutes | Cook time: 4 to 5 hours | Serves 4

2⅓ cup pineapple juice
½ cup packed brown sugar
½ cup ketchup
¼ cup lime juice (2 limes)
¼ cup soy sauce
6 garlic cloves, minced
2 tablespoons grated fresh ginger
4 (10-ounce / 283-g) chicken leg quarters, trimmed
Salt and pepper, to taste

1. Bring pineapple juice, sugar, ketchup, lime juice, soy sauce, garlic, and ginger to simmer in a medium saucepan over medium heat and cook until thickened and measures 1 cup, 15 to 20 minutes.
2. Lightly coat crock pot with vegetable oil spray. Transfer ½ cup sauce to prepared crock pot; reserve remaining sauce separately. Season chicken with salt and pepper, add to the crock pot, and turn to coat evenly with sauce. Cover and cook until chicken is tender, 4 to 5 hours on low.
3. Adjust oven rack 6 inches from broiler element and heat broiler. Set wire rack in aluminum foil-lined rimmed baking sheet and coat with vegetable oil spray. Transfer chicken to prepared rack; discard cooking liquid. Broil chicken until browned, about 10 minutes, flipping chicken halfway through broiling.
4. Brush chicken with ¼ cup reserved sauce and continue to broil until chicken is lightly charred, about 5 minutes, flipping and brushing chicken with remaining ¼ cup sauce halfway through broiling. Serve.

Lemon Garlic Chicken

Prep time: 15 minutes | Cook time: 3 to 4 hours | Serves 6

1 cup vegetable broth
1½ teaspoons grated lemon peel
3 tablespoons lemon juice
2 tablespoons capers, drained
3 garlic cloves, minced
½ teaspoon pepper
6 boneless skinless chicken breast halves (6 ounces / 170 g each)
2 tablespoons butter
2 tablespoons all-purpose flour
½ cup heavy whipping cream
Hot cooked rice

1. In a small bowl, combine the first six ingredients. Place chicken in a crock pot; pour broth mixture over chicken. Cook, covered, on low 3 to 4 hours or until chicken is tender.
2. Remove chicken from crock pot; keep warm. In a large saucepan, melt butter over medium heat. Stir in flour until smooth; gradually whisk in cooking juices. Bring to a boil, stirring constantly; cook and stir 1-2 minutes or until thickened. Remove from heat and stir in cream. Serve chicken and rice with sauce.

Apple Balsamic Chicken

Prep time: 15 minutes | Cook time: 4 to 5 hours | Serves 4

4 bone-in chicken thighs (about 1½ pounds / 680 g), skin removed
½ cup chicken broth
¼ cup apple cider or juice
¼ cup balsamic vinegar
2 tablespoons lemon juice
½ teaspoon salt
½ teaspoon garlic powder
½ teaspoon dried thyme
½ teaspoon paprika
½ teaspoon pepper
2 tablespoons butter
2 tablespoons all-purpose flour

1. Place chicken in a crock pot. In a small bowl, combine the broth, cider, vinegar, lemon juice and seasonings; pour over meat. Cover and cook on low for 4 to 5 hours or until chicken is tender.
2. Remove chicken; keep warm. Skim fat from cooking liquid. In a small saucepan, melt butter; stir in flour until smooth. Gradually add cooking liquid. Bring to a boil; cook and stir for 2 to 3 minutes or until thickened. Serve with chicken.

Mango Pineapple Chicken Tacos

Prep time: 25 minutes | Cook time: 5 to 6 hours | Serves 16

2 medium mangoes, peeled and chopped
1½ cups cubed fresh pineapple or canned pineapple chunks, drained
2 medium tomatoes, chopped
1 medium red onion, finely chopped
2 small Anaheim peppers, deseeded and chopped
2 green onions, finely chopped
1 tablespoon lime juice
1 teaspoon sugar
4 pounds (1.8 kg) bone-in chicken breast halves, skin removed
3 teaspoons salt
¼ cup packed brown sugar
32 taco shells, warmed
¼ cup minced fresh cilantro

1. In a large bowl, combine the first eight ingredients. Place chicken in a crock pot; sprinkle with salt and brown sugar. Top with mango mixture. Cover and cook on low for 5 to 6 hours or until chicken is tender.
2. Remove chicken; cool slightly. Strain cooking juices, reserving mango mixture and ½ cup juices. Discard remaining juices. When cool enough to handle, remove chicken from bones; discard bones.
3. Shred chicken with two forks. Return chicken and reserved mango mixture and cooking juices to crock pot; heat through. Serve in taco shells; sprinkle with cilantro.

Mushroom Chicken Alfredo

Prep time: 20 minutes | Cook time: 4 to 5 hours | Serves 4

4 bone-in chicken breast halves (12 to 14 ounces / 340 to 397 g each), skin removed
2 tablespoons canola oil
1 (10¾-ounce / 305-g) can condensed cream of chicken soup, undiluted
1 (10¾-ounce / 305-g) can condensed cream of mushroom soup, undiluted
1 cup chicken broth
1 small onion, chopped
1 (6-ounce / 170-g) jar sliced mushrooms, drained
¼ teaspoon garlic salt
¼ teaspoon pepper
8 ounces (227 g) fettuccine
1 (8-ounce / 227-g) package cream cheese, softened and cubed
Shredded Parmesan cheese (optional)

1. In a large skillet, brown chicken in oil in batches. Transfer to a crock pot. In a large bowl, combine the soups, broth, onion, mushrooms, garlic salt and pepper; pour over meat. Cover and cook on low for 4 to 5 hours or until chicken is tender.
2. Cook fettuccine according to package directions; drain. Remove chicken from crock pot and keep warm. Turn crock pot off and stir in cream cheese until melted. Serve with fettucine. Top with Parmesan cheese if desired.

Jamaican-Inspired Brown Chicken Stew

Prep time: 25 minutes | Cook time: 6 to 8 hours | Serves 8

¼ cup ketchup
3 garlic cloves, minced
1 tablespoon sugar
1 tablespoon hot pepper sauce
1 teaspoon browning sauce (optional)
1 teaspoon dried basil
1 teaspoon dried thyme
1 teaspoon paprika
½ teaspoon salt
½ teaspoon dried oregano
½ teaspoon ground allspice
½ teaspoon pepper
8 bone-in chicken thighs (about 3 pounds / 1.4 kg), skin removed
1 pound (454 g) fully cooked andouille chicken sausage links, sliced
1 medium onion, finely chopped
2 medium carrots, finely chopped
2 celery ribs, finely chopped

1. In a large resealable plastic bag, combine ketchup, garlic, sugar, pepper sauce and, if desired, browning sauce; stir in seasonings. Add chicken thighs, sausage and vegetables. Seal bag and turn to coat. Refrigerate 8 hours or overnight.
2. Transfer contents of bag to a crock pot. Cook, covered, on low 6 to 8 hours or until chicken is tender.

Lemon-Dill Chicken

Prep time: 20 minutes | Cook time: 4 to 5 hours | Serves 6

2 medium onions, coarsely chopped
2 tablespoons butter, softened
¼ teaspoon grated lemon peel
1 broiler/fryer chicken (4 to 5 pounds / 1.8 to 2.3 kg)
¼ cup chicken stock
4 sprigs fresh parsley
4 fresh dill sprigs
3 tablespoons lemon juice
1 teaspoon salt
1 teaspoon paprika
½ teaspoon dried thyme
¼ teaspoon pepper

1. Place onions on the bottom of a crock pot. In a small bowl, mix butter and lemon peel.
2. Tuck wings under chicken; tie drumsticks together. With fingers, carefully loosen skin from chicken breast; rub butter mixture under the skin. Secure skin to underside of breast with toothpicks. Place chicken over onions, breast side up. Add stock, parsley and dill.
3. Drizzle lemon juice over the chicken; sprinkle with seasonings. Cook, covered, on low 4 to 5 hours (a thermometer inserted in thigh should read at least 175ºF (79ºC)).
4. Remove chicken from crock pot; tent with foil. Let stand 15 minutes before carving.

Cornbread Chicken Bake

Prep time: 20 minutes | Cook time: 3 to 4 hours | Serves 6

5 cups cubed cornbread
¼ cup butter, cubed
1 large onion, chopped (about 2 cups)
4 celery ribs, chopped (about 2 cups)
3 cups shredded cooked chicken
1 (10¾-ounce / 305-g) can condensed cream of chicken soup, undiluted
1 (10¾-ounce / 305-g) can condensed cream of mushroom soup, undiluted
½ cup reduced-sodium chicken broth
1 teaspoon poultry seasoning
½ teaspoon salt
½ teaspoon rubbed sage
¼ teaspoon pepper

1. Preheat oven to 350ºF (180ºC). Place bread cubes on an ungreased 15x10-in. baking pan. Bake 20 to 25 minutes or until toasted. Cool on baking pan.
2. In a large skillet, heat butter over medium-high heat. Add onion and celery; cook and stir 6 to 8 minutes or until tender. Transfer to a greased crock pot. Stir in corn bread, chicken, soups, broth and seasonings.
3. Cook, covered, on low 3 to 4 hours or until heated through.

Thai Sesame Chicken Thighs

Prep time: 20 minutes | Cook time: 5 to 6 hours | Serves 8

8 bone-in chicken thighs (about 3 pounds / 1.4 kg), skin removed
½ cup salsa
¼ cup creamy peanut butter
2 tablespoons lemon juice
2 tablespoons reduced-sodium soy sauce
1 tablespoon chopped deseeded jalapeño pepper
2 teaspoons Thai chili sauce
1 garlic clove, minced
1 teaspoon minced fresh ginger
2 green onions, sliced
2 tablespoons sesame seeds, toasted
Hot cooked basmati rice (optional)

1. Place chicken in a crock pot. In a small bowl, combine the salsa, peanut butter, lemon juice, soy sauce, jalapeño, Thai chili sauce, garlic and ginger; pour over chicken.
2. Cover and cook on low for 5 to 6 hours or until chicken is tender. Sprinkle with green onions and sesame seeds. Serve with rice if desired.

Chicken with Apple and Chardonnay Gravy

Prep time: 20 minutes | Cook time: 6 to 8 hours | Serves 6

6 chicken leg quarters
½ teaspoon salt
¼ teaspoon pepper
2 large sweet apples, peeled and cut into wedges
1 large sweet onion, chopped
2 celery ribs, chopped
½ cup chardonnay
1 envelope brown gravy mix
2 large garlic cloves, minced
1 teaspoon each minced fresh oregano, rosemary and thyme
Hot mashed potatoes

1. Sprinkle chicken with salt and pepper. Place half of the chicken in a crock pot. In a bowl, combine the apples, onion and celery; spoon half of the mixture over chicken. Repeat layers.
2. In the same bowl, whisk wine, gravy mix, garlic and herbs until blended; pour over top. Cover and cook on low for 6 to 8 hours or until chicken is tender.
3. Remove chicken to a serving platter; keep warm. Cool the apple mixture slightly; skim fat. In a blender, cover and process apple mixture in batches until smooth. Transfer to a saucepan and heat through over medium heat, stirring occasionally. Serve with chicken and mashed potatoes.

Sour Cream Chicken Enchiladas

Prep time: 10 minutes | Cook time: 2 hours | Serves 8

1 tablespoon vegetable oil
1 large yellow onion, chopped
1 (24- to 32-ounce / 680- to 907-g) can green chile enchilada sauce
1 dozen soft corn tortillas, each one cut into 4 strips
2½ to 3 cups cooked boneless, skinless chicken, cut into ¾-inch pieces
4 cups finely shredded Monterey Jack cheese
2 cups sour cream (reduced fat is okay)

1. In a large skillet, heat the oil over medium-high heat, then add the onion and cook, stirring, until softened, about 5 minutes. Set aside.
2. Pour about ½ cup of the enchilada sauce into the crock pot; tilt to spread it around. In layers, add one-quarter of the tortilla strips, one-quarter of the remaining sauce, one-third of the sautéed onion, one-third of the chicken, and one-quarter of the cheese. Repeat the layers two more times, ending with the cheese. Finish the casserole with the remaining tortilla strips, sauce, and cheese.
3. Spoon the sour cream over the surface of the casserole in big dollops. Use a spatula or the back of a large spoon to gently spread it all around without disturbing the layers. Cover and cook on high for 2 hours, or on low for 4 to 5 hours.
4. To serve, use a long-handled spoon to reach down through all the layers for each serving. Make sure each diner gets some of the sour cream.

Rotisserie-Style Chicken with Carrots

Prep time: 25 minutes | Cook time: 6 to 7 hours | Serves 6

4 teaspoons seasoned salt
4 teaspoons poultry seasoning
1 tablespoon paprika
1½ teaspoons onion powder
1½ teaspoons brown sugar
1½ teaspoons salt-free lemon-pepper seasoning
¾ teaspoon garlic powder
1 broiler/fryer chicken (4 pounds / 1.8 kg)
1 pound (454 g) carrots, halved lengthwise and cut into 1½-inch lengths
2 large onions, chopped
2 tablespoons cornstarch

1. In a small bowl, combine the first seven ingredients. Carefully loosen skin from chicken breast; rub 1 tablespoon spice mixture under the skin. Rub remaining spice mixture over chicken. In another bowl, toss carrots and onions with cornstarch; transfer to a crock pot. Place chicken on vegetables.
2. Cover and cook on low for 6 to 7 hours or until a thermometer inserted in thigh reads 180°F (82°C). Remove chicken and vegetables to a serving platter; cover and let stand for 15 minutes before carving. Skim fat from cooking juices. Serve with chicken and vegetables.

Mushroom Chicken Cacciatore

Prep time: 10 minutes | Cook time: 4½ to 5½ hours | Serves 6 to 8

4 tablespoons extra-virgin olive oil
1 pound (454 g) cremini mushrooms, quartered
2 teaspoons salt
Pinch red pepper flakes
1 teaspoon dried oregano
3 cloves garlic, minced
¼ cup dried porcini mushrooms, crumbled
¼ cup red wine
1 (28- to 32-ounce / 794- to 907-g) can crushed tomatoes, with their juice
10 chicken thighs, skin and bones removed

1. Heat 2 tablespoons of the oil in a large skillet over high heat. Add the mushrooms, 1 teaspoon of the salt, red pepper flakes, oregano, and garlic and sauté until the liquid in the pan has evaporated, about 7 to 10 minutes.
2. Add the porcini and the wine to a small bowl and allow the porcini to soften. Add the wine mixture and the tomatoes to the skillet.
3. Transfer the contents of the pan to the insert of a crock pot.
4. Sprinkle the chicken evenly with the remaining 1 teaspoon salt. Heat the remaining 2 tablespoons oil in the same skillet over high heat. Add the chicken to the skillet and brown on all sides, 15 to 20 minutes.
5. Transfer the browned meat to the crock pot insert, submerging it in the sauce. Cover and cook on low for 4 to 5 hours, until the chicken is tender and cooked through. Skim off any fat from the top of the sauce.
6. Serve from the crock pot set on warm.

Tandoori Chicken

Prep time: 5 minutes | Cook time: 4 hours | Serves 6

1½ cups plain yogurt
2 teaspoons fresh lemon juice
1 teaspoon ground coriander
½ teaspoon ground cumin
½ teaspoon ground cardamom
½ teaspoon turmeric
1 teaspoon sweet paprika
2 cloves garlic, minced
1 teaspoon freshly grated ginger
1 (3- to 4-pound / 1.4- to 1.8-kg) chicken, cut into 8 pieces and skin removed

1. Combine the yogurt, lemon juice, coriander, cumin, cardamom, turmeric, paprika, garlic, and ginger in a 1-gallon zipper-top plastic bag.
2. Add the chicken in the bag and marinate for at least 8 hours and up to 24 hours. Put the chicken and the marinade in the insert of a crock pot.
3. Cover and cook on high for 4 hours, until the chicken is cooked through. Remove the chicken from the pot and serve warm or at room temperature.

Ginger Peach Glazed Chicken Thighs

Prep time: 15 minutes | Cook time: 4 to 5 hours | Serves 10

10 boneless skinless chicken thighs (about 2½ pounds / 1.1 kg)
1 cup sliced peeled fresh or frozen peaches
1 cup golden raisins
1 cup peach preserves
1⅓ cup chili sauce
2 tablespoons minced crystallized ginger
1 tablespoon reduced-sodium soy sauce
1 tablespoon minced garlic
Hot cooked rice (optional)

1. Place chicken in a crock pot coated with cooking spray. Top with peaches and raisins. In a small bowl, combine the preserves, chili sauce, ginger, soy sauce and garlic. Spoon over the top.
2. Cover and cook on low for 4 to 5 hours or until chicken is tender. Serve with rice if desired.

Orange-Hoisin Chicken

Prep time: 15 minutes | Cook time: 5 to 6 hours | Serves 4 to 6

2 tablespoons frozen orange juice concentrate, thawed
¼ cup honey
2 tablespoons soy sauce
2 tablespoons hoisin sauce
3 slices peeled fresh ginger, about ¼ inch thick
3 cloves garlic, minced or pressed
1 tablespoon toasted sesame oil
6 individually frozen boneless, skinless chicken breast halves (do not thaw)
2 teaspoons cornstarch
2 teaspoons cold water
1 tablespoon sesame seeds (optional), toasted in a dry skillet over medium heat until fragrant

1. In a zipper-top plastic bag, combine the orange juice concentrate, honey, soy sauce, hoisin sauce, ginger, garlic, and sesame oil. One at a time, put the chicken pieces in the bag, seal, and gently shake to coat with the sauce. Transfer the coated chicken to the crock pot, then pour the remaining sauce over the chicken. Cover and cook on low until the chicken is tender and cooked through, 5 to 6 hours.
2. Transfer the chicken to a warm platter. Strain the sauce through a fine-mesh strainer into a small saucepan. In a cup or small bowl, stir together the cornstarch and cold water. Bring the sauce to a boil over high heat, add the slurry, and cook, stirring a few times, until thickened, 1 or 2 minutes. Pour some of the sauce over the chicken and pass the rest on the side. If desired, sprinkle the sesame seeds over the top.

Filipino Chicken Adobo

Prep time: 15 minutes | Cook time: 3 to 3½ hours | Serves 6

¾ cup plain rice vinegar
½ cup low-sodium soy sauce
4 cloves garlic, pressed
1 (2- to 3-inch) piece fresh ginger, peeled and grated (optional)
1 tablespoon light brown sugar
1 teaspoon black peppercorns
2 bay leaves
2½ pounds (1.1 kg) bone-in, skin-on chicken thighs (about 8), trimmed of fat
1 pound (454 g) red or Yukon gold potatoes, scrubbed and cut into eighths
2 medium-size carrots, sliced, or 2 cups baby carrots
4 ounces (113 g) green beans, ends trimmed
2 tablespoons olive oil
¾ cup water

1. In a shallow glass baking dish, stir together the vinegar, soy sauce, garlic, ginger (if using), brown sugar, peppercorns, and bay leaves. Add the chicken and turn to coat. Cover and marinate in the refrigerator for at least 1 hour or as long as overnight.
2. Place the potatoes, carrots, and green beans in the crock pot. Lift the chicken out of the marinade and pat dry with paper towels. Heat the oil in a large skillet over medium-high heat and cook the chicken, skin side down, until it is a golden brown on both sides, about 2 minutes per side. Transfer the chicken thighs to the crock. Pour the marinade and water into the skillet and bring to a boil. Pour the sauce into the crock.
3. Cover and cook on high for 3 to 3½ hours, or until the juice of the chicken runs clear. Discard the bay leaves. Serve the chicken and vegetables with the sauce.

Jerk Chicken

Prep time: 5 minutes | Cook time: 2½ to 3 hours | Serves 8

2 teaspoons jerk seasoning
1½ cups mango nectar
½ cup firmly packed light brown sugar
2 tablespoons dark corn syrup
2 tablespoons rice vinegar
8 chicken breast halves, skin and bones removed

1. Add the jerk seasoning, nectar, sugar, corn syrup, and rice vinegar to the insert of a crock pot and stir to combine.
2. Add the chicken breasts and turn to coat in the sauce. Cover and cook on high for 2½ to 3 hours, until the chicken is cooked through.
3. Serve the chicken hot, warm, or at room temperature.

Whole Roasted Mexican Chicken

Prep time: 5 minutes | Cook time: 6 to 7 hours | Serves 4 to 6

1 (3- to 4-pound / 1.4- to 1.8-kg) broiler/fryer
¾ to 1 teaspoon salt
½ teaspoon freshly ground black pepper
Juice of 1 small or ½ large lime
½ cup fresh cilantro sprigs
2 cloves garlic, peeled

1. Remove the chicken giblets and neck and reserve for another use. Cut off any lumps of fat. Season the chicken inside and out with salt and pepper. Place in the crock pot, breast side up. Squeeze the juice of the lime over the chicken and put the rind, cilantro sprigs, and garlic into the cavity. Cover and cook on low until an instant-read thermometer inserted into the thickest part of the thigh registers 180°F (82°C), 6 to 7 hours.
2. Transfer the chicken to a platter. Pour the liquid from the crock pot into a separate container and refrigerate; then skim off the fat after it congeals. Or pour the cooking juices into a gravy separator and then into a container and refrigerate if not using. When the chicken is cool enough to handle, remove the skin, and cut or shred the meat from the carcass. Refrigerate the meat if not using it immediately.

Tarragon Chicken Marsala

Prep time: 15 minutes | Cook time: 3 to 4 hours | Serves 6

¾ cup all-purpose flour or rice flour, for dredging
6 boneless, skin-on chicken breast halves (about 2 pounds / 907 g)
3 tablespoons unsalted butter or ghee
2 medium-size shallots, minced
8 ounces (227 g) sliced white or cremini mushrooms
1 (14½-ounce / 411-g) can low-sodium chicken broth
Sea salt and freshly ground black pepper, to taste
Marsala Gravy:
2 (1.2-ounce / 34-g) packages chicken gravy mix, such as Knorr
1⅓ cup dry Marsala wine
2 teaspoons finely chopped fresh tarragon

1. Put the flour in a shallow dish or pie plate. One piece at a time, dredge the chicken in the flour, coating both sides and shaking off any excess flour.
2. Heat the butter in a large skillet over medium-high heat. When the butter is foaming, add the chicken, skin side down. Cook the chicken until it is a deep golden brown on both sides, about 5 minutes per side.
3. Transfer the chicken pieces to the crock pot. Add the shallots and mushrooms to the skillet and cook over high heat, stirring, until they are slightly brown. Transfer to the crock. Add the broth to the skillet and bring to a boil, stirring, to dissolve any brown particles that are stuck to the pan. Pour the broth over the chicken in the crock. Season with salt and pepper. Cover and cook on high for 3 to 4 hours, until the chicken pulls apart easily.
4. Ladle 2 cups of the liquid out of the crock pot and into a saucepan. Discard any remaining liquid. Add the two gravy packets, Marsala, and tarragon to the saucepan and whisk well. Cook over medium-high heat, whisking constantly, and bring to a boil. Reduce the heat to a simmer and cook for 2 minutes, until thickened and smooth. While the gravy simmers, remove the chicken breasts and mushrooms from the crock, discard the skin, and shred or chop the meat into large pieces. Serve the gravy over the warm chicken and mushrooms.

Garlicky Lemon-Thyme Turkey Legs

Prep time: 10 minutes | Cook time: 6 to 8 hours | Serves 6

8 cloves garlic, peeled
Grated zest of 4 lemons
2 teaspoons fresh thyme leaves
Salt and freshly ground black pepper, to taste
¼ cup extra-virgin olive oil
6 turkey legs, skin removed
½ cup dry white wine
1 cup chicken broth

1. Put the garlic, zest, thyme, 1½ teaspoons salt, ½ teaspoon pepper, and oil in a food processor or blender and blend to a paste. Rub the paste on the turkey and put the turkey in the crock pot.
2. Pour the wine and chicken broth in the insert of a crock pot.
3. Cover and cook on low for 6 to 8 hours, until the turkey is cooked through and registers 175°F (79°C) on an instant-read thermometer.
4. Remove the legs from the sauce and cover with aluminum foil. Strain the sauce through a fine-mesh sieve into a saucepan and bring to a boil.
5. Season with salt and pepper before serving.

Turkey Teriyaki Thighs

Prep time: 10 minutes | Cook time: 3 to 4 hours | Serves 6

½ cup soy sauce
2 tablespoons hoisin sauce
2 cloves garlic, minced
1 teaspoon freshly grated ginger
2 tablespoons rice wine (mirin) or dry sherry
¼ firmly packed light brown sugar
4 turkey thighs, skin removed

1. Blend the soy sauce, hoisin, garlic, ginger, rice wine, and brown sugar in a mixing bowl and stir to combine.
2. Pour the marinade in a zipper-top plastic bag. Add the turkey thighs to the bag. Seal the bag and refrigerate for at least 8 hours or overnight. Pour the contents of the bag in the insert of a crock pot.
3. Cover and cook on high for 3 to 4 hours, until the turkey is cooked through and registers 175°F (79°C) on an instant-read thermometer.
4. Remove the turkey from the crock pot, cover with aluminum foil, and allow to rest for 20 minutes before serving.

Apricot Glazed Turkey with Herbs

Prep time: 20 minutes | Cook time: 3 to 3½ hours | Serves 4

4 turkey legs or thighs, skinned (see headnote)
1 teaspoon paprika
1 teaspoon salt
¼ teaspoon freshly ground black pepper
½ teaspoon dried rosemary, crushed, or 1½ tablespoons chopped fresh rosemary
½ teaspoon dried thyme, or 1½ tablespoons chopped fresh thyme
¼ cup apricot jam
2 tablespoons honey
1 tablespoon fresh lemon juice
1 tablespoon barbecue sauce
1 tablespoon soy sauce
1 teaspoon cornstarch
1 teaspoon cold water

1. In a small bowl, combine the paprika, salt, pepper, rosemary, and thyme. Rub all over the turkey legs. Set aside for 15 minutes or refrigerate, covered, for 2 to 3 hours.
2. Coat the crock pot with nonstick cooking spray. Put the turkey in the crock pot. In a small bowl, combine the jam, honey, lemon juice, barbecue sauce, and soy sauce. Pour over the turkey; stir if necessary to coat the turkey. Cover and cook on high until the turkey is tender, 3 to 3½ hours.
3. Preheat the oven to 375°F (190°C). Transfer the turkey to a baking dish, tent with aluminum foil, and keep warm in the oven while you finish the sauce.
4. Pour the sauce from the crock pot into a small saucepan. Combine the cornstarch and cold water in a small bowl, stirring to remove any lumps. Bring the sauce to a boil and continue boiling for 2 to 3 minutes to reduce the sauce and concentrate the flavors. Add the slurry and cook for 2 or 3 minutes more, until thickened.
5. Remove the turkey from the oven, pour the glaze over the turkey, and serve.

Tea Smoked Turkey Legs

Prep time: 10 minutes | Cook time: 5 hours | Serves 6

2 cups chicken broth
8 bags Lapsang Souchong or black tea
4 slices fresh ginger
1 cinnamon stick
½ cup soy sauce
¼ cup hoisin sauce
6 turkey legs, skin removed

1. Bring the broth to a boil in a saucepan and add the tea bags, ginger, and cinnamon. Allow the broth to cool, about 45 minutes. Strain the broth through a fine-mesh sieve into a bowl and whisk in the soy sauce and hoisin.
2. Brush some of the sauce on the turkey legs with a silicone pastry brush. Pour the remaining sauce in the insert of a crock pot. Fit the rack in the crock pot and place the turkey legs on the rack.
3. Cover and cook on high for 5 hours, basting the turkey a few times during cooking.
4. Slice the turkey legs into serving-size pieces and serve.

Mexican Turkey

Prep time: 15 minutes | Cook time: 3 to 3½ hours | Serves 6 to 8

2 pounds (907 g) turkey thighs, skinned
1 (8-ounce / 227-g) can tomato sauce
1 (4-ounce / 113-g) can chopped roasted green chiles, with their juice
2 medium-size or 3 small white onions, chopped
2 tablespoons Worcestershire sauce
2 tablespoons chili powder
Pinch of ground cumin
1 clove garlic, crushed

For Serving:
8 large flour tortillas, at room temperature
¾ cup shredded Cheddar cheese
2⅓ cup sour cream
Diced fresh tomatoes
Shredded iceberg lettuce

1. Put the turkey thighs in the crock pot. Add the tomato sauce, chiles, onions, Worcestershire, chili powder, cumin, and garlic and stir to coat the thighs with the mixture. Cover and cook on high until the turkey is tender, 3 to 3½ hours.
2. Remove the turkey from the crock pot and, once it cools a bit, pick the meat off the bones. Shred the meat, return it to the crock pot, and stir to combine well with the sauce. Spoon the meat and sauce onto a tortilla and roll up. Top with cheese, sour cream, tomatoes, and lettuce. Repeat with the remaining tortillas and toppings and serve immediately.

Turkey Taco Salad

Prep time: 15 minutes | Cook time: 4 to 6 hours | Serves 6

Meat Sauce:
1½ pounds (680 g) ground dark turkey meat
1 (16-ounce / 454-g) jar tomato salsa

Salad:
1 medium firm-ripe avocado
6 cups thick shredded or chopped iceberg or romaine lettuce
3 cups corn chips
1 (15-ounce / 425-g) can pinto beans, rinsed, drained, and heated in a saucepan or microwave
1½ cups shredded Cheddar cheese
1 (16-ounce / 454-g) jar tomato salsa
2 medium-size ripe tomatoes, coarsely chopped
1 cup cold sour cream, stirred
1 (4-ounce / 113-g) can sliced ripe California black olives, drained

1. Coat the crock pot with nonstick cooking spray. To make the meat sauce, put the ground turkey and salsa in the crock pot. Cover and cook on low until cooked thoroughly, 4 to 6 hours. Stir the sauce.
2. To make the salad, slice the avocado and put all the salad components in separate containers. On each individual plate layer some lettuce, a handful of corn chips, some of the hot meat, a spoonful or two of hot pinto beans, shredded cheese, some salsa, diced tomatoes, sour cream, avocado, and olives.

Stuffed Turkey Cutlets with Artichokes

Prep time: 20 minutes | Cook time: 2 to 3 hours | Serves 6

4 tablespoons (½ stick) unsalted butter
2 cloves garlic, minced
1 (16-ounce / 454-g) package frozen artichoke hearts, thawed and coarsely chopped
½ cup pine nuts
1 cup fresh bread crumbs
2⅓ cup freshly grated Parmigiano-Reggiano cheese
4 leaves fresh basil, finely chopped
8 turkey breast cutlets (¾ to 1 pound / 340 to 454 g)
1½ teaspoons salt
½ teaspoon freshly ground black pepper
½ cup finely chopped onion
1 teaspoon dried sage
2 tablespoons all-purpose flour
1 cup dry white wine or vermouth
1 cup chicken broth

1. Melt 2 tablespoons of the butter in a large skillet over medium-high heat. Add the garlic and artichoke hearts and sauté until the liquid in the pan evaporates, 5 to 7 minutes.
2. Transfer to a mixing bowl. Add the pine nuts, bread crumbs, cheese, and basil to the bowl and stir to combine. Place the cutlets on a cutting board, sprinkle evenly with the salt and pepper, and spread 2 tablespoons of the filling on each turkey breast.
3. Roll the cutlets lengthwise and place seam-side down in the insert of a crock pot. Melt the remaining 2 tablespoons butter in the same skillet. Add the onion and sage and sauté until the onion is softened, about 3 minutes.
4. Add the flour and cook for 3 minutes, stirring constantly. Deglaze the pan with the wine and chicken broth, scraping up any browned bits, and bring to a boil, whisking constantly. Pour the sauce over the turkey rolls.
5. Cover and cook on high for 2 to 3 hours, until the turkey is tender.
6. Serve from the crock pot set on warm.

Duck Breasts with Port and Orange Sauce

Prep time: 10 minutes | Cook time: 6 to 7 hours | Serves 4

2 tablespoons unsalted butter
4 boneless duck breast halves, with skin (about 1½ pounds / 680 g total)
1⅓ cup port wine
Grated zest of 1 orange
1 teaspoon salt
⅛ teaspoon freshly ground black pepper
2 tablespoons cornstarch
¼ cup milk

1. Melt the butter in a large skillet (not a nonstick one) over medium-high heat. When it foams, add the duck, skin side down, and cook until deep golden brown on both sides, 2 to 3 minutes per side. Add the port and bring to a boil. Being careful of long sleeves and dangling hair, touch a long lit match to the liquid in the pan and turn off the heat. The liquid will catch fire and burn for about 30 seconds, then the flames will die out. With a slotted spoon, transfer the duck to the crock pot. Return the liquid in the pan to a boil and cook briefly, scraping up any browned bits stuck to the pan. Pour over the duck, then sprinkle with the orange zest, salt, and pepper. Cover and cook on low for 6 to 7 hours.
2. Preheat the oven to 375ºF (190ºC). With a slotted spoon, transfer the duck to a shallow baking dish. Tent with aluminum foil and keep warm in the oven while you finish the sauce.
3. Skim and discard as much fat as possible from the liquid in the crock pot, then pour into a small saucepan. In a small bowl, stir the cornstarch into the milk to make a smooth slurry. Bring the sauce to a boil, add the slurry, and cook, stirring, until it thickens, 3 to 4 minutes. Taste for salt and pepper. Serve the duck with the sauce.

Italian-Style Braised Chicken and Veggies

Prep time: 10 minutes | Cook time: 4 hours | Serves 8

8 boneless, skinless chicken breast halves
Black pepper, to taste
1 teaspoon garlic powder
1 (16-ounce / 454-g) bottle fat-free Italian salad dressing, divided
2 (15-ounce / 425-g) cans whole potatoes, drained
1 pound (454 g) frozen Italian veggies or green beans, thawed
1 (8-ounce / 227-g) can water chestnuts (optional)

1. Sprinkle the chicken with pepper and garlic powder.
2. Put the chicken in a crock pot. Pour half of the salad dressing over meat, making sure that all pieces are glazed.
3. Add the potatoes, vegetables, and water chestnuts (if desired). Pour the remaining salad dressing over, again making sure that the vegetables are all lightly coated.
4. Cover. Cook on high for 4 hours, or on low for 7 to 8 hours.
5. Serve warm.

Chicken Cacciatore

Prep time: 10 minutes | Cook time: 6 to 6½ hours | Serves 4 to 5

2 onions, sliced
2½ to 3 pounds (1.1 to 1.4 kg) chicken legs
2 garlic cloves, minced
1 (16-ounce / 454-g) can stewed tomatoes
1 (8-ounce / 227-g) can tomato sauce
1 teaspoon salt
¼ teaspoon pepper
1 to 2 teaspoons dried oregano
½ teaspoon dried basil
1 bay leaf
¼ cup white wine
Hot buttered spaghetti, linguini, or fettucini, for serving

1. Place the onions in a crock pot.
2. Lay the chicken legs over the onions.
3. Combine the remaining ingredients in a bowl. Pour over the chicken.
4. Cover. Cook on low for 6 to 6½ hours.
5. Remove the bay leaf. Serve over hot buttered spaghetti, linguini, or fettucini.

Classic Chicken Casablanca

Prep time: 20 minutes | Cook time: 4½ to 6½ hours | Serves 6 to 8

2 tablespoons oil
2 large onions, sliced
1 teaspoon ground ginger
3 garlic cloves, minced
3 large carrots, diced
2 large potatoes, diced
3 pounds (1.4 kg) skinless chicken pieces
½ teaspoon ground cumin
½ teaspoon salt
½ teaspoon pepper
¼ teaspoon cinnamon
2 tablespoons raisins
1 (14½-ounce / 411-g) can chopped tomatoes
3 small zucchini, sliced
1 (15-ounce / 425-g) can garbanzo beans, drained
2 tablespoons chopped parsley
Cooked rice or couscous, for serving

1. Sauté the onions, ginger, and garlic in the oil in a skillet, for 3 minutes. Reserve the oil. Transfer to a crock pot. Add the carrots and potatoes.
2. Brown the chicken over medium heat in the reserved oil, for 12 to 15 minutes. Transfer to the crock pot. Mix gently with the vegetables.
3. Combine the seasonings in a separate bowl. Sprinkle over the chicken and vegetables. Add the raisins and tomatoes.
4. Cover. Cook on high for 4 to 6 hours.
5. Add the sliced zucchini, beans, and parsley at the last 30 minutes.
6. Serve over cooked rice or couscous.

Authentic Con Pollo

Prep time: 5 minutes | Cook time: 8 to 10 hours | Serves 4 to 6

3 to 4 pounds (1.4 to 1.8 kg) whole chicken
Salt, to taste
Pepper, to taste
Paprika, as needed
Garlic salt, to taste
1 (6-ounce / 170-g) can tomato paste
½ cup beer
1 (3-ounce / 85-g) jar stuffed olives, with liquid
Cooked rice or noodles, for serving

1. Wash the chicken. Sprinkle all over with salt, pepper, paprika, and garlic salt. Place in a crock pot.
2. Combine the tomato paste and beer. Pour over the chicken. Add the olives.
3. Cover. Cook on low for 8 to 10 hours, or on high for 3 to 4 hours.
4. Serve over cooked rice or noodles.

Chicken and Turkey Sausage Jambalaya

Prep time: 20 minutes | Cook time: 6 hours | Serves 6

1 pound (454 g) uncooked boneless, skinless chicken breast, cubed
3 cups fat-free chicken broth
¾ cup water
1½ cups uncooked brown rice
4 ounces (113 g) reduced-fat, smoked turkey sausage, diced
½ cup thinly sliced celery with leaves
½ cup chopped onion
½ cup chopped green bell pepper
2 teaspoons Cajun seasoning
2 garlic cloves, minced
⅛ teaspoon hot pepper sauce (optional)
1 bay leaf
1 (14½-ounce / 411-g) can no-salt diced tomatoes, undrained

1. In a large nonstick skillet, sauté the chicken for 2 to 3 minutes.
2. Stir together the remaining ingredients in a crock pot.
3. Add the sautéed chicken to the crock pot.
4. Cover. Cook on high for 6 hours.
5. Serve warm.

Chicken Cheese Parmigiana

Prep time: 5 minutes | Cook time: 6$^{1/3}$ to 8$^{1/3}$ hours | Serves 6

1 egg, beaten
1 teaspoon salt
¼ teaspoon pepper
1 cup Italian bread crumbs
6 boneless, skinless chicken breast halves
2 to 4 tablespoons butter
1 (14-ounce / 397-g) jar pizza sauce
6 slices Mozzarella cheese
Grated Parmesan cheese, for topping

1. Combine the egg, salt, and pepper together in a bowl. Place the bread crumbs in a separate bowl.
2. Dip the chicken into the egg and coat with the bread crumbs. Sauté the chicken in the butter in a skillet for 5 minutes. Arrange the chicken in a crock pot.
3. Pour the pizza sauce over the chicken.
4. Cover. Cook on low for 6 to 8 hours.
5. Layer the Mozzarella cheese over top and sprinkle with the Parmesan cheese. Cook for an additional 15 minutes.
6. Serve warm.

Chicken Chili

Prep time: 5 minutes | Cook time: 6 to 8 hours | Serves 4

4 boneless, skinless chicken breast halves
1 (16-ounce / 454-g) jar salsa
2 (16-ounce / 454-g) cans Great Northern beans, drained
8 ounces (227 g) shredded cheese, Colby Jack or Pepper Jack
Cooked rice or noodles, for serving

1. Place the chicken in a crock pot.
2. Cover with the salsa.
3. Cover and cook on low for 5½ to 7½ hours, or until the chicken is tender but not dry.
4. Shred or cube the chicken in the sauce.
5. Stir in the beans and cheese.
6. Cover and cook for another 30 minutes on low.
7. Serve over cooked rice or noodles.

Chicken Tamales

Prep time: 20 minutes | Cook time: 3 to 4 hours | Serves 6

1 medium onion, chopped
1 (4-ounce / 113-g) can chopped green chilies
2 tablespoons oil
1 (10¾-ounce / 305-g) can cream of chicken soup
2 cups sour cream
1 cup sliced ripe olives
1 cup chopped stewed tomatoes
8 chicken breast halves, cooked and chopped
1 (16-ounce / 454-g) can beef tamales, chopped
1 teaspoon chili powder
1 teaspoon garlic powder
1 teaspoon pepper
2½ cups shredded Cheddar cheese, divided
Toppings:
Fresh tomatoes
Shredded lettuce
Sour cream
Salsa
Guacamole

1. Sauté the onion and chilies in the oil in a skillet for 5 minutes.
2. Stir in all the remaining ingredients, except for ½ cup of the shredded cheese. Pour into a crock pot.
3. Top with the remaining ½ cup of the cheese.
4. Cover. Cook on high for 3 to 4 hours.
5. Serve with your choice of toppings.

BBQ Chicken Legs

Prep time: 10 minutes | Cook time: 8 hours | Serves 8

10 chicken legs, skin removed
1 teaspoon salt
½ teaspoon freshly ground black pepper
2 tablespoons unsalted butter
1 medium onion, finely chopped
1 clove garlic, minced
1 tablespoon Dijon mustard
1 tablespoon Worcestershire sauce
1½ cups ketchup
½ cup chicken broth
½ cup firmly packed light brown sugar
¼ cup molasses
½ teaspoon hot sauce
Cooking spray

1. Spray the insert of a crock pot with cooking spray.
2. Sprinkle the chicken legs evenly with the salt and pepper and transfer to the crock pot insert.
3. Melt the butter in a large saucepan over medium-high heat. Add the onion and garlic and sauté until the onion is softened, for about 3 minutes.
4. Add the remaining ingredients and stir to combine. Pour the sauce over the chicken. Cook on low for 8 hours, until the chicken is tender and cooked through. Remove the cover from the crock pot and skim off any fat.
5. Serve warm.

Garlicky Chicken

Prep time: 10 minutes | Cook time: 5 to 6 hours | Serves 6

¼ cup dry white wine
2 tablespoons chopped dried parsley
2 teaspoons dried basil leaves
1 teaspoon dried oregano
Pinch of crushed red pepper flakes
20 cloves of garlic (about 1 head)
4 celery ribs, chopped
6 boneless, skinless chicken breast halves
1 lemon, juiced and zested
Fresh herbs, for garnish (optional)

1. Combine the wine, parsley, basil, oregano, and red peppers in a large bowl.
2. Add the garlic cloves and celery to the bowl. Coat well.
3. Transfer the garlic and celery to a crock pot with a slotted spoon.
4. Add the chicken to the spice mixture. Coat well. Place the chicken on top of the vegetables in the crock pot.
5. Drizzle with the lemon juice and sprinkle with the lemon zest in the crock pot. Add any remaining spice mixture.
6. Cover. Cook on low for 5 to 6 hours, or until chicken is no longer pink in center.
7. Garnish with fresh herbs, if desired. Serve warm.

Chicken Olé Casserole

Prep time: 10 minutes | **Cook time:** 4½ to 5½ hours | **Serves 8**

1 (10¾-ounce / 305-g) can cream of mushroom soup
1 (10¾-ounce / 305-g) can cream of chicken soup
1 cup sour cream
2 tablespoons grated onion
2 cups shredded Cheddar cheese, divided
12 flour tortillas, each torn into 6 to 8 pieces
3 to 4 cups cubed, cooked chicken
1 (7-ounce / 198-g) jar salsa

1. In a bowl, combine the soups, sour cream, onion, and 1½ cups of the cheese.
2. Place one-third of each of the following ingredients in layers in a crock pot: torn tortillas, soup mixture, chicken, and salsa. Repeat layers 2 more times.
3. Cover. Cook on low for 4 to 5 hours.
4. Gently stir. Sprinkle with remaining ½ cup of the cheese. Cover. Cook on low for another 15 to 30 minutes.
5. Serve warm.

Chicken Breast with Peas

Prep time: 5 minutes | **Cook time:** 3 hours | **Serves 6**

1½ pounds (680 g) uncooked boneless, skinless chicken breast
1 (10¾-ounce / 305-g) can fat-free, low-sodium cream of chicken soup
3 tablespoons flour
¼ teaspoon black pepper
1 (9-ounce / 255-g) package frozen peas and onions, thawed and drained
2 tablespoons chopped pimentos
½ teaspoon paprika

1. Cut the chicken into bite-sized pieces and place in a crock pot.
2. Combine the soup, flour, and pepper in a bowl. Pour over the chicken. Do not stir.
3. Cover. Cook on high for 2½ hours, or on low for 5 to 5½ hours.
4. Stir in the peas and onions, pimentos, and paprika.
5. Cover. Cook on high for 20 to 30 minutes.
6. Serve warm.

Chicken Tetrazzini

Prep time: 10 minutes | **Cook time:** 6 to 8 hours | **Serves 4**

2 to 3 cups diced cooked chicken
2 cups chicken broth
1 small onion, chopped
¼ cup sauterne, white wine, or milk
½ cup slivered almonds
2 (4-ounce / 113-g) cans sliced mushrooms, drained
1 (10¾-ounce / 305-g) can cream of mushroom soup
1 pound (454 g) spaghetti, cooked
Grated Parmesan cheese, for topping

1. Combine all the ingredients, except for the spaghetti and cheese, in a crock pot.
2. Cover. Cook on low for 6 to 8 hours.
3. Serve over the spaghetti. Sprinkle with the Parmesan cheese.

Veggie Ketchup Chicken

Prep time: 15 minutes | **Cook time:** 8 hours | **Serves 6**

¼ cup flour
3 whole boneless, skinless chicken breasts, cut in half
¼ cup oil
1 medium onion, sliced
1 green or yellow pepper, sliced
½ cup chopped celery
2 tablespoons Worcestershire sauce
1 cup ketchup
2 cups water
¼ teaspoon salt
¼ teaspoon paprika

1. Place the flour in a bowl. Roll the chicken breasts in the flour. Brown the chicken in the oil in a skillet, for 7 to 12 minutes. Transfer the chicken to a crock pot.
2. Sauté the onion, pepper, and celery in the skillet, for 5 minutes, or until tender. Add the remaining ingredients and bring to a boil. Pour over the chicken.
3. Cover. Cook on low for 8 hours.
4. Serve warm.

California Chicken

Prep time: 10 minutes | Cook time: 8½ to 9½ hours | Serves 4 to 6

3 pounds (1.4 kg) chicken, quartered
1 cup orange juice
1⅓ cup chili sauce
2 tablespoons soy sauce
1 tablespoon molasses
1 teaspoon dry mustard
1 teaspoon garlic salt
2 tablespoons chopped green peppers
3 medium oranges, peeled and separated into slices

1. Arrange the chicken in a crock pot.
2. In a bowl, combine the orange juice, chili sauce, soy sauce, molasses, dry mustard, and garlic salt. Pour over the chicken.
3. Cover. Cook on low for 8 to 9 hours.
4. Stir in the green peppers and oranges. Cook for 30 minutes longer.
5. Serve warm.

Tex-Mex Chicken and Rice

Prep time: 15 minutes | Cook time: 4 to 4½ hours | Serves 8

1 cup uncooked converted white rice
1 (28-ounce / 794-g) can diced peeled tomatoes
1 (6-ounce / 170-g) can tomato paste
3 cups hot water
1 package dry taco seasoning mix
4 whole boneless, skinless chicken breasts, cut into ½-inch cubes
2 medium onions, chopped
1 green pepper, chopped
1 (4-ounce / 113-g) can diced green chilies
1 teaspoon garlic powder
½ teaspoon pepper

1. Combine all the ingredients, except for the chilies and seasonings, in a crock pot.
2. Cover. Cook on low for 4 to 4½ hours, or until the rice is tender, and the chicken is cooked.
3. Stir in the green chilies and seasonings and serve.

Tender Chicken with BBQ-Soda Sauce

Prep time: 5 minutes | Cook time: 8 to 10 hours | Serves 4 to 6

3 to 4 pounds (1.4 to 1.8 kg) broiler chicken
1 medium onion, thinly sliced
1 medium lemon, thinly sliced
1 (18-ounce / 510-g) bottle barbecue sauce
¾ cup cola-flavored soda

1. Place the chicken in a crock pot.
2. Top with the onion and lemon.
3. Combine the barbecue sauce and cola in a bowl. Pour into the crock pot.
4. Cover. Cook on low for 8 to 10 hours, or until chicken juices run clear.
5. Cut into serving-sized pieces and serve with barbecue sauce.

Turkey Macaroni with Corn

Prep time: 10 minutes | Cook time: 3 to 4 hours | Serves 6

1 teaspoon vegetable oil
1½ pounds (680 g) 99% fat-free ground turkey
2 (10¾-ounce / 305-g) cans condensed low-sodium tomato soup, undiluted
1 (16-ounce / 454-g) can corn, drained
½ cup onions, chopped
1 (4-ounce / 113-g) can sliced mushrooms, drained
2 tablespoons ketchup
1 tablespoon mustard
¼ teaspoon black pepper
¼ teaspoon garlic powder
2 cups dry macaroni, cooked and drained

1. Heat the oil in a medium skillet. Add the turkey and brown for 12 to 15 minutes. Drain.
2. Combine all the remaining ingredients, except for macaroni, in a crock pot. Stir to blend.
3. Cover. Cook on high for 3 to 4 hours, or on low for 4 to 6 hours. Stir in the cooked macaroni 15 minutes before serving.
4. Serve warm.

Southwestern Chicken with Corn

Prep time: 5 minutes | Cook time: 3 to 4 hours | Serves 6

2 (15¼-ounce / 432-g) cans corn, drained
1 (15-ounce / 425-g) can black beans, rinsed and drained
1 (16-ounce / 454-g) jar chunky salsa, divided
6 boneless, skinless chicken breast halves
1 cup low-fat shredded Cheddar cheese

1. Combine the corn, black beans, and ½ cup of the salsa in a crock pot.
2. Top with the chicken. Pour the remaining ½ cup of the salsa over the chicken.
3. Cover. Cook on high for 3 to 4 hours, or on low for 7 to 8 hours.
4. Sprinkle with the cheese. Cover for 5 minutes until the cheese is melted.
5. Serve warm.

Greek Chicken with Potatoes

Prep time: 10 minutes | Cook time: 5 to 6 hours | Serves 8

6 medium potatoes, quartered
3 pounds (1.4 kg) chicken pieces, skin removed
2 large onions, quartered
1 whole bulb garlic, minced
½ cup water
3 teaspoons dried oregano
1 teaspoon salt
½ teaspoon black pepper
1 tablespoon olive oil

1. Place the potatoes in a crock pot. Add the chicken, onions, and garlic.
2. In a small bowl, mix the water with oregano, salt, and pepper.
3. Pour over the chicken and potatoes. Drizzle with the oil.
4. Cover. Cook on high for 5 to 6 hours, or on low for 9 to 10 hours.
5. Serve warm.

Red Pepper Chicken with Black Beans

Prep time: 10 minutes | Cook time: 4 to 6 hours | Serves 4

4 boneless, skinless chicken breast halves
1 (15-ounce / 425-g) can black beans, drained
1 (12-ounce / 340-g) jar roasted red peppers, undrained
1 (14½-ounce / 411-g) can Mexican stewed tomatoes, undrained
1 large onion, chopped
½ teaspoon salt
Pepper, to taste

1. Place the chicken in a crock pot.
2. Combine the beans, red peppers, stewed tomatoes, onion, salt, and pepper in a bowl. Pour over the chicken.
3. Cover. Cook on low for 4 to 6 hours, or until chicken is cooked through.
4. Serve warm.

Mediterranean Chicken with Artichokes

Prep time: 10 minutes | Cook time: 4 to 6 hours | Serves 4

1 yellow onion, thinly sliced
1 (14-ounce / 397-g) jar marinated artichoke hearts, drained
1 (14-ounce / 397-g) can low-sodium peeled tomatoes
6 tablespoons red wine vinegar
1 teaspoon minced garlic
½ teaspoon salt
½ teaspoon black pepper
4 boneless, skinless chicken breast halves

1. Combine all the ingredients, except for the chicken, in a crock pot.
2. Place the chicken in the crock pot, pushing down into vegetables and sauce until it's as covered as possible.
3. Cover. Cook on low for 4 to 6 hours.
4. Serve warm.

Peanut Butter Chicken Thighs

Prep time: 10 minutes | Cook time: 5 to 6 hours | Serves 4

1½ cups water
2 teaspoons chicken bouillon granules
2 ribs celery, thinly sliced
2 onions, thinly sliced
1 red bell pepper, sliced
1 green bell pepper, sliced
½ cup extra crunchy peanut butter
8 chicken thighs, skinned
Crushed chili pepper of your choice

1. Combine the water, chicken bouillon granules, celery, onions, and peppers in a crock pot.
2. Spread the peanut butter over both sides of the chicken pieces. Sprinkle with the chili pepper. Place on top of the ingredients in the crock pot.
3. Cover. Cook on low for 5 to 6 hours.
4. Serve warm.

Toasted Sesame Chicken Wings

Prep time: 5 minutes | Cook time: 5 hours | Serves 6 to 8

3 pounds (1.4 kg) chicken wings
Salt, to taste
Pepper, to taste
1¾ cups honey
1 cup soy sauce
½ cup ketchup
2 tablespoons canola oil
2 tablespoons sesame oil
2 garlic cloves, minced
Toasted sesame seeds, for topping

1. Rinse the wings. Cut at the joint. Sprinkle with salt and pepper. Place on a broiler pan.
2. Broil at 180ºF (82ºC) for 10 minutes on each side. Place the chicken in a crock pot.
3. Combine the remaining ingredients, except for sesame seeds, in a bowl. Pour over the chicken.
4. Cover. Cook on low for 5 hours, or on high for 2½ hours.
5. Sprinkle the sesame seeds over top just before serving.

Chicken Wings in Plum Sauce

Prep time: 5 minutes | Cook time: 4 to 5 hours | Serves 6 to 8

3 pounds (1.4 kg) chicken wings (about 16)
1 cup bottled plum sauce
2 tablespoons butter, melted
1 teaspoon five-spice powder
Orange wedges, thinly sliced (optional)
Pineapple slices (optional)

1. In a foil-lined baking pan, arrange the wings in a single layer. Bake at 375ºF (190ºC) in the oven for 20 minutes.
2. Meanwhile, combine the plum sauce, melted butter, and five-spice powder in a crock pot. Add the wings. Then stir to coat the wings with the sauce.
3. Cover and cook on low for 4 to 5 hours, or on high for 2 to 2½ hours.
4. Garnish with orange wedges and pineapple slices to serve, if desired.

Sweet and Sour Chicken Wings

Prep time: 10 minutes | Cook time: 5 to 6 hours | Serves 8

4 pounds (1.8 kg) chicken wings
2 large onions, chopped
2 (6-ounce / 170-g) cans tomato paste
2 large garlic cloves, minced
¼ cup Worcestershire sauce
¼ cup cider vinegar
½ cup brown sugar
½ cup sweet pickle relish
½ cup red or white wine
2 teaspoons salt
2 teaspoons dry mustard

1. Cut off the wing tips. Cut the wings at the joint. Place in a crock pot.
2. Combine the remaining ingredients in a bowl. Add to the crock pot and stir.
3. Cover. Cook on low for 5 to 6 hours.
4. Serve warm.

Turkey-Broccoli Supreme

Prep time: 10 minutes | Cook time: 2 to 2½ hours | Serves 8

4 cups cooked turkey breast, cubed
1 (10¾-ounce / 305-g) can condensed cream of chicken soup
1 (10-ounce / 284-g) package frozen broccoli florets, thawed and drained
1 (6.9-ounce / 196-g) package low-sodium plain rice mix
1½ cups fat-free milk
1 cup fat-free chicken broth
1 cup chopped celery
1 (8-ounce / 227-g) can sliced water chestnuts, drained
¾ cup low-fat mayonnaise
½ cup chopped onions

1. Combine all the ingredients in a crock pot.
2. Cook, uncovered, on high for 2 to 2½ hours, or until the rice is tender.
3. Serve warm.

BBQ Turkey Cutlets

Prep time: 10 minutes | Cook time: 4 hours | Serves 6 to 8

6 to 8 turkey cutlets (1½ to 2 pounds / 680 to 907 g)
¼ cup molasses
¼ cup cider vinegar
¼ cup ketchup
3 tablespoons Worcestershire sauce
1 teaspoon garlic salt
3 tablespoons chopped onion
2 tablespoons brown sugar
¼ teaspoon pepper

1. Place the turkey cutlets in a crock pot.
2. Combine the remaining ingredients. Pour over the turkey.
3. Cover. Cook on low for 4 hours.
4. Serve warm.

Ground Turkey with Potatoes

Prep time: 15 minutes | Cook time: 4 hours | Serves 6

1 pound (454 g) ground turkey
5 cups raw sliced potatoes
1 onion, sliced
½ teaspoon salt
Dash of black pepper
1 (14½-ounce / 411-g) can cut green beans, undrained
1 (4-ounce / 113-g) can mushroom pieces, undrained (optional)
1 (10¾-ounce / 305-g) can cream of chicken soup

1. Crumble the uncooked ground turkey in a crock pot.
2. Add the potatoes, onions, salt, and pepper.
3. Add the beans and mushrooms. Pour the soup over top.
4. Cover. Cook on high for 4 hours, or on low for 6 to 8 hours.
5. Serve warm.

Turkey Loaf

Prep time: 5 minutes | Cook time: 6 to 7 hours | Serves 10

2 pounds (907 g) fat-free ground turkey
2 tablespoons poultry seasoning
2 slices bread, cubed
1 egg

1. Combine all the ingredients in a bowl. Form the mixture into a round or oval loaf and place in a crock pot.
2. Cook for 6 to 7 hours on low. Remove the dish from the crock pot and allow to sit for 15 minutes before slicing and serving.

Turkey Sloppy Joes

Prep time: 10 minutes | Cook time: 4½ to 6 hours | Makes 6 sandwiches

1 red onion, chopped
1 sweet pepper, chopped
1½ pounds (680 g) boneless turkey, finely chopped
1 cup chili sauce or ketchup
¼ teaspoon salt
1 garlic clove, minced
1 teaspoon Dijon-style mustard
⅛ teaspoon pepper
Bread or sandwich rolls, for serving

1. Place the onion, sweet pepper, and turkey in a crock pot.
2. Combine the chili sauce, salt, garlic, mustard, and pepper in a bowl. Pour over the turkey mixture. Mix well.
3. Cover. Cook on low for 4½ to 6 hours.
4. Serve on bread or sandwich rolls.

Chapter 10 Red Meat

Cabbage and Beef Stew

Prep time: 20 minutes | Cook time: 6 to 8 hours | Serves 6

½ pound (227 g) 90% lean ground beef
3 cups shredded cabbage or angel hair coleslaw mix
1 (16-ounce / 454-g) can red beans, rinsed and drained
1 (14½-ounce / 411-g) can diced tomatoes, undrained
1 (8-ounce / 227-g) can tomato sauce
¾ cup salsa or picante sauce
1 medium green pepper, chopped
1 small onion, chopped
3 garlic cloves, minced
1 teaspoon ground cumin
½ teaspoon pepper

1. In a large skillet, cook beef over medium heat 4 to 6 minutes or until no longer pink, breaking into crumbles; drain.
2. Transfer meat to a crock pot. Stir in remaining ingredients. Cook, covered, on low 6 to 8 hours or until cabbage is tender.

Beef and Baby Carrot Stew

Prep time: 20 minutes | Cook time: 6½ to 8½ hours | Serves 8

1½ pounds (680 g) boneless beef chuck roast, cut into 1-inch cubes
3 medium potatoes, peeled and cubed
3 cups hot water
1½ cups fresh baby carrots
1 (10¾-ounce / 305-g) can condensed tomato soup, undiluted
1 medium onion, chopped
1 celery rib, chopped
2 tablespoons Worcestershire sauce
1 tablespoon browning sauce (optional)
2 teaspoons beef bouillon granules
1 garlic clove, minced
1 teaspoon sugar
¾ teaspoon salt
¼ teaspoon pepper
¼ cup cornstarch
¾ cup cold water
2 cups frozen peas, thawed

1. Place the beef, potatoes, hot water, carrots, soup, onion, celery, Worcestershire sauce, browning sauce if desired, bouillon granules, garlic, sugar, salt and pepper in a crock pot. Cover and cook on low for 6 to 8 hours or until meat is tender.
2. Combine cornstarch and cold water in a small bowl until smooth; gradually stir into stew. Stir in peas. Cover and cook on high 30 minutes or until thickened.

Beer-Braised Beef Brisket

Prep time: 20 minutes | Cook time: 6 to 9 hours | Serves 8 to 10

1 (4- to 5-pound / 1.8- to 2.3-kg) brisket or boneless chuck roast, trimmed off as much fat as possible and blotted dry
3 medium-size yellow onions, cut in half and thinly sliced into half-moons
2 ribs celery, chopped
1 cup prepared chili sauce
1 (12-ounce / 340-g) bottle beer (not dark)
½ cup water
1 package dried onion soup mix
1 teaspoon salt
¼ teaspoon freshly ground black pepper

1. Put the roast in the crock pot. If the meat is too big to lie flat in your crock pot, cut it in half and stack the pieces one atop the other. Add the sliced onions and the celery.
2. In a medium-size bowl, combine the chili sauce, beer, water, onion soup mix, salt, and pepper; pour it over the meat and vegetables. Cover and cook on low for 6 to 9 hours.
3. Skim off as much fat as possible from the sauce, slice the meat, and serve with the sauce.

Sweet and Sour Tomato Brisket

Prep time: 25 minutes | Cook time: 5 to 7 hours | Serves 6 to 8

3 ounces (85 g) tomato paste (half of a 6-ounce / 170-g can)
¼ cup firmly packed light brown sugar
2 tablespoons cider vinegar
½ teaspoon Worcestershire sauce
⅛ teaspoon dry mustard
2 to 3 large cloves garlic, pressed
1 (3- to 4-pound / 1.4- to 1.8-kg) brisket, trimmed off as much fat as possible and blotted dry
Salt and freshly ground black pepper, to taste
Paprika, to taste
1 tablespoon oil of your choice
2 large or 3 small yellow onions, cut in half and thinly sliced into half-moons

1. In a small bowl, stir together the tomato paste, brown sugar, vinegar, Worcestershire, mustard, and garlic.
2. If the meat is too big to lie flat in your crock pot, cut it in half. Season the meat generously with salt, pepper, and paprika.
3. In a large, heavy skillet, preferably one without a nonstick coating, heat the oil over high heat. When hot, brown the brisket very well, about 3 minutes per side. Transfer to a plate. Add the onions to the pan and cook, stirring a few times, until browned or even a bit blackened on the edges, 5 to 7 minutes.
4. Put half the onions in the crock pot. (If you have cut your brisket into 2 pieces, place one-third of the onions in the crock pot.) Smear the tomato paste mixture thickly on both sides of the brisket and place in the crock pot, with the fattier side facing up. Top with the remaining onions. (If you have cut your brisket into 2 pieces, place one-third of the onions between the two pieces of brisket, and the remaining onions on top of the second piece.) Pour any meat juices from the plate over the brisket. Cover and cook on low until the brisket is tender when pierced with a fork, 5 to 7 hours.
5. Transfer to a cutting board and cut on the diagonal, against the grain, into thin slices. Pour the sauce into a bowl and allow to settle so that you can skim the fat. Serve the meat with the sauce and sliced onions.

Lamb with Artichokes

Prep time: 20 minutes | Cook time: 8 hours | Serves 6 to 8

½ cup olive oil
1½ teaspoons salt
1 teaspoon ground cumin
Pinch of cayenne pepper
1 teaspoon sweet paprika
3 pounds (1.4 kg) lamb shoulder meat, fat trimmed and cut into 1-inch chunks
4 leeks, cut into ½-inch pieces, using the white and tender green parts
4 garlic cloves, minced
1 cup dry white wine
½ cup chicken broth
Grated zest of 2 lemons
1 (16-ounce / 454-g) package frozen artichoke hearts, thawed and drained

1. Mix ¼ cup of the oil, the salt, cumin, cayenne, and paprika in a large bow. Add the meat and toss to coat with the spice mixture. Heat the remaining oil in a large skillet over medium-high heat. Add the meat a few pieces at a time and brown on all sides. Transfer the browned meat to the insert of a crock pot.
2. Add the leeks and garlic to the same skillet and sauté until the leeks are softened, 3 to 4 minutes. Add the wine, broth, and zest and heat, scraping up any browned bits from the bottom of the pan.
3. Pour the contents of the skillet over the lamb and add the artichokes, stirring to distribute the ingredients in the pot. Cover and cook on low for 8 hours, until the lamb is tender.
4. Using a slotted spoon, carefully transfer the lamb and artichokes to a serving bowl. Strain the sauce through a fine-mesh sieve into a saucepan. Skim off any fat from the top and bring to a boil. Boil until the sauce is reduced to about 1½ cups to concentrate the flavor. Taste and adjust the seasoning.
5. Spoon the sauce over the lamb and artichokes and serve.

Vinegary Steak with Green Chilies

Prep time: 20 minutes | Cook time: 6 to 8 hours | Serves 4

1 tablespoon canola oil
1 beef flank steak (1½ pounds / 680 g)
1 large onion, sliced
1⅓ cup water
1 (4-ounce / 113-g) can chopped green chilies
2 tablespoons cider vinegar
2 to 3 teaspoons chili powder
1 teaspoon garlic powder
1 teaspoon sugar
½ teaspoon salt
⅛ teaspoon pepper

1. In a large skillet, heat oil over medium-high heat; brown steak on both sides. Transfer to a crock pot.
2. Add onion to same skillet; cook and stir 1 to 2 minutes or until crisp-tender. Add water to pan; cook 30 seconds, stirring to loosen browned bits from pan. Stir in remaining ingredients; return to a boil. Pour over steak.
3. Cook, covered, on low 6 to 8 hours or until meat is tender. Slice steak across the grain; serve with onion mixture.

Pork Chops with Plum Sauce

Prep time: 10 minutes | Cook time: 3½ to 4 hours | Serves 6

¼ cup olive oil
1 teaspoon salt
½ teaspoon freshly ground black pepper
6 (1-inch-thick) pork loin chops
2 medium onions, finely chopped
1 cup plum preserves
2 tablespoons Dijon mustard
2 tablespoons fresh lemon juice
Grated zest of 1 lemon
½ cup ketchup

1. Heat the oil in a large skillet over high heat. Sprinkle the salt and pepper evenly over the pork chops and add to the skillet. Brown the pork on all sides.
2. Transfer to the insert of a crock pot. lower heat to medium-high. Add the onions to the skillet and sauté until the onions are softened, about 3 to 5 minutes. Add the preserves to the skillet and scrape up any browned bits from the bottom of the pan. Transfer the contents of the skillet to the crock pot insert.
3. Add the mustard, lemon juice and zest, and ketchup and stir to combine. Cover and cook on high for 3½ to 4 hours or on low for 6 to 8 hours. Skim off any fat from the surface of the sauce.
4. Serve the pork chops from the crock pot set on warm.

Flank Steak Fajitas

Prep time: 25 minutes | Cook time: 6 to 8 hours | Serves 6

¾ cup prepared chunky salsa, such as a fire-roasted one
1 tablespoon tomato paste
1 tablespoon olive oil
1 clove garlic, minced
3 tablespoons fresh lime juice
1 teaspoon freshly ground black pepper
½ teaspoon salt
1 (1½-pound / 680-g) flank steak, trimmed of excess fat and silver skin
1 large white onion, cut in half and thinly sliced into half-moons
3 red bell peppers, deseeded and cut into ¼-inch-wide strips
For Serving:
Warm flour tortillas (the small ones, not the grandes for burritos)
1 cup guacamole
1 cup chopped plum tomatoes
½ bunch fresh cilantro, chopped

1. In a small bowl, combine salsa, tomato paste, olive oil, garlic, lime juice, pepper, and salt. Lay the flank steak in the crock pot and pour the mixture over it, making sure to coat all exposed surfaces well. Lay the onion and bell peppers on top. Cover and cook on low for 6 to 8 hours, until the meat is tender.
2. Remove the steak and vegetables from the juice and transfer to a serving platter. Cover with aluminum foil and let stand 10 minutes. Cut the meat across the grain into ½-inch-thick slices. Serve it heaped over warm tortillas, with the peppers and onions on top. Garnish with a dab of guacamole, some chopped tomatoes, and the cilantro on top.

Asian Baby Back Ribs

Prep time: 10 minutes | Cook time: 7½ to 8½ hours | Serves 6

½ cup soy sauce
¼ cup hoisin sauce
2 teaspoons grated fresh ginger
2 cloves garlic, minced
¼ cup firmly packed light brown sugar
1 tablespoon toasted sesame oil
½ cup chicken broth
4 green onions, finely chopped, using the white and tender green parts
4 pounds (1.8 kg) baby back ribs (about 3 slabs), cut to fit the crock pot

1. Stir the soy sauce, hoisin, ginger, garlic, sugar, sesame oil, broth, and green onions together in the insert of a crock pot. Add the ribs and push them down into the sauce.
2. Cover and cook on low for 7 to 8 hours, until the meat is tender. Remove cover and cook for an additional 30 to 35 minutes.
3. Serve the ribs with the remaining sauce on the side.

Maple Pork Chops in Bourbon

Prep time: 10 minutes | Cook time: 3 to 4 hours | Serves 6

2 tablespoons olive oil
1½ teaspoons salt
½ teaspoon freshly ground black pepper
6 (1-inch-thick) pork loin chops
2 tablespoons unsalted butter
2 medium onions, finely chopped
½ cup ketchup
½ cup bourbon
¼ cup pure maple syrup
1 teaspoon Tabasco sauce
1 teaspoon dry mustard
½ cup beef broth

1. Heat the oil in a large skillet over high heat. Sprinkle the salt and pepper evenly over the pork chops and add to the skillet.
2. Brown the chops on both sides, adding a few at a time, being careful not to crowd the pan, and transfer to the insert of a crock pot.
3. Melt the butter in the skillet over medium-high heat. Add the onions and sauté until they begin to soften, about 5 minutes. Add the remaining ingredients and scrape up any browned bits from the bottom of the pan. Transfer the contents of the skillet to the crock pot insert.
4. Cover and cook on high for 3 to 4 hours or on low for 6 to 8 hours. Skim off any fat from the top of the sauce.
5. Serve from the crock pot set on warm.

Mediterranean Beef Roast

Prep time: 30 minutes | Cook time: 8 to 10 hours | Serves 8

2 pounds (907 g) potatoes (about 6 medium), peeled and cut into 2-inch pieces
5 medium carrots (about ¾ pound / 340 g), cut into 1-inch pieces
2 tablespoons all-purpose flour
1 boneless beef chuck roast (3 to 4 pounds / 1.4 to 1.8 kg)
1 tablespoon olive oil
8 large fresh mushrooms, quartered
2 celery ribs, chopped
1 medium onion, thinly sliced
¼ cup sliced Greek olives
½ cup minced fresh parsley, divided
1 (14½-ounce / 411-g) can fire-roasted diced tomatoes, undrained
1 tablespoon minced fresh oregano or 1 teaspoon dried oregano
1 tablespoon lemon juice
2 teaspoons minced fresh rosemary or ½ teaspoon dried rosemary, crushed
2 garlic cloves, minced
¾ teaspoon salt
¼ teaspoon pepper
¼ teaspoon crushed red pepper flakes (optional)

1. Place potatoes and carrots in a crock pot. Sprinkle flour over all surfaces of roast. In a large skillet, heat oil over medium-high heat. Brown roast on all sides. Place over vegetables.
2. Add mushrooms, celery, onion, olives and ¼ cup parsley to crock pot. In a small bowl, mix remaining ingredients; pour over top.
3. Cook, covered, on low 8 to 10 hours or until the meat and vegetables are tender. Remove beef. Stir remaining parsley into vegetables. Serve beef with vegetables.

Asian-Flavored Braised Spareribs

Prep time: 5 minutes | Cook time: 8 to 10 hours | Serves 6

2 cups soy sauce
1 cup rice wine (mirin)
1 teaspoons freshly grated ginger
¼ cup hoisin sauce
¼ cup rice vinegar
2 tablespoons sugar
3 pounds (1.4 kg) country-style spareribs

1. Stir the soy sauce, rice wine, ginger, hoisin, rice vinegar, and sugar together in the insert of a crock pot.
2. Add the ribs to the pot and spoon the liquid over the ribs. Cover and cook on low for 8 to 10 hours, until the ribs are tender. Skim off any fat from the sauce.
3. Serve the ribs from the crock pot set on warm.

Balsamic Beef with Cranberry Gravy

Prep time: 20 minutes | Cook time: 7 to 9 hours | Serves 6

1 boneless beef chuck roast (3 to 4 pounds / 1.4 to 1.8 kg)
2 teaspoons salt
1 teaspoon pepper
2 tablespoons canola oil
2 medium carrots, finely chopped
1 medium onion, chopped
2 garlic cloves, minced
1 cup cranberry juice
¾ cup water
½ cup fresh or frozen cranberries
½ cup balsamic vinegar
2 fresh thyme sprigs
1 bay leaf
3 tablespoons cornstarch
3 tablespoons cold water

1. Sprinkle beef with salt and pepper. In a large skillet, heat oil over medium heat. Brown roast on all sides. Transfer to a crock pot.
2. Add carrots and onion to drippings; cook and stir over medium heat 4 to 5 minutes or until tender. Add garlic; cook 1 minute longer. Spoon vegetables around roast; add cranberry juice, ¾ cup water, cranberries, vinegar, thyme and bay leaf. Cook, covered, on low 7 to 9 hours or until meat is tender.
3. Using a slotted spoon, remove roast and vegetables to a serving platter; keep warm. Pour cooking juices into a small saucepan; skim fat. Discard thyme and bay leaf. Bring cooking juices to a boil. Mix cornstarch and water until smooth; gradually stir into pan. Return to a boil, stirring constantly; cook and stir 1 to 2 minutes or until thickened. Serve with roast.

Mexican Beef Enchilada

Prep time: 10 minutes | Cook time: 6 to 7 hours | Serves 10

1½ pounds (680 g) 90% lean ground beef
1 small onion, chopped
1 garlic clove, minced
1 envelope taco seasoning
½ teaspoon salt
½ teaspoon pepper
9 corn tortillas (6 inches)
½ cup chicken broth
½ cup tomato sauce
1 (10-ounce / 283-g) can enchilada sauce
1½ cups shredded Cheddar cheese
2 (15-ounce / 425-g) cans pinto beans, rinsed and drained
1 (11-ounce / 312-g) can Mexicorn, drained
1 (4-ounce / 113-g) can chopped green chilies, drained
1 (2¼-ounce / 64-g) can chopped ripe olives, drained
Sour cream and avocado slices, for serving

1. In a large skillet, cook the beef, onion and garlic over medium heat until meat is no longer pink; drain. Stir in the taco seasoning, salt and pepper.
2. In a greased crock pot, layer three tortillas, beef mixture, broth, tomato sauce and enchilada sauce; sprinkle with ½ cup cheese. Add three tortillas, beans, Mexicorn, green chilies, half of the olives and ½ cup cheese. Top with remaining tortillas, cheese and olives.
3. Cover and cook on low for 6 to 7 hours. Serve with sour cream and avocado if desired.

Beef Roast Sandwiches

Prep time: 5 minutes | Cook time: 10 to 12 hours | Serves 6 to 8

3 to 4 pounds (1.4 to 1.8 kg) lean rump roast
2 teaspoons salt, divided
4 garlic cloves
2 teaspoons Romano or Parmesan cheese, divided
1 (12-ounce / 340-g) can beef broth
1 teaspoon dried oregano
Buns, for serving

1. Place the roast in a crock pot. Cut 4 slits in top of roast. Fill each slit with ½ teaspoon salt, 1 garlic clove, and ½ teaspoon cheese.
2. Pour the broth over the meat. Sprinkle with the oregano.
3. Cover. Cook on low for 10 to 12 hours, or on high for 4 to 6 hours.
4. Remove the meat and slice or shred. Serve on buns with meat juices on the side.

Beef Ragoût with Veggies

Prep time: 25 minutes | Cook time: 7 to 8 hours | Serves 4 to 5

2 tablespoons olive oil
2 pounds (907 g) lean beef stew meat or beef cross rib roast, trimmed of fat, cut into 1½-inch chunks, and blotted dry
2 medium-size onions, coarsely chopped
2 large tomatoes, peeled, deseeded, and chopped, or 1 (14½-ounce / 411-g) can diced tomatoes, with their juice
1 cup dry red wine
1 cup baby carrots
2 cloves garlic, minced
2 tablespoons quick-cooking tapioca
1 teaspoon dried Italian herb seasoning
½ teaspoon salt
¼ teaspoon freshly ground black pepper
2 medium-size zucchini, ends trimmed, cut in half lengthwise and sliced crosswise into ¼-inch-thick half-moons
8 ounces (227 g) fresh mushrooms, thickly sliced

1. In a large skillet over medium-high heat, heat 1 tablespoon of the oil until very hot. Add half of the beef and brown on all sides, 3 to 4 minutes total. Transfer to the crock pot. Add the remaining 1 tablespoon of oil and brown the remaining beef.
2. Add the onions to the skillet and brown slightly over medium-high heat. Add the tomatoes and wine and bring to a boil, scraping up any browned bits stuck to the pan; pour into the crock pot. Add the carrots, garlic, tapioca, and Italian herbs to the crock pot. Cover and cook on low for 6 to 7 hours.
3. Add the salt, pepper, zucchini, and mushrooms, cover, turn the crock pot to high, and cook for about 45 minutes, until the meat, mushrooms, and zucchini are tender. Serve in shallow bowls or on rimmed dinner plates.

Pork Loin with Cran-Orange Sauce

Prep time: 20 minutes | Cook time: 4 hours | Serves 6 to 8

2 tablespoons olive oil
1 (3- to 4-pound / 1.4- to 1.8-kg) pork loin roast, tied
Salt and freshly ground black pepper, to taste
1 large sweet onion, such as Vidalia, coarsely chopped
2 (16-ounce / 454-g) cans whole-berry cranberry sauce
Grated zest of 2 oranges
Juice of 2 oranges (about 1 cup)
2 teaspoons dried thyme leaves
½ cup beef broth

1. Spray the insert of a crock pot with nonstick cooking spray or line it with a crock pot liner according to the manufacturer's directions.
2. Heat the oil in a large sauté pan over high heat. Sprinkle the roast with 1½ teaspoons salt and 1 teaspoon pepper and add to the pan.
3. Sauté the pork on all sides until browned. Transfer the roast to the crock pot insert. Add the remaining ingredients and stir to combine. Cover the crock pot and cook the roast on high for 4 hours or on low for 8 hours.
4. Remove the cover, transfer the roast to a cutting board, and cover loosely with aluminum foil. Let the meat rest for 15 minutes. Skim off any fat from the top of the sauce. Stir the sauce and season with salt and pepper.
5. Slice the roast and nap with some of the sauce. Serve the remaining sauce in a gravy boat on the side.

Smoked Sausages with BBQ Sauce

Prep time: 10 minutes | Cook time: 4 hours | Serves 6 to 8

2 cups yellow mustard
1 cup apple cider
¾ cup firmly packed light brown sugar
¼ cup molasses
1 tablespoon sweet paprika
1 teaspoon Worcestershire sauce
½ teaspoon cayenne pepper
½ teaspoon ground white pepper
3 pounds (1.4 kg) smoked sausages, such as kielbasa, cut into 3-inch lengths
6 to 8 hot dog rolls

1. Mix the mustard, cider, sugar, molasses, paprika, Worcestershire, cayenne, and white pepper in the insert of a crock pot.
2. Add the sausages, pushing them into the sauce, cover, and cook on high for 4 hours, until the sausages are heated through and the sauce is thickened.
3. Serve the sausage in hot dog rolls with some of the sauce.

Cider Pork Loin

Prep time: 20 minutes | Cook time: 4 hours | Serves 6 to 8

2 tablespoons olive oil
½ cup Dijon mustard
½ cup firmly packed light brown sugar
1 (2½- to 3-pound / 1.1- to 1.4-kg) pork loin roast, rolled and tied
1 large onion, finely sliced
2 teaspoons dried thyme
½ cup apple cider
1 cup beef stock
4 large Gala or Braeburn apples, peeled, cored, and cut into 8 wedges each
¾ cup heavy cream
Salt and freshly ground black pepper, to taste
1 pound (454 g) buttered cooked wide egg noodles, for serving

1. Heat the oil in a large sauté pan over medium-high heat. Make a paste of the mustard and sugar and spread over the roast on all sides. Add the roast to the pan and brown on all sides. Add the onion and thyme to the sauté pan and cook until the onion is softened, 3 to 5 minutes.
2. Transfer the roast, onion, and any bits from the bottom of the pan to the insert of a crock pot. Add the cider and beef stock. Cover the crock pot and cook on high for 3 hours. Remove the cover and add the apples and cream. Cover and cook on high for an additional 1 hour.
3. Remove the pork from the crock pot insert, cover with aluminum foil, and allow to rest for 15 minutes. Season the sauce with salt and pepper. Remove the strings from the roast, cut into thin slices, and serve the pork on the buttered noodles, napping both with some of the sauce.

Pork Tenderloin with Mango Sauce

Prep time: 20 minutes | Cook time: 3 hours | Serves 6

4 tablespoons (½ stick) unsalted butter, melted
2 large mangoes, peeled, pitted, and coarsely chopped
2 navel oranges, peeled and sectioned
2 tablespoons soy sauce
½ cup dark rum
½ cup beef broth
2 (1-pound / 454-g) pork tenderloins
2 tablespoons Jamaican jerk seasoning
6 green onions, finely chopped, using the white and tender green parts for garnish

1. Stir the butter, mangoes, oranges, soy sauce, rum, and broth together in the insert of a crock pot. Remove the silver skin from the outside of the pork with a boning knife and discard.
2. Rub the jerk seasoning on the pork and arrange it in the crock pot. Cover and cook on high for 3 hours, until the pork is tender and cooked through. (The pork should register 175ºF (79ºC) on an instant-read thermometer.)
3. Remove the pork from the sauce, cover with aluminum foil, and allow to rest for 20 minutes. Skim off any fat from the top of the sauce.
4. Slice the meat and garnish with the green onions. Serve the sauce on the side.

Sausage and Peppers in Wine

Prep time: 15 minutes | Cook time: 6 to 8 hours | Serves 4 to 6

3 large assorted colored bell peppers, such as red, yellow, and orange, deseeded and cut into chunks
1 large yellow onion, cut into wedges
3 cloves garlic, peeled
Salt and freshly ground black pepper, to taste
1 tablespoon minced fresh thyme
2 tablespoons olive oil
2 pounds (907 g) assorted sausages, such as hot and sweet Italian and chicken basil
1⅓ cup dry red wine

1. Put the peppers in the crock pot. Add the onion and garlic and toss to combine. Sprinkle with a small amount of salt and pepper and all the thyme.
2. In a large skillet, heat the olive oil over medium-high heat and brown the sausages all over, 3 to 5 minutes, pricking them with a fork. Place them on top of the vegetables in the crock pot. Add the wine to the skillet and bring to a boil, scraping up any browned bits stuck to the pan. Pour into the crock pot. Cover and cook on low for 6 to 8 hours. Serve the sausage and peppers hot.

Sweet and Spiced Pork Loin

Prep time: 25 minutes | Cook time: 4 to 5 hours | Serves 6 to 8

2 medium sweet potatoes, peeled and cut into 1-inch chunks or wedges
2 medium Yukon gold potatoes, peeled and cut into 1-inch chunks or wedges
2 medium red onions, cut into quarters
½ cup olive oil
1 teaspoon ground cumin
1½ teaspoons fennel seeds
½ teaspoon ground cinnamon
½ teaspoon ground ginger
¼ cup firmly packed light brown sugar
2 teaspoons salt
1 teaspoon freshly ground black pepper
1 (4-pound / 1.8-kg) pork loin roast, rolled and tied
½ cup chicken broth

1. Arrange the vegetables in the insert of a crock pot. Drizzle ¼ cup of the oil over the vegetables and toss to coat. Combine the cumin, fennel seeds, cinnamon, ginger, sugar, salt, and pepper in a small bowl. Sprinkle 1 tablespoon of the rub over the vegetables and toss again.
2. Pat the rest of the rub over the meat, place the meat on the vegetables, and drizzle with the remaining ¼ cup olive oil. Pour in the chicken broth. Cover and cook on high for 4 to 5 hours or on low for 8 to 10 hours, until the pork and vegetables are tender. The roast should register 175°F (79°C) on an instant-read thermometer.
3. Transfer the pork to a cutting board, cover with aluminum foil, and let rest for 20 minutes. Cut the meat into ½-inch-thick slices and arrange on the center of a platter. Spoon the vegetables around the meat and serve.

Teriyaki Pork Tenderloin

Prep time: 5 minutes | Cook time: 3 hours | Serves 6

2 tablespoons vegetable oil
2 cloves garlic, minced
1 teaspoon grated fresh ginger
1 cup soy sauce
¼ cup rice vinegar
3 tablespoons light brown sugar
2 (1-pound / 454-g) pork tenderloins

1. Whisk the oil, garlic, ginger, soy sauce, vinegar, and sugar together in a bowl until blended. Remove the silver skin from the outside of the pork with a boning knife and discard.
2. Place the tenderloins in a 1-gallon zipper-top plastic bag or 13-by-9-inch baking dish. Pour the marinade over the tenderloins and seal the bag or cover the dish with plastic wrap.
3. Marinate for at least 4 hours or overnight, turning the meat once or twice during that time. Place the marinade and pork in the insert of a crock pot. Cover and cook on high for 3 hours.
4. Remove the meat from the sauce, cover loosely with aluminum foil, and allow the meat to rest for about 10 minutes. Skim off any fat from the top of the sauce.
5. Cut the meat diagonally in ½-inch-thick slices. Nap each serving of pork with some of the sauce.

Country-Style Spareribs

Prep time: 10 minutes | Cook time: 8 to 10 hours | Serves 6

3 pounds (1.4 kg) country-style spareribs
1½ teaspoons salt
2 tablespoons extra-virgin olive oil
3 medium onions, finely chopped
⅛ teaspoon red pepper flakes
3 cloves garlic, minced
1 teaspoon dried oregano
½ cup red wine, such as Chianti or Barolo
1 (28- to 32-ounce / 794- to 907-g) can crushed tomatoes, with their juice

1. Sprinkle the ribs with the salt and arrange in the insert of a crock pot. Heat the oil in a large skillet over medium-high heat. Add the onions, red pepper flakes, garlic, and oregano and sauté until the onions are softened, about 5 minutes.
2. Add the wine to the skillet and stir up any browned bits from the bottom of the pan. Transfer the contents of the skillet to the crock pot insert and stir in the tomatoes. Cover and cook on low for 8 to 10 hours, until the meat is tender. Skim off any fat from the surface of the sauce.
3. Serve the ribs from the crock pot set on warm.

Braised Lamb with Eggplant

Prep time: 25 minutes | Cook time: 3 to 4 hours | Serves 8

¼ cup extra-virgin olive oil
3 pounds (1.4 kg) lamb shoulder, fat trimmed and cut into 1-inch chunks
1½ teaspoons salt
½ teaspoon freshly ground black pepper
2 large onions, coarsely chopped
4 cloves garlic, sliced
4 Japanese eggplants (about 1 pound / 454 g), cut into ½-inch cubes
1 teaspoon dried oregano
½ cup dry white wine or vermouth
1 (28- to 32-ounce / 794- to 907-g) can chopped tomatoes, with their juice
½ cup finely chopped fresh Italian parsley
1 cup crumbled feta cheese, for garnish

1. Heat the oil in a large skillet over medium-high heat. Sprinkle the lamb evenly with the salt and pepper, add a few pieces at a time to the skillet, and brown on all sides. Transfer the browned meat to the insert of a crock pot.
2. Add the onions, garlic, eggplants, and oregano to the skillet and sauté until the onions begin to soften and turn translucent, 5 to 7 minutes. Add the wine to the skillet and heat, scraping the browned bits from the bottom of the pan. Transfer the contents of the skillet to the crock pot insert and stir in the tomatoes.
3. Cover and cook on high 3 to 4 hours or low for 7 to 8 hours. Skim off any fat from the top of the stew and stir in the parsley. Keep the stew in the crock pot set on warm until ready to serve.
4. Garnish each serving with a sprinkling of feta.

Mediterranean Lamb and Lentils

Prep time: 20 minutes | Cook time: 8 to 10 hours | Serves 6 to 8

¼ cup extra-virgin olive oil
2 pounds (907 g) lamb shoulder meat, fat trimmed and cut into 1-inch chunks
1½ teaspoons salt
½ teaspoon freshly ground black pepper
2 medium onions, coarsely chopped
3 medium carrots, cut into 1-inch lengths
3 stalks celery, coarsely chopped
2 teaspoons dried thyme
1 (14- to 15-ounce / 397- to 425-g) can crushed tomatoes, with their juice
1 cup green lentils
2 cups chicken broth

1. Heat the oil in a large skillet over medium-high heat. Sprinkle the lamb evenly with the salt and pepper. Add the meat a few pieces at a time to the skillet and brown on all sides. Transfer the meat to the insert of a crock pot.
2. Add the onions, carrots, celery, and thyme to the same skillet and sauté until the vegetables begin to soften and the onions begin to turn translucent. Add the tomatoes and heat, scraping up any browned bits from the bottom of the pan.
3. Transfer the contents of the skillet to the crock pot insert and stir in the lentils and chicken broth. Cover and cook on low for 8 to 10 hours, until the meat and lentils are tender. Skim any fat from the top of the stew.
4. Serve from the crock pot set on warm.

Lamb Chops and White Beans

Prep time: 20 minutes | Cook time: 5 to 7 hours | Serves 4

1 to 2 tablespoons olive oil
4 shoulder lamb chops
1 medium-size yellow onion, chopped
½ cup chicken broth
½ cup dry white wine
¼ cup chopped oil-packed sun-dried tomatoes, drained
½ teaspoon dried marjoram or thyme
Pinch of ground cumin
1 (15-ounce / 425-g) can small white beans, rinsed and drained
Salt and freshly ground black pepper, to taste
Hot cooked rice, for serving

1. In a large nonstick skillet, heat the oil and brown the lamb on both sides over medium-high heat; transfer to the crock pot. Add the onion to the skillet and cook for a few minutes until limp; add to the crock pot. Add the broth, wine, tomatoes, marjoram, and cumin, cover, and cook on low for 2½ to 3½ hours.
2. Add the beans, cover, and continue to cook on low until the lamb is very tender, another 2½ to 3½ hours. Season with salt and pepper and serve over rice.

Leg of Lamb with Pinto Beans

Prep time: 20 minutes | Cook time: 8 to 10 hours | Serves 8

2 cups pinto beans, soaked overnight and drained
¼ cup olive oil
3 pounds (1.4 kg) leg of lamb, cut into 1-inch chunks
½ teaspoon chili powder
2 medium onions, coarsely chopped
2 Anaheim chiles, deseeded and coarsely chopped
1 teaspoon ground cumin
½ teaspoon dried oregano
1 (14- to 15-ounce / 397- to 425-g) can chopped tomatoes, with their juice
1½ cups beef broth

1. Put the beans in the bottom of the insert of a crock pot. Heat the oil in a large skillet over medium-high heat.
2. Sprinkle the meat with the chili powder. Add the meat a few pieces at a time to the skillet and brown on all sides. Transfer the browned meat to the crock pot insert. Add the onions, chiles, cumin, and oregano to the same skillet and cook until the onions are softened, about 5 minutes.
3. Add the tomatoes to the skillet and heat, stirring up any browned bits from the bottom of the pan.
4. Transfer the contents of the skillet to the crock pot and stir in the broth. Cover and cook on low for 8 to 10 hours, until the meat and beans are tender.
5. Remove any fat from the top of the stew and serve from the crock pot set on warm.

Indian Tandoori Lamb

Prep time: 20 minutes | Cook time: 3 hours | Serves 8

1½ cups plain yogurt
2 tablespoons fresh lemon juice
4 cloves garlic, minced
1½ teaspoons ground cumin
1½ teaspoons garam masala
1 teaspoon ground coriander
Pinch of cayenne pepper
1 teaspoon salt
3 pounds (1.4 kg) lamb shoulder, fat trimmed and cut into 1-inch chunks
4 medium Yukon gold potatoes, cut into quarters
3 medium carrots, cut into 1-inch lengths
½ cup chicken broth

1. Whisk together the yogurt, lemon juice, garlic, and spices in a large bowl. Add the lamb and toss to coat well with the marinade. Cover and refrigerate for at least 2 hours or overnight.
2. Drain the marinade and add the lamb to the insert of a crock pot. Add the vegetables and broth and stir to combine. Cover and cook on high for 3 hours, until the lamb is tender and the vegetables are cooked through. Skim off any fat from the top of the sauce.
3. Serve from the crock pot set on warm.

Sweet and Savory Brisket

Prep time: 10 minutes | Cook time: 8 to 10 hours | Serves 8 to 10

3 to 3½ pounds (1.4 to 1.5 kg) fresh beef brisket, cut in half, divided
1 cup ketchup
¼ cup grape jelly
1 envelope dry onion soup mix
½ teaspoon pepper

1. Place half of the brisket in a crock pot.
2. In a bowl, combine the ketchup, jelly, dry soup mix, and pepper.
3. Spread half the mixture over half the meat. Top with the remaining meat and then the remaining ketchup mixture.
4. Cover and cook on low for 8 to 10 hours or until meat is tender but not dry.
5. Allow meat to rest for 10 minutes. Then slice and serve with the cooking juices.

Leg of Lamb and Cabbage

Prep time: 10 minutes | Cook time: 5^1/3 to 6^1/3 hours | Serves 4 to 6

½ teaspoon allspice berries
½ teaspoon black peppercorns
½ teaspoon whole cloves
1 small leg of lamb (about 2 pounds / 907 g), bone-in or boned and tied
2 cups hot chicken broth (optional)
½ cup dry white wine (optional)
¾ teaspoon to 1 teaspoon salt, to your taste
1 head cabbage, cored and cut into 8 wedges

1. Put the allspice berries, peppercorns, and cloves in a cheesecloth bag or tea ball and set aside.
2. Put the lamb in the crock pot. If you are using a round crock pot, put the lamb in meaty end down. Add the broth and wine, if using. Add hot water to cover the lamb by an inch. Add the salt, using the lesser amount if you used salted chicken broth. Add the spice ball. Cover and cook on high for 1 hour.
3. Turn the crock pot to low and cook until the lamb is fork-tender, 4 to 5 hours. About 20 minutes before it is done, preheat the oven to 200ºF (93ºC).
4. Transfer the lamb to a platter, tent with aluminum foil, and place in the oven to keep warm. Put the cabbage wedges in the hot broth remaining in the crock pot, cover, and turn the heat to high. Cook until tender, 20 to 30 minutes.
5. Just before cabbage is done, carve the meat. Serve the lamb in shallow bowls with 1 or 2 wedges of cabbage and some of the broth.

Corned Beef Braised in Riesling

Prep time: 15 minutes | Cook time: 8 to 10 hours | Serves 6

12 small Yukon gold potatoes, scrubbed
2 cups baby carrots
3 medium sweet onions, coarsely chopped
2 cups Riesling wine
½ cup whole-grain mustard
¼ cup Dijon mustard
¼ cup firmly packed light brown sugar
4 whole black peppercorns
2 bay leaves
1 (3½- to 4-pound / 1.5- to 1.8-kg) corned beef, rinsed and fat trimmed
1 large head green cabbage, cut in half, cored and thickly sliced

1. Layer the potatoes, carrots, and onions in the insert of a crock pot. Whisk together the Riesling, whole-grain mustard, Dijon mustard, and sugar in a large bowl. Stir in the peppercorns and bay leaves.
2. Place the brisket on top of the vegetables in the crock pot insert. Pour the Riesling mixture over the brisket and strew the cabbage over the top of the brisket.
3. Cover the crock pot and cook on low for 8 to 10 hours. Remove the brisket from the crock pot, cover with aluminum foil, and allow to rest for about 20 minutes.
4. Using a slotted spoon, remove the vegetables and arrange them on a platter. Slice the brisket across the grain and arrange over the vegetables. Strain the liquid from the crock pot through a fine-mesh sieve and ladle a bit over the meat and vegetables before serving.

Brisket Braised with Dried Fruits

Prep time: 15 minutes | Cook time: 4 to 5 hours | Serves 8

Salt and freshly ground black pepper, to taste
¼ cup Dijon mustard
¼ cup firmly packed light brown sugar
1 (3- to 4-pound / 1.4- to 1.8-kg) first-cut or flat-cut brisket, fat trimmed
3 tablespoons olive oil
3 large sweet onions, thinly sliced
2 teaspoons dried thyme
½ cup red wine
½ cup beef broth
1 cup dried figs, halved
½ cup dried plums, halved
½ cup dried apricots, halved
2 tablespoons cornstarch dissolved in ¼ cup water or beef broth

1. Combine 2 teaspoons salt, 1 teaspoon pepper, the mustard, and brown sugar in a small bowl. Rub the mixture over the brisket. Heat the oil in a large skillet over medium-high heat.
2. Add the brisket and brown on all sides for 4 minutes. Remove the brisket and transfer to the insert of a crock pot. Add the onions and thyme to the same skillet over medium-high heat and sauté until the onions are softened, for 2 to 3 minutes. Deglaze the pan with the wine and broth, scraping up any browned bits, and bring the liquid to a boil.
3. Pour the mixture into the crock pot insert and add the dried fruits around the brisket. Cover and cook on high for 4 to 5 hours or on low for 8 to 10 hours, until the meat is fork tender. Remove the brisket and fruits from the insert and cover with aluminum foil.
4. Transfer the liquid to a saucepan or saucier. Skim off any fat from the top of the sauce.
5. Bring the sauce to a boil, add the cornstarch and stir, bringing the sauce back to a boil. Season with salt and pepper.
6. Trim any fat from the brisket and thinly slice it across the grain. Serve the brisket surrounded with the fruit and napped with some of the sauce. Serve the remaining sauce on the side.

Chicago-Style Flank Steaks

Prep time: 15 minutes | Cook time: 8 hours | Serves 8

3 (1½- to 2-pound / 680- to 907-g) flank steaks
4 cloves garlic
1 teaspoon dried oregano
1 teaspoon dried basil
1 bay leaf
2 shallots, coarsely chopped
½ cup soy sauce
½ cup red wine vinegar
½ teaspoon freshly ground black pepper
¼ cup extra-virgin olive oil, divided
4 large onions, cut into half rounds
2 medium green bell peppers, deseeded and thinly sliced
2 medium red bell peppers, deseeded and thinly sliced
2 (15-ounce / 425-g) cans double-strength beef broth
8 crusty rolls

1. Put the flank steaks into a 2-gallon zipper-top plastic bag. Mix the garlic, oregano, basil, bay leaf, shallots, soy sauce, vinegar, pepper, and 2 tablespoons of the oil together in a bowl. Pour the marinade into the bag and toss with the meat to coat. Seal the bag and refrigerate for at least 6 hours or overnight.
2. Remove the meat from the marinade and discard the marinade. Roll the steaks from the short side and place them in the bottom of the insert of a crock pot.
3. Heat the remaining 2 tablespoons of the oil in a large skillet over medium-high heat. Add the onions and sauté until they are softened and begin to turn translucent, for 5 to 7 minutes. Add the bell peppers and sauté until they are softened, for about 5 minutes.
4. Transfer the onions and bell peppers to the crock pot and stir in the broth. Cover and cook on low for 8 hours, until the meat is tender.
5. Remove the meat from the crock pot, cover with aluminum foil, and allow to rest for at least 15 minutes. Skim off any fat from the top of the sauce. Unroll the meat on a cutting board and cut across the grain into thin slices. Return the meat to the crock pot.
6. Serve the meat, onions, and peppers from the crock pot along with the crusty rolls.

BBQ Short Ribs

Prep time: 5 minutes | Cook time: 3½ to 4 hours | Serves 4 to 6

2 cups ketchup
1 tablespoon Dijon mustard
½ cup firmly packed light brown sugar
2 tablespoons Worcestershire sauce
½ teaspoon cayenne pepper
1½ tablespoons vegetable oil
4½ pounds (2.0 kg) boneless short ribs, fat trimmed
1 cup coarsely chopped red onion

1. Combine the ketchup, mustard, brown sugar, Worcestershire, and cayenne in the insert of a crock pot. Cover and set on low while you brown the meat.
2. Heat the oil in a large skillet over high heat.
3. Add the short ribs a few at a time and brown on all sides for 4 minutes. Transfer them to the crock pot insert. Add the onion to the same skillet and sauté until it begins to soften, for 3 to 5 minutes.
4. Transfer the onion to the insert and stir the sauce to combine. Cover, and cook on high for 3½ to 4 hours or on low for 8 hours. Remove the meat from the crock pot insert and cover with aluminum foil. Let the meat rest for 10 to 15 minutes. Skim off any fat from the sauce.
5. Serve the beef with the sauce.

Osso Buco

Prep time: 15 minutes | Cook time: 5 hours | Serves 6

½ cup all-purpose flour
1 teaspoon salt
½ teaspoon freshly ground black pepper
6 meaty slices veal shank, cut into 1½ to 2 inches thick
2 tablespoons olive oil
2 tablespoons unsalted butter
1 medium onion, finely chopped
3 medium carrots, finely chopped
¼ cup tomato paste
2⅓ cup dry white wine or vermouth
1 cup chicken broth
½ cup beef broth
2 cloves garlic, minced
Grated zest of 2 lemons
Grated zest of 1 orange
½ cup finely chopped Italian parsley

1. Mix the flour, salt, and pepper in a large zipper-top plastic bag. Coat the veal shanks in the flour mixture and shake off the excess. Heat the oil and butter in a large skillet over high heat. Add the shanks a few at a time and brown on all sides for 4 minutes.
2. Transfer the shanks to the insert of a crock pot. Add the onion and carrots to the same skillet and sauté until the onion is softened, for about 3 minutes. Add the tomato paste and stir to combine. Add the wine and bring to a boil.
3. Transfer the contents of the skillet to the crock pot insert Add the broths and stir. Cover and cook on low for 4 hours. Combine the garlic, citrus zests, and parsley in a small bowl. Add the garlic mixture to the stew and stir to combine. Cook the stew for another hour, until the veal is tender.
4. Taste and adjust the seasoning and serve.

Texas-Style Smoked Beef Brisket

Prep time: 10 minutes | Cook time: 10¹⁄₃ hours | Serves 8

4 medium onions, cut into half rounds
2 tablespoons sweet paprika
2 chipotle chiles in adobo, minced
1 teaspoon freshly ground black pepper
1 teaspoon ground cumin
¼ cup firmly packed light brown sugar
2 tablespoons Worcestershire sauce
2 tablespoons apple cider vinegar
1 (4-pound / 1.8-kg) brisket, fat trimmed
1 cup ketchup

1. Spread the onions on the bottom of the insert of a crock pot and turn the machine on low. Stir the paprika, chiles, pepper, cumin, sugar, Worcestershire, and vinegar together in a small bowl.
2. Rub the mixture over the brisket and place the brisket on top of the onions in the crock pot. Cover and cook for 10 hours on low, until the brisket is tender. Remove the brisket from the crock pot and cover with aluminum foil.
3. Skim off any fat from the cooking liquid and strain through a fine-mesh sieve into a saucepan. Stir in the ketchup and simmer for 20 minutes, until thickened.
4. Slice the brisket across the grain to serve, accompanied by some of the sauce.

Mexican Beef Brisket

Prep time: 15 minutes | Cook time: 10 to 12 hours | Serves 6 to 8

3 pounds (1.4 kg) beef brisket, cubed
2 tablespoons oil
½ cup slivered almonds
2 cups mild picante sauce, or hot, if you prefer
2 tablespoons vinegar
1 teaspoon garlic powder
½ teaspoon salt
¼ teaspoon cinnamon
¼ teaspoon dried thyme
¼ teaspoon dried oregano
⅛ teaspoon ground cloves
⅛ teaspoon pepper
½ to ¾ cup water, as needed

1. Brown the beef in the oil in a skillet, for 4 minutes. Place in a crock pot.
2. Combine the remaining ingredients in a bowl. Pour over the meat.
3. Cover. Cook on low for 10 to 12 hours. Add the water as needed.
4. Serve warm.

Onion Beef Short Ribs

Prep time: 15 minutes | Cook time: 8 hours | Serves 4 to 6

1½ tablespoons vegetable oil
½ cup firmly packed light brown sugar, divided
4½ pounds (2.0 kg) boneless short ribs, fat trimmed
4 cups sliced sweet onions, such as Vidalia or red onions (about 4 medium to large)
6 cloves garlic, minced
1 teaspoon freshly grated ginger
2 tablespoons hoisin sauce
½ cup soy sauce
1½ cups chicken broth
½ teaspoon freshly ground black pepper
Chopped green onions, for garnish
Toasted sesame seeds, for garnish

1. Heat the oil in a large skillet over medium-high heat. Pat half of the brown sugar onto the ribs. Add the ribs a few at a time to the skillet and brown on all sides for 4 minutes, being careful not to burn the sugar.
2. Transfer the ribs to the insert of a crock pot. Add the onions, garlic, and ginger to the skillet over medium-high heat and sauté until the onions and garlic are fragrant, for about 4 minutes.
3. Transfer the contents of the skillet to the crock pot insert and stir in the remaining half of the sugar, the hoisin, soy sauce, and broth. Sprinkle with the pepper. Cover the crock pot and cook on high for 8 hours or on low for 3½ to 4 hours, until the meat is tender.
4. Remove the meat from the crock pot insert. Skim off any fat from the sauce and pour some of the sauce over the meat. Serve any remaining sauce on the side. Garnish the ribs with the green onions and sesame seeds.

Zinfandel-Braised Beef Short Ribs

Prep time: 10 minutes | Cook time: 3½ to 4 hours | Serves 4

4½ pounds (2.0 kg) boneless short ribs, fat trimmed
2 teaspoons salt
1 teaspoon freshly ground black pepper
2 tablespoons extra-virgin olive oil
2 cups red onions, cut into half rounds
6 cloves garlic, minced
1 tablespoon dried thyme
2 cups Zinfandel wine
4 dried porcini mushrooms, crumbled

1. Sprinkle the beef ribs evenly with the salt and pepper. Heat the oil in a large skillet over medium-high heat. Add the beef a few pieces at a time and brown on all sides for 4 minutes. Transfer the meat to the insert of a crock pot.
2. Add the onions, garlic, and thyme to the skillet and sauté until the onions are softened and fragrant, for about 3 minutes. Stir in the wine and mushrooms, stirring up any browned bits from the bottom of the skillet, and then transfer to the crock pot insert.
3. Cover and cook on high for 3½ to 4 hours or on low for 8 hours.
4. Remove the beef from the crock pot and cover with aluminum foil. Let the meat rest for 10 to 15 minutes. Skim off any fat from the sauce.
5. Serve the meat with the sauce.

Sweet and Sour Pork

Prep time: 20 minutes | Cook time: 7½ to 8½ hours | Serves 6

1 (15-ounce / 425-g) can tomato sauce
1 medium onion, halved and sliced
1 medium green pepper, cut into strips
1 (4½-ounce / 128-g) can sliced mushrooms, drained
3 tablespoons brown sugar
4½ teaspoons white vinegar
2 teaspoons steak sauce
1 teaspoon salt
1½ pounds (680 g) pork tenderloin, cut into 1-inch cubes
1 tablespoon olive oil
1 (8-ounce / 227-g) can unsweetened pineapple chunks, drained
Hot cooked rice, for serving

1. In a large bowl, combine the first eight ingredients and set aside.
2. In a large skillet, brown the pork in the oil for 4 minutes, in batches. Transfer to a crock pot. Pour the tomato sauce mixture over the pork. Cover and cook on low for 7 to 8 hours or until meat is tender.
3. Add the pineapple. Cover and cook for 30 minutes longer or until heated through. Serve with rice.

Garlicky Veal Stew

Prep time: 15 minutes | Cook time: 6 to 7 hours | Serves 6

½ cup all-purpose flour
1½ teaspoons salt
½ teaspoon freshly ground black pepper
2½ pounds (1.1 kg) boneless veal shoulder or shank, cut into 1-inch pieces
3 tablespoons extra-virgin olive oil
¼ cup tomato paste
1 teaspoon dried thyme
½ cup dry white wine or vermouth
1 cup chicken broth
½ cup beef broth
1 bay leaf
40 cloves garlic, peeled

1. Mix the flour, salt, and pepper in a large zipper-top plastic bag. Add the veal, toss to coat, and shake off any excess. Heat the oil in a large skillet over high heat. Add the veal a few pieces at a time and sauté until browned on all sides for 4 minutes.
2. Transfer the browned meat to the insert of a crock pot. When all the veal is browned, add the tomato paste, thyme, and white wine to the skillet and scrape up any browned bits from the bottom of the pan. Add both broths and stir to combine.
3. Pour the contents of the skillet over the veal in the crock pot, add the bay leaf and garlic, and stir to distribute the ingredients. Cover and cook the veal on low for 6 to 7 hours, until it is tender. Remove the veal from the crock pot with a slotted spoon.
4. Mash the garlic cloves and stir them into the sauce. Taste and adjust the seasoning. Return the veal to the crock pot and serve the stew.

Beef Roast with Stewed Tomatoes

Prep time: 5 minutes | Cook time: 8 to 10 hours | Serves 10

4 to 5 pounds (1.8 to 2.3 kg) beef roast
3 tablespoons oil
2 (14½-ounce / 411-g) cans Mexican-style stewed tomatoes
1 (16-ounce / 454-g) jar salsa
2 or 3 medium onions, cut in chunks
1 or 2 green or red bell peppers, sliced

1. Brown the roast in the oil in a skillet, for 4 minutes. Place in a crock pot.
2. In a bowl, combine the stewed tomatoes and salsa. Spoon over the meat.
3. Cover and cook on low for 8 to 10 hours, or until the meat is tender but not dry.
4. Add the onions halfway through cooking time in order to keep fairly crisp. Push down into the sauce.
5. One hour before serving, add the pepper slices. Push down into the sauce.
6. Remove the meat from the crock pot and allow to rest for 10 minutes before slicing. Place the slices on a serving platter and top with the vegetables and sauce.

German Sauerbraten

Prep time: 15 minutes | Cook time: 8 hours | Serves 6

1½ tablespoons extra-virgin olive oil
1 (4-pound / 1.8-kg) boneless beef chuck roast
2 tablespoons tomato paste
1 cup dry red wine
¾ cup cider vinegar
1½ tablespoons white sugar, plus more as needed
1 tablespoon pickling spices, wrapped in a sachet
4 carrots, chopped
1 large onion, chopped
1 cup low-sodium beef bone broth
8 gingersnap cookies, crushed
1 teaspoon kosher salt, plus more for seasoning
½ teaspoon freshly ground black pepper, plus more for seasoning
1½ tablespoons cornstarch
1½ tablespoons cold water

1. In a pan over medium-high heat, heat the oil until shimmering. Season the roast with salt and pepper, and brown for about 3 minutes per side. Transfer the meat to a plate. Add the tomato paste and cook, stirring, for 1 minute. Whisk in the wine, vinegar, and sugar. Bring to a boil and simmer for 5 minutes.
2. Add the tomato-wine mixture to a crock pot. Add the pickling spice sachet, carrots, onion, bone broth, gingersnaps, salt, and pepper. Stir to combine. Place the meat in the crock pot. Cover and cook on low for 8 hours.
3. About 30 minutes before serving, remove the pickling spice sachet and discard. In a small bowl, whisk together the cornstarch and water. Add to the crock pot and gently stir. Leave the lid slightly ajar and continue cooking until the liquid is thickened and the meat is tender. Using a ladle or large spoon, skim the fat from the top of the liquid and discard the spice packet. Season with additional salt and pepper, as needed, and add more sugar if the cooking juices taste too tart. Slice the meat and serve immediately with vegetables and gravy.

Chinese-Style Cumin Lamb

Prep time: 15 minutes | Cook time: 6 to 8 hours | Serves 6

1 tablespoon extra-virgin olive oil
½ tablespoon sesame oil
2 pounds (907 g) boneless lamb shoulder, cut into ½-inch-by-2-inch strips
Black pepper, to taste
1 large onion, sliced
2 garlic cloves, minced
½ cup low-sodium chicken stock
2 teaspoons soy sauce
2 tablespoons ground cumin
1 tablespoon packed brown sugar
1 tablespoon Chinese black vinegar, or white vinegar
½ teaspoon red pepper flakes
½ teaspoon kosher salt, plus more for seasoning
1½ teaspoons cornstarch
3 cups cooked white rice, for serving
3 scallions, white and green parts sliced, for garnish

1. In a pan over medium-high heat, heat the olive oil and the sesame oil until shimmering. Season the lamb shoulder with salt and pepper, and brown on all sides, for about 5 minutes total.
2. Put the lamb in a crock pot, along with the onion and garlic. In a medium bowl, whisk together the chicken stock, soy sauce, cumin, brown sugar, vinegar, red pepper flakes, and salt. Pour over the lamb. Cover and cook on low for 6 to 8 hours.
3. Season with additional salt, as needed. About 30 minutes before serving, whisk in the cornstarch, taking care that there are no lumps. Cover and continue cooking until the sauce is thickened. Serve over the rice, garnished with the scallions.

Chapter 10 Red Meat | 113

Apple and Cranberry Pork Roast

Prep time: 10 minutes | Cook time: 6 to 8 hours | Serves 8

2 pounds (907 g) pork tenderloin, fat trimmed
2 tablespoons canola oil
3 cups apple juice
3 Granny Smith apples
1 cup fresh cranberries
¾ teaspoon salt
½ teaspoon black pepper

1. Brown the roast on all sides in a skillet in the canola oil, for 4 minutes. Place in a crock pot.
2. Add the remaining ingredients.
3. Cover. Cook on low for 6 to 8 hours.
4. Serve warm.

Pork-Beef Patties with Cabbage

Prep time: 15 minutes | Cook time: 5 to 6 hours | Serves 8

1 (32-ounce / 907-g) can tomato purée
¼ cup granulated sugar
¼ cup white vinegar
½ cup golden raisins
8 ounces (227 g) lean ground pork
8 ounces (227 g) 85% lean ground beef
½ cup cooked rice
½ cup finely chopped shallot
½ cup ketchup
1 teaspoon salt
½ teaspoon freshly ground black pepper
1 large head green cabbage, cut into ½-inch-thick slices
1 large onion, sliced into half rounds
1 (15-ounce / 425-g) can sauerkraut, drained and rinsed

1. Stir the tomato purée, sugar, vinegar, and raisins together in the insert of a crock pot. Stir the pork, beef, rice, shallot, ketchup, salt, and pepper together in a large mixing bowl. Form the mixture into 3-inch oval patties and set aside.
2. Lay half of the cabbage, onion, and sauerkraut in the bottom of the crock pot with the sauce. Top with all the meat patties and spread the remaining cabbage, onion, and sauerkraut on top of the meat.
3. Cover the crock pot and cook on high for 1 hour. Spoon some of the sauce over the top of the cabbage and cook on low for 4 to 5 hours, until the meat registers 165ºF (74ºC) on an instant-read thermometer.
4. Serve from the crock pot set on warm.

Pork Roast in Apricot Glaze

Prep time: 5 minutes | Cook time: 4 to 6 hours | Serves 10 to 12

1 (10½-ounce / 298-g) can condensed chicken broth
1 (18-ounce / 510-g) jar apricot preserves
1 large onion, chopped
2 tablespoons Dijon mustard
3½ to 4 pounds (1.5 to 1.8 kg) boneless pork loin

1. Mix the broth, preserves, onion, and mustard in a bowl.
2. Cut the roast to fit, if necessary, and place in a crock pot. Pour the glaze over the meat.
3. Cover and cook on low for 4 to 6 hours, or on high for 3 hours, or until tender.
4. Remove the pork loin from the crock pot to a serving platter. Discard the juices or thicken for gravy. Serve warm.

Sumptuous Pork with Veggies

Prep time: 10 minutes | Cook time: 6 to 8 hours | Serves 6

1 pound (454 g) pork roast, cut into strips ½-inch thick
1 large onion, chopped
1 small green bell pepper, sliced
8 ounces (227 g) fresh mushrooms, sliced
1 (8-ounce / 227-g) can low-sodium tomato sauce
4 carrots, sliced
1½ tablespoons vinegar
1 teaspoon salt
2 teaspoons Worcestershire sauce
Hot rice, for serving

1. Brown the pork in a skillet over medium heat for 4 minutes. Transfer to a crock pot.
2. Combine all the remaining ingredients in the crock pot.
3. Cover. Cook on low for 6 to 8 hours.
4. Serve over hot rice.

Beef Roast with Tangy Au Jus

Prep time: 10 minutes | Cook time: 6 to 8 hours | Serves 8

1½ tablespoons extra-virgin olive oil
1 (3- to 4-pound / 1.4- to 1.8-kg) boneless chuck roast
1¼ teaspoons kosher salt
1½ teaspoons freshly ground black pepper
¼ cup all-purpose flour
4 tablespoons unsalted butter
10 pepperoncini
2 tablespoons mayonnaise
1 tablespoon sour cream
2 teaspoons apple cider vinegar
1 teaspoon buttermilk
½ teaspoon dried dill
½ teaspoon dried chives

1. In a pan over medium-high heat, heat the oil until shimmering. Season the roast with and pepper, and coat with the flour. Brown the roast on both sides to create a crust, for about 4 minutes per side.
2. Place the roast in the crock pot, along with the butter, pepperoncini, mayonnaise, sour cream, cider vinegar, buttermilk, dill, and chives. Cover and cook on low for 6 to 8 hours, until tender.
3. Transfer the meat to a cutting board. Using two forks, shred the meat and discard any fat. Return the meat to the crock pot and mix the meat with the liquid inside, or plate the meat and drizzle the tangy au jus on top.

Texas-Style Pork Burritos

Prep time: 20 minutes | Cook time: 6½ to 8½ hours | Serves 10

1 boneless pork shoulder butt roast, cubed (3 to 4 pounds / 1.4 to 1.8 kg)
1 teaspoon salt
½ teaspoon pepper
2 tablespoons canola oil
2 (10-ounce / 284-g) cans green enchilada sauce
1 large onion, thinly sliced
2 medium carrots, thinly sliced
2 (2¼-ounce / 64-g) cans sliced ripe olives, drained
½ cup chicken broth
2 tablespoons ground cumin
3 garlic cloves, minced
2 teaspoons dried oregano
2 tablespoons all-purpose flour
1 cup sour cream
½ cup minced fresh cilantro
10 flour tortillas (8 inches), warmed
2 cups shredded Mexican cheese blend

1. Sprinkle the pork with salt and pepper. In a large skillet, brown the meat in the oil for 4 minutes, in batches. Transfer to a crock pot. Combine the enchilada sauce, onion, carrots, olives, broth, cumin, garlic and oregano in a bowl. Pour over the meat. Cover and cook on low for 6 to 8 hours or until meat is tender.
2. Combine the flour and sour cream. Stir into the meat mixture. Cover and cook on high for 30 minutes or until thickened. Stir in the cilantro.
3. Spoon ²⁄₃ cup of the pork mixture onto each tortilla. Top with about 3 tablespoons cheese. Roll up tightly and serve.

Pork Wraps with Hoisin Sauce

Prep time: 10 minutes | Cook time: 7 to 8 hours | Serves 15

1 boneless pork loin roast (3 pounds / 1.4 kg)
1 cup hoisin sauce, divided
1 tablespoon minced fresh ginger
6 cups shredded red cabbage
1½ cups shredded carrots
¼ cup thinly sliced green onions
3 tablespoons rice vinegar
4½ teaspoons sugar
15 flour tortillas (8 inches), warmed

1. Cut the roast in half. Combine 1⅓ cup of the hoisin sauce and ginger in a bowl. Rub over the pork. Transfer to a crock pot. Cover and cook on low for 7 to 8 hours or until the pork is tender.
2. Meanwhile, in a large bowl, combine the cabbage, carrots, onions, vinegar and sugar. Chill until serving.
3. Shred the meat with two forks and return to the crock pot. Heat through. Place 2 teaspoons of the hoisin sauce down the center of each tortilla. Top with 1⅓ cup shredded pork and 1⅓ cup coleslaw. Roll up and serve.

Oregano Lamb Chops

Prep time: 10 minutes | Cook time: 4 to 6 hours | Serves 6 to 8

1 medium onion, sliced
1 teaspoon dried oregano
½ teaspoon dried thyme
½ teaspoon garlic powder
¼ teaspoon salt
⅛ teaspoon pepper
8 loin lamb chops (1¾ to 2 pounds / 794 to 907 g)
2 garlic cloves, minced
¼ cup water

1. Place the onion in a crock pot.
2. Combine the oregano, thyme, garlic powder, salt, and pepper in a bowl. Rub over the lamb chops. Place in the crock pot. Top with the garlic. Pour the water down alongside of the crock pot, so as not to disturb the rub on the chops.
3. Cover. Cook on low for 4 to 6 hours.
4. Serve warm.

Pork and Butternut Stew

Prep time: 20 minutes | Cook time: 8½ to 10½ hours | Serves 6

1⅓ cup plus 1 tablespoon all-purpose flour, divided
1 tablespoon paprika
1 teaspoon salt
1 teaspoon ground coriander
1½ pounds (680 g) boneless pork shoulder butt roast, cut into 1-inch cubes
1 tablespoon canola oil
2¾ cups peeled, cubed butternut squash
1 (14½-ounce / 411-g) can diced tomatoes, undrained
1 cup frozen corn, thawed
1 medium onion, chopped
2 tablespoons cider vinegar
1 bay leaf
2½ cups reduced-sodium chicken broth
1⅔ cups frozen shelled edamame, thawed

1. In a large resealable plastic bag, combine 1⅓ cup of the flour, paprika, salt and coriander. Add the pork, a few pieces at a time, and shake to coat.
2. In a large skillet, brown the pork in the oil for 4 minutes, in batches. Drain. Transfer to a crock pot. Add the squash, tomatoes, corn, onion, vinegar and bay leaf. In a small bowl, combine the broth and remaining flour until smooth. Stir into the crock pot.
3. Cover and cook on low for 8 to 10 hours or until pork and vegetables are tender. Stir in the edamame. Cover and cook for 30 minutes longer. Discard the bay leaf. Serve warm.

Italian Pork Sausage Lasagna Soup

Prep time: 15 minutes | Cook time: 8 hours | Serves 6

1 tablespoon extra-virgin olive oil
¾ pound (340 g) hot or sweet Italian pork sausage, casings removed
1 medium onion, finely chopped
3 garlic cloves, minced
6 cups low-sodium chicken stock
1 (28-ounce / 794-g) can puréed tomatoes
¾ cup dry red wine
2 teaspoons dry Italian seasoning
½ teaspoon kosher salt, plus more for seasoning
½ teaspoon freshly ground black pepper, plus more for seasoning
¼ teaspoon red pepper flakes
8 ounces (227 g) dried elbow macaroni or ditalini
½ cup ricotta cheese, plus more for garnish
½ cup shredded Parmesan cheese

1. In a pan over medium-high heat, heat the oil until shimmering. Brown the Italian sausage for 10 minutes, breaking it up into small bits until no pink remains.
2. Put the Italian sausage in a crock pot, along with the onion, garlic, chicken stock, tomatoes, wine, Italian seasoning, salt, pepper, and red pepper flakes. Cover and cook on low for 8 hours.
3. During the final hour of cooking, add the macaroni. Cover and continue cooking until tender.
4. In a small bowl, combine the ricotta and Parmesan. Season with salt and pepper and stir to combine. Season the soup with additional salt and pepper, as needed. Ladle the soup into bowls and top with a dollop of the ricotta mixture before serving.

Garlic Braised Lamb Shanks

Prep time: 10 minutes | Cook time: 7 to 8 hours | Serves 2 to 3

1½ tablespoons olive oil
2 lamb shanks (about 2½ pounds / 1.1 kg total), trimmed of fat, and each cut crosswise into 3 pieces
¾ cup dry white wine
3 heads garlic, separated into cloves, unpeeled
2 medium-size fresh or canned tomatoes, coarsely chopped
1½ teaspoons chopped fresh rosemary
Salt and freshly ground black pepper, to taste
¼ cup chopped lemon zest, for garnish

1. In a large skillet, heat the oil over medium-high heat and cook the shanks until golden brown on all sides, for about 5 minutes total. As they brown, transfer the shanks to a crock pot. Add the wine to the skillet and bring to a boil, scraping up any browned bits stuck to the pan. Add the garlic, tomatoes, and rosemary, bring to a boil, and pour over the lamb. Cover and cook on low for 7 to 8 hours, until the lamb is very tender and falling off the bone.
2. Season with salt and pepper, sprinkle with the lemon zest, and serve warm.

Pork Shoulder Chili Con Carne

Prep time: 15 minutes | Cook time: 10 hours | Serves 8

2 canned chipotle chiles en adobo, minced, plus 1 tablespoon adobo sauce
1 (28-ounce / 794-g) can puréed tomatoes
1 large onion, finely chopped
4 garlic cloves, minced
1½ tablespoons chili powder, preferably ancho
1 tablespoon ground cumin
2 teaspoons dried oregano
2 teaspoons ground paprika
½ teaspoon ground cinnamon
½ teaspoon kosher salt
½ teaspoon freshly ground black pepper
2 teaspoons apple cider vinegar
1 (4-pound / 1.8-kg) boneless pork shoulder
2 teaspoons coarse cornmeal
½ cup chopped fresh cilantro, for garnish

1. Put the chipotle chiles, adobo sauce, tomatoes, onion, garlic, chili powder, cumin, oregano, paprika, cinnamon, salt, pepper, and vinegar in a crock pot and stir to combine. Place the pork shoulder in the crock pot and spoon the sauce on top. Cover and cook on low for 10 hours.
2. About 30 minutes before serving, transfer the pork to a cutting board. Stir the cornmeal into the chili, cover with the lid, and continue cooking. Using two forks, shred the meat, discarding any undesirable bits of fat. Return the meat to the crock pot and stir it into the sauce. Ladle the chili into bowls and garnish with the cilantro. Serve warm.

Hungarian Pork Paprikash

Prep time: 15 minutes | Cook time: 6 hours | Serves 6

3 pounds (1.4 kg) pork stew meat
1 large onion, finely chopped
1 large red or yellow bell pepper, deseeded and chopped
2 garlic cloves, minced
1 cup low-sodium chicken stock
3 tablespoons red wine vinegar
1 tablespoon Worcestershire sauce
¼ cup tomato paste
1 tablespoon paprika
½ teaspoon kosher salt, plus more for seasoning
½ teaspoon freshly ground black pepper, plus more for seasoning
¼ teaspoon ground caraway
½ cup sour cream
1 pound (454 g) egg noodles, cooked

1. To a crock pot, add the pork, onion, bell pepper, garlic, chicken stock, vinegar, Worcestershire sauce, tomato paste, paprika, salt, pepper, and caraway. Stir to combine. Cover and cook on low for 6 hours.
2. About 20 minutes before the end of the cooking time, season with additional salt and pepper, if desired. Add the sour cream and stir to combine. Continue cooking until the ingredients are warmed through. Serve on top of the egg noodles.

Lamb Goulash au Blanc

Prep time: 10 minutes | Cook time: 5 to 6 hours | Serves 4 to 6

3 tablespoons unsalted butter, softened
1 medium-size yellow onion, chopped
2 pounds (907 g) fresh spring lamb stew meat, such as shoulder, cut into 1½-inch cubes
1 lemon, deseeded and very thinly sliced
1 teaspoon caraway seeds
2 teaspoons dried marjoram
1 clove garlic, peeled
1 cup vegetable broth
Salt and freshly ground black pepper, to taste

1. Smear the bottom of a crock pot with the butter and sprinkle with the onion. Put the lamb in the crock pot and arrange the lemon slices over it.
2. In a mortar, mash together the caraway seeds, marjoram, and garlic with a pestle. Stir into the broth. Add the broth to the crock pot, cover, and cook on low for 5 to 6 hours, until the lamb is fork-tender. Season with salt and pepper and serve.

Irish Lamb Stew

Prep time: 10 minutes | Cook time: 8 hours | Serves 2

12 ounces (340 g) boneless lamb shoulder or stew meat, cut into 1-inch pieces
⅛ teaspoon sea salt
Freshly ground black pepper, to taste
1 cup diced and peeled parsnips
1 cup diced and peeled potatoes
½ cup diced onions
1 tablespoon minced garlic
1 cup low-sodium beef broth
½ cup dark beer, such as Guinness Stout
½ tablespoon tomato paste

1. Season the lamb with salt and black pepper. Put the lamb, parsnips, potatoes, onions, and garlic into a crock pot.
2. In a measuring cup or small bowl, whisk together the beef broth, beer, and tomato paste. Pour this over the lamb and vegetables.
3. Cover and cook on low for 8 hours.
4. Serve warm.

Soy-Honey Lamb and Brown Rice

Prep time: 10 minutes | Cook time: 8 hours | Serves

1 teaspoon extra-virgin olive oil
½ cup brown rice
1 cup low-sodium chicken broth or water
1 scallion, white and green parts, sliced thin on a bias
2 tablespoons low-sodium soy sauce
2 tablespoons honey
1 tablespoon freshly squeezed lime juice
Pinch of red pepper flakes
12 ounces (340 g) boneless lamb shoulder, cut into 1-inch cubes

1. Grease the inside of a crock pot with the olive oil.
2. Put the brown rice, broth, and scallion in the crock pot. Stir to mix the ingredients and make sure the rice is submerged in the liquid.
3. In a large bowl, whisk together the soy sauce, honey, lime juice, and red pepper flakes. Add the lamb cubes and toss to coat them in this mixture.
4. Place the lamb over the rice in the crock pot.
5. Cover and cook on low for 8 hours.
6. Serve warm.

Chapter 11 Fish and Seafood

Basil Perch with Potatoes

Prep time: 10 minutes | Cook time: 1 to 2 hours | Serves 4

1 (10¾-ounce / 305-g) can cream of celery soup
½ cup water
1 pound (454 g) perch fillet, fresh or thawed
2 cups cooked, diced potatoes, drained
¼ cup grated Parmesan cheese
1 tablespoon chopped parsley
½ teaspoon salt
½ teaspoon dried basil
¼ teaspoon dried oregano

1. Combine soup and water. Pour half in the crock pot. Spread fillet on top. Place potatoes on fillet. Pour remaining soup mix over top.
2. Combine cheese and herbs. Sprinkle over ingredients in a crock pot.
3. Cover. Cook on high 1 to 2 hours, being careful not to overcook fish.

Herbed Braised Flounder

Prep time: 5 minutes | Cook time: 3 to 4 hours | Serves 6

2 pounds (907 g) flounder fillets, fresh or frozen
½ teaspoon salt
¾ cup chicken broth
2 tablespoons lemon juice
2 tablespoons dried chives
2 tablespoons dried minced onion
½ to 1 teaspoon leaf marjoram
4 tablespoons chopped fresh parsley

1. Wipe fish as dry as possible. Cut fish into portions to fit crock pot.
2. Sprinkle with salt.
3. Combine broth and lemon juice. Stir in remaining ingredients.
4. Place a meat rack in the crock pot. Lay fish on the rack. Pour liquid mixture over each portion.
5. Cover. Cook on high 3 to 4 hours.

Red Snapper Feast

Prep time: 15 minutes | Cook time: 2 to 3 hours | Serves 8

3 pounds (1.4 kg) red snapper fillets
1 tablespoon minced garlic
1 large onion, sliced
1 green bell pepper, cut into 1-inch pieces
2 unpeeled zucchini, sliced
1 (14-ounce / 397-g) can low-sodium diced tomatoes
½ teaspoon dried basil
½ teaspoon dried oregano
¼ teaspoon salt
¼ teaspoon black pepper
¼ cup dry white wine or white grape juice

1. Rinse snapper and pat dry. Place in a crock pot sprayed with non-fat cooking spray.
2. Mix remaining ingredients together and pour over fish.
3. Cover. Cook on high 2 to 3 hours, being careful not to overcook the fish.

Five-Ingredient Tuna Loaf

Prep time: 5 minutes | Cook time: 1 hour | Serves 4

1 (10¾-ounce / 305-g) can cream of mushroom soup, divided
¾ cup milk, divided
2 eggs, beaten
2 cups dry stuffing mix
1 (12-ounce / 340-g) can tuna, drained and flaked

1. Place ²⁄₃ of the undiluted soup and ½ cup of the milk in a small saucepan. Blend together; then set aside.
2. Grease the interior of the crock pot with nonstick cooking spray. Mix the rest of the ingredients together in the crock pot.
3. Cover and cook on high for 1 hour. Allow to stand for 15 minutes before serving.
4. Meanwhile, heat the reserved soup and milk in the saucepan. Serve over the cooked tuna as a sauce.

Salmon with Chili-Garlic Glaze

Prep time: 20 minutes | Cook time: 1 to 2 hours | Serves 4

1²⅓ cups boiling water
1½ cups instant brown rice
3 tablespoons vegetable oil
Salt and pepper, to taste
4 scallions, white parts minced, green parts sliced on bias ½ inch thick
3 tablespoons toasted sesame oil
2 tablespoons Asian chili-garlic sauce
2 tablespoons honey
4 (6- to 8-ounce / 170- to 227-g) skin-on salmon fillets, 1 to 1½ inches thick
2 oranges
¼ cup rice vinegar
1 teaspoon grated fresh ginger

1. Lightly coat crock pot with vegetable oil spray. Combine boiling water, rice, 1 tablespoon vegetable oil, ½ teaspoon salt, and ½ teaspoon pepper in prepared crock pot. Gently press 16 by 12-inch sheet of parchment paper onto surface of water, folding down edges as needed.
2. Combine scallion whites, sesame oil, chili-garlic sauce, and honey in bowl; measure out and reserve half of scallion mixture in medium bowl until ready to use. Season salmon with salt and pepper, brush with remaining scallion mixture, and arrange, skin side down, in even layer on top of parchment. Cover and cook until salmon is opaque throughout when checked with tip of paring knife and registers 135°F (57°C) (for medium), 1 to 2 hours on low.
3. Cut away peel and pith from oranges. Cut oranges into 8 wedges, then slice wedges crosswise into ½-inch-thick pieces. Using 2 metal spatulas, transfer salmon to serving dish; discard parchment and remove any white albumin from salmon. Whisk vinegar, ginger, and remaining 2 tablespoons vegetable oil into reserved scallion mixture. Fluff rice with fork, then gently fold in oranges (adding any accumulated juices), scallion greens, and half of vinaigrette. Season with salt and pepper to taste. Serve salmon with salad, passing remaining vinaigrette separately.

Spinach-Stuffed Sole

Prep time: 25 minutes | Cook time: 1 to 2 hours | Serves 4

1 lemon, sliced ¼ inch thick, plus ½ teaspoon grated lemon zest plus 1 tablespoon juice
¼ cup chopped fresh basil, stems reserved
¼ cup dry white wine
10 ounces (283 g) frozen chopped spinach, thawed and squeezed dry
4 ounces (113 g) whole-milk ricotta cheese
Pinch of nutmeg
Salt and pepper, to taste
8 (2- to 3-ounce / 57- to 85-g) skinless sole fillets, ¼ to ½ inch thick
8 ounces (227 g) cherry tomatoes
1 shallot, peeled and quartered
2 tablespoons extra-virgin olive oil

1. Fold sheet of aluminum foil into 12 by 9-inch sling and press widthwise into a crock pot. Arrange lemon slices in single layer in bottom of prepared crock pot. Scatter basil stems over lemon slices. Add wine to crock pot, then add water until liquid level is even with lemon slices (about ¼ cup).
2. Combine spinach, ricotta, lemon zest, 2 tablespoons chopped basil, nutmeg, ¼ teaspoon salt, and ¼ teaspoon pepper in a bowl. Season sole with salt and pepper and place skinned side up on the cutting board. Mound filling evenly in center of fillets, fold tapered ends tightly over filling, then fold over thicker ends to make tidy bundles. Arrange bundles seam side down in an even layer on top of basil sprigs. Cover and cook until sole flakes apart when gently prodded with a paring knife, 1 to 2 hours on low.
3. Process tomatoes, shallot, oil, and lemon juice in blender until smooth, about 2 minutes, scraping down sides of the blender jar as needed. Strain sauce through fine-mesh strainer into bowl, pressing on solids to extract as much liquid as possible; discard solids. Season with salt and pepper to taste.
4. Using sling, transfer sole bundles to a baking sheet. Gently lift and tilt bundles with spatula to remove basil stems and lemon slices; transfer to serving dish. Discard poaching liquid and remove any white albumin from bundles. Spoon sauce over bundles and sprinkle with remaining 2 tablespoons basil. Serve.

Halibut Tacos

Prep time: 25 minutes | Cook time: 1 to 2 hours | Serves 4

1 lime, sliced ¼ inch thick, plus 3 tablespoons lime juice plus lime wedges for serving
6 tablespoons minced fresh cilantro, stems reserved
¼ cup dry white wine
2 tablespoons extra-virgin olive oil
1 tablespoon minced canned chipotle chile in adobo sauce
½ teaspoon ground coriander
¼ teaspoon ground cumin
Salt and pepper, to taste
4 (6- to 8-ounce / 170- to 227-g) skinless halibut fillets, 1 to 1½ inches thick
4 cups shredded green cabbage
3 scallions, thinly sliced
¼ cup mayonnaise
¼ cup sour cream
2 garlic cloves, minced
12 (6-inch) corn tortillas, warmed

1. Fold sheet of aluminum foil into 12 by 9-inch sling and press widthwise into a crock pot. Arrange lime slices in single layer in bottom of prepared crock pot. Scatter cilantro stems over lime slices. Add wine to crock pot, then add water until liquid level is even with lime slices (about ¼ cup).
2. Microwave 1 tablespoon oil, 2 teaspoons chipotle, coriander, cumin, ½ teaspoon salt, and ¼ teaspoon pepper in bowl until fragrant, about 30 seconds; let cool slightly. Rub halibut with spice mixture, then arrange in an even layer on top of cilantro stems. Cover and cook until halibut flakes apart when gently prodded with a paring knife and registers 140°F (60°C), 1 to 2 hours on low.
3. Combine cabbage, scallions, 2 tablespoons lime juice, ¼ cup cilantro, ¼ teaspoon salt, and remaining 1 tablespoon oil in the bowl. In a separate bowl, combine mayonnaise, sour cream, garlic, remaining 1 tablespoon lime juice, remaining 2 tablespoons cilantro, and remaining 1 teaspoon chipotle. Season with salt and pepper to taste.
4. Using sling, transfer halibut to cutting board. Gently lift and tilt fillets with spatula to remove cilantro stems and lime slices; discard poaching liquid and remove any white albumin from halibut. Cut each fillet into 3 equal pieces. Spread sauce evenly onto warm tortillas, top with fish and cabbage mixture, and serve with lime wedges.

Swordfish with Tomato and Olive Relish

Prep time: 20 minutes | Cook time: 1 to 2 hours | Serves 4

1 lemon, sliced ¼ inch thick
2 tablespoons minced fresh parsley, stems reserved
¼ cup dry white wine
4 (6- to 8-ounce / 170- to 227-g) skinless swordfish steaks, 1 to 1½ inches thick
Salt and pepper, to taste
1 pound (454 g) cherry tomatoes, halved
½ cup pitted salt-cured black olives, rinsed and halved
3 garlic cloves, minced
¼ cup extra-virgin olive oil

1. Fold sheet of aluminum foil into 12 by 9-inch sling and press widthwise into a crock pot. Arrange lemon slices in single layer in bottom of prepared crock pot. Scatter parsley stems over lemon slices. Add wine to crock pot, then add water until liquid level is even with lemon slices (about ¼ cup). Season swordfish with salt and pepper and arrange in an even layer on top of parsley stems. Cover and cook until swordfish flakes apart when gently prodded with a paring knife and registers 140°F (60°C), 1 to 2 hours on low.
2. Microwave tomatoes, olives, and garlic in bowl until tomatoes begin to break down, about 4 minutes. Stir in oil and minced parsley and season with salt and pepper to taste. Using sling, transfer swordfish to baking sheet. Gently lift and tilt steaks with spatula to remove parsley stems and lemon slices; transfer to serving dish. Discard poaching liquid and remove any white albumin from swordfish. Serve with relish.

Salmon and Mushroom Bake

Prep time: 10 minutes | Cook time: 2½ to 3½ hours | Serves 6

1 (14¾-ounce / 418-g) can salmon with liquid
1 (4-ounce / 113-g) can mushrooms, drained
1½ cups bread crumbs
1⅓ cup eggbeaters
1 cup shredded fat-free cheese
1 tablespoon lemon juice
1 tablespoon minced onion

1. Flake fish in a bowl, removing bones. Stir in remaining ingredients. Pour into lightly greased crock pot.
2. Cover. Cook on low 2½ to 3½ hours.

Cod with Garlic Edamame

Prep time: 15 minutes | Cook time: 1 to 2 hours | Serves 4

2 shallots, minced
4 garlic cloves, minced
1 tablespoon grated fresh ginger
1 tablespoon vegetable oil
⅛ teaspoon red pepper flakes
2 cups frozen edamame, thawed
½ cup canned coconut milk
2 tablespoons fish sauce, plus extra for seasoning
4 (6- to 8-ounce / 170- to 227-g) skinless cod fillets, 1 to 1½ inches thick
Salt and pepper, to taste
¼ cup chopped fresh cilantro
1 teaspoon rice vinegar

1. Microwave shallots, garlic, ginger, oil, and pepper flakes in bowl, stirring occasionally, until shallots are softened, about 2 minutes; transfer to a crock pot. Stir edamame, coconut milk, and fish sauce into a crock pot. Season cod with salt and pepper and nestle into a crock pot. Spoon portion of sauce over cod. Cover and cook until cod flakes apart when gently prodded with a paring knife and registers 140ºF (60ºC), 1 to 2 hours on low.
2. Using 2 metal spatulas, transfer cod to serving dish. Stir cilantro and vinegar into edamame and season with extra fish sauce to taste. Spoon edamame and sauce over cod. Serve.

Cheddar Salmon Soufflé

Prep time: 5 minutes | Cook time: 2 to 3 hours | Serves 4

1 (15-ounce / 425-g) can salmon, drained and flaked
2 eggs, beaten well
2 cups seasoned croutons
1 cup shredded Cheddar cheese
2 chicken bouillon cubes
1 cup boiling water
¼ teaspoon dry mustard (optional)

1. Grease the interior of your crock pot with nonstick cooking spray.
2. Combine salmon, eggs, croutons, and cheese in the crock pot.
3. Dissolve bouillon cubes in boiling water in a small bowl. Add mustard, if you wish, and stir. Pour over salmon mixture and stir together lightly.
4. Cover and cook on high 2 to 3 hours, or until mixture appears to be set. Allow to stand 15 minutes before serving.

Sweet and Sour Tuna

Prep time: 15 minutes | Cook time: 1 hour | Serves 3

Half a green bell pepper, cut into ¼-inch strips
1 small onion, thinly sliced
2 teaspoons olive oil
1⅓ cup unsweetened pineapple juice
1½ teaspoons cornstarch
2⅓ cup canned unsweetened pineapple chunks, drained
1 tablespoon sugar (scant)
1 tablespoon vinegar
1 (6-ounce / 170-g) can solid, water-packed tuna, drained and flaked
⅛ teaspoon black pepper
Dash of Tabasco sauce

1. Cook green pepper and onion with oil in a skillet over medium heat, leaving the vegetables slightly crisp.
2. Mix pineapple juice with cornstarch. Add to green pepper mixture.
3. Cook, stirring gently until thickened.
4. Add remaining ingredients. Pour into a crock pot.
5. Cover. Cook on low 1 hour.

Tuna and Veggie Casserole with Almonds

Prep time: 15 minutes | Cook time: 7 to 9 hours | Serves 6

2 (6½-ounce / 184-g) cans water-packed tuna, drained
2 (10½-ounce / 298-g) cans cream of mushroom soup
1 cup milk
2 tablespoons dried parsley
1 (10-ounce/ 283-g) package frozen mixed vegetables, thawed
1 (10-ounce / 283-g) package noodles, cooked and drained
½ cup toasted sliced almonds

1. Combine tuna, soup, milk, parsley, and vegetables. Fold in noodles. Pour into greased crock pot. Top with almonds.
2. Cover. Cook on low 7 to 9 hours, or on high 3 to 4 hours.

Fish Tagine with Artichokes

Prep time: 25 minutes | Cook time: 7 to 8 hours | Serves 4 to 6

2 onions, finely chopped
2 tablespoons tomato paste
4 garlic cloves, minced
1 tablespoon vegetable oil
2 teaspoons garam masala
1½ teaspoons paprika
¼ teaspoon cayenne pepper
3 cups jarred whole baby artichokes packed in water, halved, rinsed, and patted dry
2 cups chicken broth
1 (14½-ounce / 411-g) can diced tomatoes, drained
¼ cup dry white wine
Salt and pepper, to taste
1½ pounds (680 g) skinless cod fillets, 1 to 1½ inches thick, cut into 2-inch pieces
½ cup pitted kalamata olives, coarsely chopped
2 tablespoons minced fresh parsley

1. Microwave onions, tomato paste, garlic, oil, garam masala, paprika, and cayenne in bowl, stirring occasionally, until onions are softened, about 5 minutes; transfer to a crock pot. Stir in artichokes, broth, tomatoes, wine, and ½ teaspoon salt. Cover and cook until flavors meld, 7 to 8 hours on low or 4 to 5 hours on high.
2. Stir cod and olives into tagine, cover, and cook on high until cod flakes apart when gently prodded with a paring knife, 30 to 40 minutes. Gently stir in parsley and season with salt and pepper to taste. Serve.

Salmon with White Rice Salad

Prep time: 20 minutes | Cook time: 1 to 2 hours | Serves 4

1²⁄₃ cups boiling water
1½ cups instant white rice
1⅓ cup extra-virgin olive oil
Salt and pepper, to taste
4 (6- to 8-ounce / 170- to 227-g) skin-on salmon fillets, 1 to 1½ inches thick
¼ cup red wine vinegar
1 tablespoon honey
2 teaspoons minced fresh oregano
2 garlic cloves, minced
8 ounces (227 g) cherry tomatoes, quartered
½ cup fresh parsley leaves
2 ounces (57 g) feta cheese, crumbled (½ cup)
Lemon wedges, for serving

1. Lightly coat crock pot with vegetable oil spray. Combine boiling water, rice, 1 tablespoon oil, ½ teaspoon salt, and ½ teaspoon pepper in prepared crock pot. Gently press 16 by 12-inch sheet of parchment paper onto surface of water, folding down edges as needed.
2. Season salmon with salt and pepper and arrange, skin side down, in even layer on top of parchment. Cover and cook until salmon is opaque throughout when checked with tip of paring knife and registers 135ºF (57ºC) (for medium), 1 to 2 hours on low.
3. Using 2 metal spatulas, transfer salmon to serving dish; discard parchment and remove any white albumin from salmon. Whisk vinegar, honey, oregano, garlic, and remaining oil together in a bowl. Fluff rice with fork, then gently fold in tomatoes, parsley, feta, and ½ cup vinaigrette. Season with salt and pepper to taste. Drizzle remaining vinaigrette over salmon and serve with salad and lemon wedges.

Chapter 11 Fish and Seafood | 123

BBQ Tuna

Prep time: 10 minutes | Cook time: 8 to 10 hours | Serves 4

1 (12-ounce / 340-g) can tuna, drained
2 cups tomato juice
1 medium green pepper, finely chopped
2 tablespoons onion flakes
2 tablespoons Worcestershire sauce
3 tablespoons vinegar
2 tablespoons sugar
1 tablespoon prepared mustard
1 rib celery, chopped
Dash chili powder
½ teaspoon cinnamon
Dash of hot sauce (optional)

1. Combine all ingredients in a crock pot.
2. Cover. Cook on low 8 to 10 hours, or on high 4 to 5 hours. If mixture becomes too dry while cooking, add ½ cup tomato juice.
3. Serve on buns.

Halibut with Green Bean Salad

Prep time: 20 minutes | Cook time: 1 to 2 hours | Serves 4

1 (15-ounce / 425-g) can small white beans, rinsed
1 shallot, thinly sliced
2 (2-inch) strips lemon zest, plus 1 tablespoon juice
2 bay leaves
4 (6- to 8-ounce / 170- to 227-g) skinless halibut fillets, 1 to 1½ inches thick
2 tablespoons extra-virgin olive oil
Salt and pepper, to taste
8 ounces (227 g) green beans, trimmed and cut into 1-inch lengths
2 tablespoons minced fresh tarragon
1 teaspoon Dijon mustard
1 teaspoon honey
2 tablespoons chopped pitted kalamata olives

1. Stir white beans, ½ cup water, shallot, lemon zest, and bay leaves into crock pot. Rub halibut with 1 tablespoon oil and season with salt and pepper. Nestle halibut into a crock pot. Cover and cook until halibut flakes apart when gently prodded with a paring knife and registers 140°F (60°C), 1 to 2 hours on low.
2. Microwave green beans with 1 tablespoon water in the covered bowl, stirring occasionally, until tender, 4 to 6 minutes. Drain green beans and return to now-empty bowl. Whisk remaining 1 tablespoon oil, lemon juice, tarragon, mustard, and honey together in a separate bowl.
3. Transfer halibut to serving dish; discard lemon zest and bay leaves. Drain white bean mixture and transfer to bowl with green beans. Add dressing and olives and toss to combine. Season with salt and pepper to taste. Serve.

Shrimp and Ham Jambalaya

Prep time: 20 minutes | Cook time: 2¼ hours | Serves 8

2 tablespoons margarine
2 medium onions, chopped
2 green bell peppers, chopped
3 ribs celery, chopped
1 cup chopped, cooked lean ham
2 garlic cloves, chopped
1½ cups minute rice, uncooked
1½ cups fat-free low sodium beef broth
1 (28-ounce / 794-g) can low-sodium chopped tomatoes
2 tablespoons fresh chopped parsley
1 teaspoon dried basil
½ teaspoon dried thyme
¼ teaspoon black pepper
⅛ teaspoon cayenne pepper
1 pound (454 g) medium-sized shrimp, shelled and deveined
1 tablespoon chopped parsley, for garnish

1. One-half hour before assembling recipe, melt margarine in a crock pot set on high. Add onions, peppers, celery, ham, and garlic. Cook 30 minutes.
2. Add rice. Cover and cook 15 minutes.
3. Add broth, tomatoes, 2 tablespoons parsley, and remaining seasonings. Cover and cook on high 1 hour.
4. Add shrimp. Cook on high 30 minutes, or until liquid is absorbed.
5. Garnish with 1 tablespoon parsley.

Tuna and Egg Casserole

Prep time: 10 minutes | Cook time: 5 to 8 hours | Serves 4

2 (7-ounce / 198-g) cans tuna
1 (10¾-ounce / 305-g) can cream of celery soup
3 hard-boiled eggs, chopped
½ to 1½ cups diced celery
½ cup diced onions
½ cup mayonnaise
¼ teaspoon ground pepper
1½ cups crushed potato chips

1. Combine all ingredients except ¼ cup potato chips in crock pot. Top with remaining chips.
2. Cover. Cook on low 5 to 8 hours.

Shrimp and Crab Gumbo

Prep time: 25 minutes | Cook time: 3 to 4 hours | Serves 10

1 pound (454 g) okra, sliced
2 tablespoons butter, melted
¼ cup butter, melted
¼ cup flour
1 bunch green onions, sliced
½ cup chopped celery
2 garlic cloves, minced
1 (16-ounce / 454-g) can tomatoes and juice
1 bay leaf
1 tablespoon chopped fresh parsley
1 fresh thyme sprig
1½ teaspoons salt
½ to 1 teaspoon red pepper
3 to 5 cups water, depending upon the consistency you like
1 pound (454 g) fresh shrimp, peeled and deveined
½ pound (227 g) fresh crab meat

1. Sauté okra in 2 tablespoons butter until okra is lightly browned. Transfer to a crock pot.
2. Combine remaining butter and flour in the skillet. Cook over medium heat, stirring constantly until roux is the color of chocolate, 20 to 25 minutes. Stir in green onions, celery, and garlic. Cook until vegetables are tender. Add to a crock pot. Gently stir in remaining ingredients.
3. Cover. Cook on high 3 to 4 hours.
4. Serve over rice.

Crab Angel Hair Pasta

Prep time: 15 minutes | Cook time: 4 to 6 hours | Serves 4 to 6

1 medium onion, chopped
½ pound (227 g) fresh mushrooms, sliced
2 (12-ounce / 340-g) cans low-sodium tomato sauce, or 1 (12-ounce / 340-g) can low-sodium tomato sauce and 1 (12-ounce / 340-g) can low-sodium chopped tomatoes
1 (6-ounce / 170-g) can tomato paste
½ teaspoon garlic powder
½ teaspoon dried basil
½ teaspoon dried oregano
½ teaspoon salt
1 pound (454 g) crab meat
16 ounces (454 g) angel hair pasta, cooked

1. Sauté onions and mushrooms in nonstick skillet over low heat. When wilted, place in a crock pot.
2. Add tomato sauce, tomato paste, and seasonings. Stir in crab.
3. Cover. Cook on low 4 to 6 hours.
4. Serve over angel-hair pasta.

Shrimp Spaghetti with Marinara

Prep time: 15 minutes | Cook time: 6¼ to 7¼ hours | Serves 6

1 (16-ounce / 454-g) can low-sodium tomatoes, cut up
2 tablespoons minced parsley
1 clove garlic, minced
½ teaspoon dried basil
½ teaspoon salt
¼ teaspoon black pepper
1 teaspoon dried oregano
1 (6-ounce / 170-g) can tomato paste
½ teaspoon seasoned salt
1 pound (454 g) shrimp, cooked and shelled
3 cups spaghetti
Grated Parmesan cheese, for serving

1. Combine tomatoes, parsley, garlic, basil, salt, pepper, oregano, tomato paste, and seasoned salt in a crock pot.
2. Cover. Cook on low 6 to 7 hours.
3. Stir shrimp into sauce.
4. Cover. Cook on low 10 to 15 minutes.
5. Serve over cooked spaghetti. Top with Parmesan cheese.

Seafood Medley

Prep time: 20 minutes | Cook time: 3 to 4 hours | Serves 10 to 12

1 pound (454 g) shrimp, peeled and deveined
1 pound (454 g) crab meat
1 pound (454 g) bay scallops
2 (10¾-ounce / 305-g) cans cream of celery soup
2 soup cans milk
2 tablespoons butter, melted
1 teaspoon Old Bay seasoning
¼ to ½ teaspoon salt
¼ teaspoon pepper

1. Layer shrimp, crab, and scallops in a crock pot.
2. Combine soup and milk. Pour over seafood.
3. Mix together butter and spices and pour over top.
4. Cover. Cook on low 3 to 4 hours.
5. Serve over rice or noodles.

Thai Green Curry Shrimp

Prep time: 25 minutes | Cook time: 4½ to 5½ hours | Serves 4 to 6

2 cups chicken broth, plus extra as needed
2 tablespoons Thai green curry paste
2 tablespoons instant tapioca
2 pounds (907 g) sweet potatoes, peeled and cut into 1-inch pieces
1 (13½-ounce / 383-g) can coconut milk
1½ pounds (680 g) large shrimp, peeled, deveined, and tails removed
Salt and pepper, to taste
2 tablespoons lime juice
1 tablespoon fish sauce
8 ounces (227 g) snow peas, strings removed and cut into 1-inch pieces
1 tablespoon vegetable oil
½ cup fresh cilantro leaves

1. Whisk broth, curry paste, and tapioca together in a crock pot, then stir in potatoes. Cover and cook until flavors meld and potatoes are tender, 4 to 5 hours on low or 3 to 4 hours on high.
2. Microwave coconut milk in bowl until hot, about 2 minutes. Season shrimp with salt and pepper. Stir shrimp, coconut milk, lime juice, and fish sauce into curry. Cover and cook on high until shrimp are opaque throughout, about 30 minutes.
3. Microwave snow peas and oil in bowl, stirring occasionally, until snow peas are tender, 3 to 5 minutes. Stir snow peas into curry. Adjust consistency with extra hot broth as needed. Stir in cilantro and season with salt and pepper to taste. Serve.

Creamy Shrimp Curry

Prep time: 5 minutes | Cook time: 2 to 3 hours | Serves 4 to 5

1 small onion, chopped
2 cups cooked shrimp
1 teaspoon curry powder
1 (10¾-ounce / 305-g) can cream of mushroom soup
1 cup sour cream

1. Combine all ingredients except sour cream in a crock pot.
2. Cover. Cook on low 2 to 3 hours.
3. Ten minutes before serving, stir in sour cream.
4. Serve over rice or puff pastry.

Citrus Swordfish Fillets

Prep time: 15 minutes | Cook time: 1½ hours | Serves 2

1½ pounds (680 g) swordfish fillets
Sea salt and black pepper, to taste
1 yellow onion, chopped
5 tablespoons chopped fresh flat-leaf parsley
1 tablespoon olive oil
2 teaspoons lemon zest
2 teaspoons orange zest
Orange and lemon slices, for garnish
Fresh parsley sprigs, for garnish
Nonstick cooking spray

1. Spritz the crock pot with nonstick cooking spray.
2. Season the fish fillets with salt and pepper. Place the fish in the crock pot.
3. Distribute the onion, parsley, olive oil, lemon zest, and orange zest over fish.
4. Cover and cook on low for 1½ hours.
5. Serve hot, garnished with orange and lemon slices and sprigs of fresh parsley.

Asian Shrimp and Rice Casserole

Prep time: 10 minutes | **Cook time:** 45 minutes | **Serves 10**

4 cups rice, cooked
2 cups cooked or canned shrimp
1 cup cooked or canned chicken
1 (1-pound / 454-g) can Chinese vegetables
1 (10¾-ounce / 305-g) can cream of celery soup
½ cup milk
½ cup chopped green peppers
1 tablespoon soy sauce
1 can Chinese noodles

1. Combine all ingredients except noodles in a crock pot.
2. Cover. Cook on low 45 minutes.
3. Top with noodles just before serving.

Green Chile and Shrimp Tacos

Prep time: 25 minutes | **Cook time:** 6 to 7 hours | **Serves 4 to 6**

4 poblano chiles, stemmed, deseeded, and cut into ½-inch-wide strips
3 onions, halved and thinly sliced
3 tablespoons extra-virgin olive oil
4 garlic cloves, thinly sliced
½ teaspoon dried oregano
Salt and pepper, to taste
1½ pounds (680 g) extra-large shrimp (21 to 25 per pound), peeled, deveined, tails removed, and cut into 1-inch pieces
2 tablespoons minced fresh cilantro
1 teaspoon grated lime zest plus 1 teaspoon juice
12 to 18 (6-inch) corn tortillas, warmed

1. Toss poblanos and onions with 2 tablespoons oil, garlic, oregano, ½ teaspoon salt, and ½ teaspoon pepper in crock pot. Cover and cook until vegetables are tender, 6 to 7 hours on low or 4 to 5 hours on high.
2. Season shrimp with salt and pepper and stir into a crock pot. Cover and cook on high until shrimp pieces are opaque throughout, 30 to 40 minutes. Strain shrimp mixture, discarding cooking liquid, and return to now-empty crock pot. Stir in cilantro, lime zest and juice, and remaining 1 tablespoon oil. Season with salt and pepper to taste. Serve with tortillas.

Scallops with Creamy Leeks

Prep time: 20 minutes | **Cook time:** 3 to 4 hours | **Serves 4**

1 pound (454 g) leeks, white and light green parts only, halved lengthwise, thinly sliced, and washed thoroughly
4 garlic cloves, minced
1 teaspoon extra-virgin olive oil
1⅓ cup heavy cream
¼ cup dry white wine
1½ pounds (680 g) large sea scallops, tendons removed
Salt and pepper, to taste
¼ cup grated Pecorino Romano cheese
2 tablespoons minced fresh parsley

1. Microwave leeks, garlic, and oil in bowl, stirring occasionally, until leeks are softened, about 5 minutes; transfer to a crock pot. Stir in cream and wine. Cover and cook until leeks are tender but not mushy, 3 to 4 hours on low or 2 to 3 hours on high.
2. Season scallops with salt and pepper and nestle into a crock pot. Spoon portion of sauce over scallops. Cover and cook on high until sides of scallops are firm and centers are opaque, 30 to 40 minutes.
3. Transfer scallops to serving dish. Stir Pecorino into sauce and season with salt and pepper to taste. Spoon sauce over scallops and sprinkle with parsley. Serve.

Monterey Jack Seafood Pasta

Prep time: 15 minutes | **Cook time:** 1 to 2 hours | **Serves 4 to 6**

2 cups sour cream
3 cups shredded Monterey Jack cheese
2 tablespoons butter, melted
½ pound (227 g) crab meat or imitation flaked crab meat
⅛ teaspoon pepper
½ pound (227 g) bay scallops, lightly cooked
1 pound (454 g) medium shrimp, cooked and peeled

1. Combine sour cream, cheese, and butter in a crock pot.
2. Stir in remaining ingredients.
3. Cover. Cook on low 1 to 2 hours.
4. Serve immediately over linguine. Garnish with fresh parsley.

Moroccan Sea Bass with Bell Pepper

Prep time: 20 minutes | Cook time: 2 hours | Serves 8

2 tablespoons extra-virgin olive oil
1 large yellow onion, finely chopped
1 medium red bell pepper, cut into ½-inch strips
1 medium yellow bell pepper, cut into ½-inch strips
4 garlic cloves, minced
1 teaspoon saffron threads, crushed
1½ teaspoons sweet paprika
¼ teaspoon hot paprika or ¼ teaspoon smoked paprika (or pimentón)
½ teaspoon ground ginger
1 (15-ounce / 425-g) can diced tomatoes, with the juice
¼ cup fresh orange juice
2 pounds (907 g) fresh sea bass fillets
¼ cup finely chopped fresh flat-leaf parsley
¼ cup finely chopped fresh cilantro
Sea salt and black pepper, to taste
1 navel orange, thinly sliced, for garnish

1. In a large skillet, heat the olive oil over medium-high heat. Add the onion, red and yellow bell peppers, garlic, saffron, sweet paprika, hot or smoked paprika, and ginger and cook, stirring often, for 3 minutes, or until the onion begins to soften.
2. Add the tomatoes and stir for another 2 minutes to blend the flavors.
3. Transfer the mixture to the crock pot and stir in the orange juice.
4. Place the sea bass fillets on top of the tomato mixture, and spoon some mixture over the fish. Cover and cook on high for 2 hours, or on low for 3 to 4 hours. At the end of the cooking time, the sea bass should be opaque in the center.
5. Carefully lift the fish out of the crock pot with a spatula and transfer to a serving platter. Cover loosely with aluminum foil.
6. Skim off any excess fat from the sauce, stir in the parsley and cilantro, and season with salt and pepper.
7. Spoon some sauce over the fish and garnish with the orange slices. Serve hot, passing the remaining sauce on the side.

Foil Pack Garlic Butter Tilapia

Prep time: 5 minutes | Cook time: 2 hours | Serves 3 to 4

2 tablespoons butter, at room temperature
2 cloves garlic, minced
2 teaspoons minced fresh flat-leaf parsley
4 tilapia fillets
Sea salt and black pepper, to taste

1. In a small bowl, mix the butter, garlic, and parsley to combine.
2. Pull out a large sheet of aluminum foil and put it on the counter. Place the fillets in the middle of the foil.
3. Season the fish generously with salt and pepper.
4. Evenly divide the butter mixture among the fillets and place on top.
5. Wrap the foil around the fish, sealing all sides and crimping the edges to make a packet. Place in the crock pot, cover, and cook on high for 2 hours. Serve hot.

Poached Tuna with Olives

Prep time: 15 minutes | Cook time: 1 hours | Serves 2

2 (1-inch-thick) tuna steaks (about 1¼ pounds / 567 g in total)
2 teaspoons coarse salt
6 (1-inch) strips orange zest
4 garlic cloves, smashed and peeled
2 dried bay leaves
1 serrano chile, halved
1 rosemary sprig
¼ cup pitted green olives, smashed
2 cups canola, safflower, or extra-virgin olive oil

1. Rub tuna all over with the salt and let sit at room temperature for 30 minutes.
2. Place the tuna (do not rinse) in the crock pot. Add orange zest, garlic, bay leaves, chile, rosemary, olives, and oil.
3. Cover and cook on high until tuna is just firm, 1 hour (flip to check underside). Remove the tuna and let sit in oil for 30 minutes.
4. Transfer tuna to a wide bowl and strain oil through a sieve over tuna, then discard solids, but reserve olives, if desired. Serve warm.

Fruit Salsa Mahi Mahi with Lentils

Prep time: 15 minutes | Cook time: 5½ to 6 hours | Serves 6

1¼ cups vegetable or chicken stock
1 cup orange juice
¾ cup orange lentils
½ cup finely diced carrot
¼ cup finely diced red onion
¼ cup finely diced celery
1 tablespoon honey
6 (4- to 5-ounce / 113- to 142-g) mahi-mahi fillets
Sea salt and black pepper, to taste
1 teaspoon lemon juice
Salsa:
¾ cup finely diced pineapple
¾ cup finely diced mango
½ cup finely diced strawberries
¼ cup finely diced red onion
2 tablespoons chopped fresh mint (or 2 teaspoons dried)
2 tablespoons orange juice
1 tablespoon lime juice
¼ teaspoon salt

1. Combine the stock, orange juice, lentils, carrot, onion, celery, and honey in the crock pot.
2. Cover and cook on low for 5 to 5½ hours, or until the lentils are tender.
3. Place 1 sheet of parchment paper over the lentils in the crock pot. Season mahimahi lightly with salt and black pepper and place it on the parchment (skin-side down, if you have not removed the skin).
4. Replace the lid and continue to cook on low for 25 minutes or until the mahimahi is opaque in the center. Remove the fish by lifting out the parchment paper and putting it on a plate.
5. Stir the lemon juice into the lentils and season with salt and pepper.
To make the salsa
1. While the fish is cooking, combine the pineapple, mango, strawberries, red onion, mint, orange juice, lime juice, and salt into a big jar. Combine and chill to give the flavors a chance to blend.
2. To serve, place about ½ cup of hot lentils on a plate and top with a mahimahi fillet and 1⅓ cup of salsa.

Lime Buttered Salmon

Prep time: 5 minutes | Cook time: 2 hours | Serves 2

2 (6-ounce / 170-g) salmon fillets
1 tablespoon olive oil
½ tablespoon lime juice
2 cloves garlic, minced
1 teaspoon finely chopped fresh parsley
¼ teaspoon black pepper

1. Spread a length of foil onto the countertop and put the salmon fillets directly in the middle.
2. In a small bowl, combine the olive oil, lime juice, garlic, parsley, and black pepper. Brush the mixture over the fillets. Fold the foil over and crimp the sides to make a packet.
3. Place the packet into the crock pot. Cover and cook on high for 2 hours.
4. Salmon is finished when it flakes easily with a fork. Serve hot.

Crayfish Creole

Prep time: 15 minutes | Cook time: 3 to 4 hours | Serves 2

1½ cups diced celery
1 large yellow onion, chopped
2 small bell peppers, any colors, chopped
1 (8-ounce / 227-g) can tomato sauce
1 (28-ounce / 794-g) can whole tomatoes, broken up, with the juice
1 clove garlic, minced
1 teaspoon sea salt
¼ teaspoon black pepper
6 drops hot pepper sauce (such as tabasco)
1 pound (454 g) precooked crayfish meat

1. Place the celery, onion, and bell peppers in the crock pot. Add the tomato sauce, tomatoes, and garlic. Sprinkle with the salt and pepper and add the hot sauce.
2. Cover and cook on high for 3 to 4 hours or on low for 6 to 8 hours.
3. About 30 minutes before the cooking time is completed, add the crayfish.
4. Serve hot.

Poached Turbot

Prep time: 5 minutes | Cook time: 40 to 50 minutes | Serves 4

1 cup vegetable or chicken stock
½ cup dry white wine
1 yellow onion, sliced
1 lemon, sliced
4 sprigs fresh dill
½ teaspoon sea salt
4 (6-ounce / 170-g) turbot fillets

1. Combine the stock and wine in the crock pot. Cover and cook on high for 20 to 30 minutes.
2. Add the onion, lemon, dill, salt, and turbot to the crock pot. Cover and cook on high for about 20 minutes, until the turbot is opaque and cooked through according to taste. Serve hot.

Lemon-Dijon Salmon

Prep time: 15 minutes | Cook time: 2 hours | Serves 6

1 medium yellow onion, diced
2 teaspoons garlic, minced
2 teaspoons olive oil
2 cups vegetable or chicken stock
1 cup quick-cooking barley
1 tablespoon minced fresh dill weed
1½ pounds (680 g) salmon fillets
Sea salt and black pepper, to taste
Lemon-Dijon Sauce:
1⅓ cup Dijon mustard
3 tablespoons olive oil
3 tablespoons fresh lemon juice
1⅓ cup plain Greek yogurt
1 clove garlic, minced

1. Combine the onion, garlic, and oil in a microwave-safe bowl. Heat in the microwave on medium-high for 4 to 5 minutes, stirring occasionally. Put into the crock pot.
2. Add the stock, barley, and dill weed to the crock pot and stir.
3. Season the salmon fillets with salt and pepper, and gently place them on top of the barley mixture.
4. Cover and cook on low for about 2 hours, until the salmon and barley are cooked through.
To make the lemon-Dijon sauce

1. In a small bowl, whisk together the Dijon mustard, olive oil, lemon juice, Greek yogurt, and garlic. Set aside and allow the flavors to blend.
2. To serve, place some barley on a plate and top with a salmon fillet. Spoon the lemon-Dijon sauce over of the salmon.

Coconut Halibut with Eggplant Relish

Prep time: 15 minutes | Cook time: 2½ hours | Serves 4

4 medium Japanese eggplants (or 2 large eggplants), cut into ½-inch cubes
¼ cup coarse salt
¼ cup extra-virgin olive oil, divided
2 onions, diced
3 garlic cloves, minced
1 (1-inch) piece fresh ginger, peeled and finely grated
2 kaffir lime leaves
1 teaspoon brown sugar
1 tablespoon rice vinegar
¼ cup fresh lime juice
1 cup packed fresh cilantro, finely chopped
1 pound (454 g) halibut, cut into 1-inch pieces
½ cup unsweetened flaked coconut, toasted, for garnish

1. Combine eggplant and salt in a colander set over a bowl, then let stand about 1 hour. Rinse well and pat dry.
2. Heat 2 tablespoons oil in a large skillet over medium. Add onions and sauté until deeply golden, about 15 minutes. Add garlic and ginger, and cook for 2 more minutes. Add eggplants and cook just until hot. Transfer vegetables to the crock pot.
3. Add remaining 2 tablespoons oil, the lime leaves, brown sugar, vinegar, and lime juice to the crock pot. Cover and cook on low until soft but not mushy, about 4 hours or on high for 2 hours.
4. Stir in cilantro. Nestle fish on top of eggplant mixture and cook on low until cooked through, about 20 minutes or on high for 10 minutes. Serve relish topped with halibut and sprinkled with toasted coconut.

Honeyed Worcestershire Salmon

Prep time: 10 minutes | Cook time: 1 hours | Serves 6

6 (6-ounce / 170-g) salmon fillets
½ cup honey
2 tablespoons lime juice
3 tablespoons Worcestershire sauce
1 tablespoon water
2 cloves garlic, minced
1 teaspoon ground ginger
½ teaspoon black pepper

1. Place the salmon fillets in the crock pot.
2. In a medium bowl, whisk the honey, lime juice, Worcestershire sauce, water, garlic, ginger, and pepper. Pour the sauce mixture over the salmon.
3. Cover and cook on high for 1 hour.
4. Serve warm.

Branzino and Potato Bake

Prep time: 15 minutes | Cook time: 4 hours | Serves 4

1 lemon, thinly sliced
½ bunch fresh thyme
½ fennel bulb, cored and thinly sliced
1 small garlic clove, thinly sliced
2 whole branzino (about 2 pounds / 907 g in total), scaled, gutted, and cleaned (head left on, if desired)
1 (3-pound / 1.4-kg) box kosher salt
2 pounds (907 g) small (1 to 1¼ inches) white potatoes, such as Honey Gold, scrubbed
1 tablespoon extra-virgin olive oil, plus more for drizzling

1. Divide lemon, thyme, fennel, and garlic between fish, stuffing each cavity.
2. Cover bottom of the crock pot with a ½-inch layer of salt. Toss potatoes with oil and arrange over salt layer. Bury potatoes in salt, adding more salt, as necessary, to cover. Cover crock pot and cook on high for 1 hour.
3. Wrap fish well in a parchment, tucking ends under, and place on top of potato-salt layer. Sprinkle about 1 cup more salt on top. Cover and cook on high until fish is cooked through, about 3 hours.
4. Carefully lift parchment package out of crock pot, brushing off salt layer. Open parchment packet and transfer fish to a serving platter.
5. Arrange potatoes around fish, drizzle fish and potatoes with oil, and top with lemon slices. Serve warm.

White Fish Curry

Prep time: 15 minutes | Cook time: 2½ hours | Serves 4 to 6

½ cup flaked unsweetened coconut
2 serrano chiles, sliced
1 teaspoon coriander seeds
½ onion, coarsely chopped
1 (1-inch) piece fresh turmeric, peeled and coarsely chopped
1 (1-inch) piece fresh ginger, peeled and coarsely chopped
2 garlic cloves, thinly sliced
2 tablespoons tamarind paste
1 teaspoon ground cumin
¼ teaspoon fenugreek seeds
1 tablespoon mild curry powder
Coarse salt, to taste
2 (13½-ounce / 383-g) cans unsweetened coconut milk
2 pounds (907 g) firm white fish fillets, such as cod or halibut, cut into 2- to 3-inch pieces
Fresh cilantro, for garnish

1. Combine coconut, chiles, coriander seeds, onion, turmeric, ginger, garlic, tamarind, cumin, fenugreek, curry powder, and 1 teaspoon salt in a food processor, then purée to form a paste.
2. Transfer paste to a saucepan, add coconut milk, and bring to a boil. Transfer coconut mixture to the crock pot. Cover and cook on high until slightly thickened, 2 hours or on low for 4 hours.
3. Season fish with salt and transfer to the crock pot, then submerge fish in coconut mixture. Reduce crock pot to low and cook until fish is flaky but does not fall apart, about 20 minutes.
4. Serve fish curry sprinkled with cilantro.

Chapter 11 Fish and Seafood | 131

Shrimp, Quinoa, and Corn Salad

Prep time: 15 minutes | Cook time: 2 to 3 hours | Serves 4

1 cup white quinoa, rinsed
2 scallions, white parts minced, green parts cut into ½-inch pieces
2 jalapeño chiles, stemmed, deseeded, and minced
5 teaspoons extra-virgin olive oil, divided
1 teaspoon chili powder
1⅓ cups water
Salt and ground black pepper, to taste
1 pound (454 g) medium-large shrimp (31 to 40 per pound), peeled, deveined, and tails removed
¾ cup frozen corn, thawed
3 tomatoes, cored and chopped
1⅓ cup minced fresh cilantro
1 tablespoon lime juice
2 ounces (57 g) Cotija cheese, crumbled (½ cup)
Cooking spray

1. Spritz the crock pot with cooking spray. Microwave quinoa, scallion whites, jalapeños, 2 teaspoons oil, and chili powder in a bowl, stirring occasionally, until vegetables are softened, about 2 minutes. Transfer to the prepared crock pot. Stir in water and ½ teaspoon salt. Cover and cook until water is absorbed and quinoa is tender, 3 to 4 hours on low or 2 to 3 hours on high.
2. Season shrimp with pepper. Fluff quinoa with fork, then nestle shrimp into quinoa and sprinkle with corn. Cover and cook on high until shrimp are opaque throughout, 30 to 40 minutes.
3. Combine tomatoes, cilantro, lime juice, scallion greens, remaining 1 tablespoon oil, ¼ teaspoon salt, and ¼ teaspoon pepper in a separate bowl. Sprinkle quinoa and shrimp with Cotija and serve, passing salsa separately.

Barbecue Shrimp and Scallops

Prep time: 15 minutes | Cook time: 1 hours | Serves 2

½ teaspoon paprika
½ teaspoon garlic powder
¼ teaspoon onion powder
¼ teaspoon cayenne pepper
¼ teaspoon dried oregano
¼ teaspoon dried thyme
½ teaspoon sea salt
½ teaspoon black pepper
2 cloves garlic, minced
½ cup olive oil
¼ cup Worcestershire sauce
1 tablespoon hot pepper sauce (such as tabasco)
Juice of 1 lemon
1 pound (454 g) scallops
1 pound (454 g) large shrimp, unpeeled
1 green onion, finely chopped

1. Combine the paprika, garlic powder, onion powder, cayenne pepper, oregano, thyme, ½ teaspoon salt, and ¼ teaspoon black pepper.
2. Combine the paprika blend, garlic, olive oil, Worcestershire sauce, hot pepper sauce, and lemon juice in the crock pot. Season with salt and pepper.
3. Cover and cook on high for 30 minutes or until hot.
4. Rinse the scallops and shrimp, and drain.
5. Spoon one-half of the sauce from the crock pot into a glass measuring cup.
6. Place the scallops and shrimp in the crock pot with the remaining sauce. Drizzle with the sauce in the measuring cup and stir to coat.
7. Cover and cook on high for 30 minutes, until the scallops and shrimp are opaque.
8. Turn the heat to warm for serving. Sprinkle with the chopped green onion to serve.

Mushroom and Tomato Mussels

Prep time: 15 minutes | Cook time: 2½ to 3½ hours | Serves 4

3 tablespoons olive oil
4 cloves garlic, minced
3 shallot cloves, minced
8 ounces (227 g) mushrooms, diced
1 (28-ounce / 794-g) can diced tomatoes, with the juice
¾ cup white wine
2 tablespoons dried oregano
½ tablespoon dried basil
½ teaspoon black pepper
1 teaspoon paprika
¼ teaspoon red pepper flakes
3 pounds (1.4 kg) mussels

1. In a large sauté pan, heat the olive oil over medium-high heat. Cook the garlic, shallots, and mushrooms for 2 to 3 minutes, until the garlic is brown and fragrant. Scrape the entire contents of the pan into the crock pot.
2. Add the tomatoes and white wine to the crock pot. Sprinkle with the oregano, basil, black pepper, paprika, and red pepper flakes.
3. Cover and cook on low for 4 to 5 hours, or on high for 2 to 3 hours. The mixture is done cooking when mushrooms are fork tender.
4. Clean and debeard the mussels. Discard any open mussels.
5. Increase the heat on the crock pot to high once the mushroom mixture is done. Add the cleaned mussels to the crock pot and secure the lid tightly. Cook for 30 more minutes.
6. To serve, ladle the mussels into bowls with plenty of broth. Discard any mussels that didn't open up during cooking. Serve hot, with crusty bread for sopping up the sauce.

Spanish Herbed Octopus

Prep time: 15 minutes | Cook time: 1¼ hours | Serves 6

2 pounds (907 g) octopus, cleaned
1 small fennel, trimmed, bulb and fronds coarsely chopped
2 small onions, thickly sliced
1 bunch fresh flat-leaf parsley
1 bunch fresh oregano
2 dried bay leaves
¼ cup plus 2 tablespoons extra-virgin olive oil
Coarse salt, to taste
2 garlic cloves, minced
¼ cup capers, drained, rinsed, and coarsely chopped
Juice of 2 lemons (about 1⅓ cup)
¼ teaspoon hot smoked paprika
¼ teaspoon sweet smoked paprika

1. Bring a large stockpot of water to a boil. Add octopus and boil briefly to tenderize, about 2 minutes. Drain and let cool, then slice octopus into 2-inch pieces.
2. Place fennel, onions, parsley, oregano, and bay leaves in the crock pot. Arrange octopus over vegetables. Drizzle with 1 tablespoon oil and ½ teaspoon salt. Cover and cook on low until octopus is tender, 2 hours, or on high for 1 hour.
3. Heat a grill or grill pan to high. Remove octopus and half the vegetables from the crock pot (discard remaining vegetables and liquid). Toss with 1 tablespoon oil and grill until charred, about 6 minutes. Transfer to a bowl.
4. Meanwhile, gently heat remaining ¼ cup oil in a small skillet. Add garlic and cook until just fragrant, about 2 minutes. Stir in capers and lemon juice.
5. Remove from heat and stir in both paprikas. Pour over octopus, toss, season with salt, and serve.

Chapter 11 Fish and Seafood | 133

Marinara Shrimp

Prep time: 15 minutes | Cook time: 6¼ to 7¼ hours | Serves 4

1 (15-ounce / 425-g) can diced tomatoes, with the juice one
1 (6-ounce / 170-g) can tomato paste
1 clove garlic, minced
2 tablespoons minced fresh flat-leaf parsley
½ teaspoon dried basil
1 teaspoon dried oregano
1 teaspoon garlic powder
1½ teaspoons sea salt
¼ teaspoon black pepper
1 pound (454 g) cooked shrimp, peeled and deveined
2 cups hot cooked spaghetti or linguine, for serving
½ cup grated Parmesan cheese, for serving

1. Combine the tomatoes, tomato paste, and minced garlic in the crock pot. Sprinkle with the parsley, basil, oregano, garlic powder, salt, and pepper.
2. Cover and cook on low for 6 to 7 hours.
3. Turn up the heat to high, stir in the cooked shrimp, and cover and cook on high for about 15 minutes longer.
4. Serve hot over the cooked pasta. Top with Parmesan cheese.

Shrimp Polenta

Prep time: 15 minutes | Cook time: 2 to 3 hours | Serves 4

3 scallions, white parts minced, green parts sliced thin on bias
1 tablespoon unsalted butter
2 garlic cloves, minced
1 teaspoon minced canned chipotle chile in adobo sauce
½ teaspoon dry mustard
4 cups water
1 cup coarse-ground cornmeal
½ cup whole milk
Salt and ground black pepper, to taste
1 cup Cheddar cheese, shredded
1 pound (454 g) extra-large shrimp (21 to 25 per pound), peeled, deveined, and tails removed
Cooking spray

1. Spritz the crock pot with cooking spray. Microwave scallion whites, butter, garlic, chipotle, and mustard in a bowl, stirring occasionally, until scallions are softened, about 2 minutes. Transfer to the prepared crock pot.
2. Whisk in water, cornmeal, milk, and ¼ teaspoon salt. Cover and cook until polenta is tender, 3 to 4 hours on low or 2 to 3 hours on high.
3. Stir Cheddar into polenta until melted, and season with salt and pepper to taste. Season shrimp with pepper and nestle into polenta.
4. Cover and cook on high until shrimp are opaque throughout, 30 to 40 minutes. Sprinkle with scallion greens and serve.

Chapter 12 Rice, Grains, and Beans

Kedgeree (Spiced Rice with Smoked Fish)

Prep time: 20 minutes | Cook time: 3 hours | Serves 6

2 cups basmati rice
1 tablespoon ghee
2 teaspoons mustard seeds
2 teaspoons ground cumin seeds
2-inch (5-cm) piece fresh ginger, grated
2 garlic cloves, finely chopped
2 fresh bay leaves
2 fresh red chiles, finely chopped
1 bunch scallions, finely chopped
1 teaspoon turmeric
2 tomatoes, finely chopped
Sea salt, to taste
3¾ cups hot water
10 ounces (283 g) smoked fish fillets
3 large eggs
2 handfuls fresh coriander leaves, chopped
Juice of 1 lemon

1. Wash the rice and soak for 10 minutes.
2. Heat the ghee in a frying pan (or in the crock pot if you have a sear setting). Add the mustard seeds and cook until they pop. Then add the cumin seeds. Once fragrant (a few seconds), add the ginger, garlic, bay leaves, chiles, scallions, turmeric, tomatoes and season with salt. Cook for 5 minutes.
3. Add the rice and hot water. Place the fish on top, skin-side down, and cook on high for 3 hours.
4. Meanwhile, on the stovetop, hard boil the eggs, and set aside.
5. After cooking for 3 hours, gently lift the fish out and remove the skin and bones.
6. When you are ready to eat, flake the fish into the rice, add the coriander leaves and lemon juice, and fold through.
7. Peel the shells from the eggs, slice into quarters, and arrange on top of the rice, and serve.

White Beans with Pancetta and Carrot

Prep time: 15 minutes | Cook time: 3½ to 4½ hours | Serves 4

1 heaping cup dried cannellini beans
A few slices of pancetta or prosciutto, chopped
¼ cup olive oil
3 shallots, halved
1 medium-size carrot, quartered
2 ribs celery, halved
1 bay leaf
Sprig of fresh thyme or savory
1 (15-ounce / 425-g) can chicken broth
Fine sea salt and freshly ground black pepper, to taste
4 ounces (113 g) fresh goat cheese, such as Chabis or Montrachet, crumbled
½ cup sliced pitted black olives, or your choice, drained

1. Put the beans in a colander and rinse under cold running water, picking over for damaged beans and small stones. Transfer to the crock pot and cover by 3 inches with cold water. Soak for 6 to 12 hours, drain, and add back to the crock pot.
2. In a medium-size skillet over medium-high heat, cook the pancetta in the olive oil, stirring, for 8 minutes. Add the shallots, carrot, and celery and cook, stirring, until just softened. Transfer the mixture to the beans in the crock pot along with the bay leaf and herb sprig. Add the broth and enough water to cover the beans by 2 inches.
3. Cover and cook on high for 3½ to 4½ hours. The beans need to be covered with liquid at all times to cook properly. Toward the end of cooking, season with salt and pepper. When done, the beans will be tender and hold their shape, rather than fall apart. Remove the bay leaf and herb sprig and discard.
4. Serve the beans in soup bowls, topped with the crumbled goat cheese and sliced olives.

Creamy Saffron Rice

Prep time: 10 minutes | Cook time: 1½ to 2 hours | Serves 6

1¹⁄₃ cups basmati rice
Pinch saffron
1 tablespoon vegetable oil
1 teaspoon cumin seeds
3¹⁄₃ cups hot water
1 teaspoon salt
1 tablespoon butter
4 tablespoons cream

1. Wash the rice in two or three changes of water until the water runs clear. Then leave it to soak in warm water while you prep the rest of the dish.
2. Grind a few threads of saffron in a mortar and pestle. Add 2 tablespoons of hot water and stir. Set aside.
3. Preheat the crock pot to high and add the oil. Add the cumin seeds and let them toast.
4. Pour the hot water, salt, butter, and cream into the crock pot. Strain the soaked rice and add to the crock pot.
5. Stir and cover with the lid. Cook on high for 1½ to 2 hours. Halfway through the cooking, very gently stir the rice.
6. Turn off the crock pot and sprinkle in the saffron water. Let it stand, uncovered, for 5 to 10 minutes. Fluff the rice with a fork and serve.

Wild Rice, Bacon, and Cherries

Prep time: 10 minutes | Cook time: 6 hours | Serves 2

1 teaspoon extra-virgin olive oil
¾ cup wild rice
½ cup minced onion
1 piece applewood-smoked bacon, cooked and crumbled
1 teaspoon minced fresh rosemary
¼ cup dried cherries
2 cups chicken broth
⅛ teaspoon sea salt

1. Grease the crock pot with the olive oil.
2. Put all the ingredients into the crock pot and stir them to mix thoroughly.
3. Cover and cook on low for 6 hours until the rice has absorbed all the water and is tender.
4. Serve warm.

Almond-Mushroom Wild Rice

Prep time: 10 minutes | Cook time: 4½ to 6 hours | Serves 6

2 cups wild rice
1 cup slivered almonds
1 to 2 shallots, finely chopped
½ cup finely chopped celery
8 ounces (227 g) fresh mushrooms, chopped or sliced
6 cups vegetable broth
Salt and freshly ground black pepper, to taste

1. Rinse the rice under cold running water until the water runs clear, then drain.
2. Place all the ingredients except the salt and pepper in the crock pot. Stir to combine. Cover and cook on low until the kernels are open and tender, but not mushy, 4½ to 6 hours. Do not remove the lid before the rice has cooked at least 4 hours.
3. Season with salt and pepper, and serve immediately.

Cranberry Sweet Potato and Wild Rice

Prep time: 10 minutes | Cook time: 6 to 8 hours | Serves 2

1 teaspoon extra-virgin olive oil
¾ cup wild rice
1 medium sweet potato, peeled and cut into 1-inch pieces
¼ cup minced celery
¼ cup minced onion
¼ cup dried cranberries
1 teaspoon minced fresh sage
1 teaspoon minced fresh thyme
2 cups low-sodium chicken broth
⅛ teaspoon sea salt

1. Grease the inside of the crock pot with the olive oil.
2. Put the remaining ingredients in the crock pot and stir them to mix thoroughly.
3. Cover and cook on low for 6 to 8 hours until the rice has absorbed all the liquid and is tender. Serve hot.

Butternut Squash Risotto with White Wine

Prep time: 10 minutes | Cook time: 2½ hours | Serves 4 to 6

½ cup (1 stick) unsalted butter, divided
2 tablespoons olive oil
½ cup finely chopped shallots (about 4 medium)
2 cups diced, peeled, and deseeded butternut squash
1½ cups Arborio or Carnaroli rice
¼ cup dry white wine or vermouth
4¼ cups chicken broth
½ cup freshly grated Parmesan cheese, divided
Cooking spray

1. Spritz the crock pot with nonstick cooking spray.
2. Heat ¼ cup of the butter with the oil in a large saucepan over medium-high heat. Add the shallots and squash and sauté until the shallots are softened, about 3 minutes.
3. Add the rice and cook, tossing to coat with the butter, until the rice is opaque. Add the wine and cook until the wine evaporates.
4. Transfer the mixture to the crock pot and stir in the broth. Cover and cook on high for 2½ hours. Check the risotto at 2 hours to make sure the broth hasn't evaporated. Stir in the remaining ¼ cup butter and ¼ cup of the cheese.
5. Serve the risotto immediately with the remaining cheese on the side.

Wild Rice and Fruit Pilaf

Prep time: 15 minutes | Cook time: 2¾ to 3¾ hours | Serves 8 to 10

2 cups wild rice, rinsed with cold water and drained twice
½ cup (1 stick) unsalted butter
1 medium onion, finely chopped
3 stalks celery, finely chopped
1 teaspoon dried marjoram
4 to 5 cups chicken broth
½ cup finely chopped dried apricots
½ cup dried cranberries
½ teaspoon freshly ground black pepper
½ cup sliced almonds, toasted
Cooking spray

1. Spritz the crock pot with nonstick cooking spray.
2. Pour the rice into the crock pot. Melt the butter in a large skillet over medium-high heat. Add the onion, celery, and marjoram and sauté until the vegetables are softened, about 4 minutes.
3. Transfer the vegetables to the crock pot. Stir in the broth, apricots, cranberries, and pepper. Cover and cook on high for 2½ to 3 hours or on low for 7 hours, until the rice is tender. Check at intervals to make sure there is still liquid in the crock pot and add more broth if needed. Uncover the crock pot and cook for another 30 to 45 minutes on low. Stir in the almonds.
4. Serve warm.

Mexican Pinto Beans

Prep time: 20 minutes | Cook time: 8 to 9 hours | Serves 6

1 onion, finely chopped
2 tablespoons extra-virgin olive oil, divided
4 garlic cloves, minced
1 tablespoon minced fresh oregano or 1 teaspoon dried
1 tablespoon chili powder
2 teaspoons minced canned chipotle chile in adobo sauce
Salt and pepper, to taste
5 cups water, plus extra as needed
1 pound (454 g) dried pinto beans, picked over and rinsed
1 cup mild lager, such as Budweiser
2 tablespoons minced fresh cilantro
1 tablespoon packed brown sugar
1 tablespoon lime juice, plus extra for seasoning

1. Microwave onion, 1 tablespoon oil, garlic, oregano, chili powder, chipotle, and 1 teaspoon salt in a bowl, stirring occasionally, until onion is softened, about 5 minutes. Transfer to a crock pot. Stir in water, beans, and beer. Cover and cook until beans are tender, 8 to 9 hours on high.
2. Drain beans, reserving 1 cup cooking liquid. Return beans and reserved cooking liquid to the crock pot. Stir in cilantro, sugar, lime juice, and remaining 1 tablespoon oil. Season with salt, pepper, and extra lime juice to taste. Serve. (Beans can be held on warm or low setting for up to 2 hours; adjust consistency with extra hot water as needed before serving.)

Aromatic Vegetable Pulao

Prep time: 10 minutes | Cook time: 2 hours | Serves 6

1½ cups basmati rice
1 tablespoon rapeseed oil
2 bay leaves
2-inch (5-cm) piece cassia bark
1 tablespoon black peppercorns
1 tablespoon cumin seeds
1 tablespoon coriander seeds
4 green cardamom pods
2 black cardamom pods
3 cloves
2 medium onions, chopped
1 teaspoon salt
1 tablespoon freshly grated ginger
1 garlic clove, chopped
2 fresh green chiles, chopped
1 teaspoon turmeric
Handful mint leaves, chopped
Handful fresh coriander leaves, chopped
2½ cups hot water
12 ounces (340 g) frozen mixed vegetables, thawed

1. Wash the rice in a few changes of water until the water runs clear. Soak the rice in warm water for 10 minutes.
2. Heat the oil in a frying pan (or in the crock pot if you have a sear setting). Add the bay leaves, cassia bark, peppercorns, cumin, and coriander seeds, green and black cardamom pods, and cloves. Sauté for 2 minutes until the spices become aromatic.
3. Add the chopped onions and cook for about 5 minutes until soft. Stir in the salt with the ginger, garlic, green chiles, turmeric, mint, and coriander leaves. Transfer to the crock pot. Then add the rice and hot water. Stir through gently.
4. Cover the crock pot and cook on high for 1½ hours or 3 hours on low. Stir the rice once during the cooking time.
5. Switch the crock pot to the warming function, add the mixed vegetables, and stir through gently. Cover and leave to steam for 20 minutes.
6. Remove the lid and leave the rice to stand for about 5 minutes before fluffing it with a fork to serve.

Lemon Thyme Pearl Barley Risotto

Prep time: 10 minutes | Cook time: 6 to 8 hours | Serves 2

1 teaspoon extra-virgin olive oil
½ cup minced onion
2 tablespoons minced preserved lemon
1 teaspoon fresh thyme leaves
¼ cup roughly chopped fresh parsley, divided
¾ cup pearl barley
2 cups low-sodium vegetable broth
⅛ teaspoon sea salt
Freshly ground black pepper, to taste
½ lemon, cut into wedges, for garnish

1. Grease the inside of the crock pot with olive oil. Add the onion, preserved lemon, thyme, 2 tablespoons of the parsley, barley, and vegetable broth. Season with the salt and pepper, and stir thoroughly.
2. Cover and cook on low for 6 to 8 hours, until the barley is tender and all the liquid is absorbed. Garnish each serving with the remaining parsley and a lemon wedge.

Brown Rice Risotto with Starch Vegetables

Prep time: 20 minutes | Cook time: 4 to 5 hours | Serves 8

1 large sweet potato, peeled and chopped
1 onion, chopped
5 garlic cloves, minced
2 cups short-grain brown rice
1 teaspoon dried thyme leaves
7 cups vegetable broth
2 cups green beans, cut in half crosswise
2 cups frozen baby peas
3 tablespoons unsalted butter
½ cup grated Parmesan cheese

1. In the crock pot, mix the sweet potato, onion, garlic, rice, thyme, and broth. Cover and cook on low for 3 to 4 hours, or until the rice is tender.
2. Stir in the green beans and frozen peas. Cover and cook on low for 30 to 40 minutes or until the vegetables are tender.
3. Stir in the butter and cheese. Cover and cook on low for 20 minutes, then stir and serve.

Pine Nut Pilaf

Prep time: 10 minutes | Cook time: 2½ hours | Serves 8 to 10

2 tablespoons unsalted butter
1 cup pine nuts
3 cups converted white rice
4½ cups chicken or vegetable broth
1 teaspoon freshly ground black pepper
½ cup finely chopped fresh basil, plus additional whole leaves for garnishing
Nonstick cooking spray

1. Spritz the crock pot with nonstick cooking spray.
2. Melt the butter in a small sauté pan over medium-high heat. Add the pine nuts and sauté until they begin to color, about 4 minutes. Set aside.
3. Combine the rice, 4½ cups broth, and the pepper in the crock pot. Cover and cook on high for 1 hour.
4. Stir in the pine nuts and chopped basil. Cover and cook for 1½ hours, until the rice is tender and liquid is absorbed.
5. Serve warm, garnished with the whole basil leaves.

Barley and Mushroom Risotto

Prep time: 15 minutes | Cook time: 7 to 8 hours | Serves 8

2¼ cups hulled barley, rinsed
1 onion, finely chopped
4 garlic cloves, minced
1 (8-ounce / 227-g) package button mushrooms, chopped
6 cups vegetable broth
½ teaspoon dried marjoram leaves
⅛ teaspoon freshly ground black pepper
⅔ cup grated Parmesan cheese

1. In the crock pot, mix the barley, onion, garlic, mushrooms, broth, marjoram, and pepper.
2. Cover and cook on low for 7 to 8 hours, or until the barley has absorbed most of the liquid and is tender, and the vegetables are tender.
3. Stir in the Parmesan cheese and serve.

Barley Risotto Primavera

Prep time: 20 minutes | Cook time: 8 hours | Serves 2

1 teaspoon extra-virgin olive oil
½ cup minced onion
½ cup diced carrot
1 cup diced zucchini
1 cup diced red bell pepper
1 teaspoon minced garlic
1 (15-ounce / 425-g) can whole plum tomatoes, undrained, hand-crushed
2 tablespoons tomato paste
1 tablespoon Italian herbs
¾ cup pearl barley
1½ cups low-sodium chicken or vegetable broth
⅛ teaspoon sea salt
½ cup roughly chopped fresh basil, for garnish

1. Grease the inside of the crock pot with the olive oil.
2. Put the onion, carrot, zucchini, bell pepper, garlic, tomatoes, tomato paste, Italian herbs, barley, broth, and salt in the crock pot, and mix thoroughly.
3. Cover and cook on low for 8 hours, until the barley is tender and all the liquid is absorbed.
4. Garnish each serving with the fresh basil.

Tex-Mex Quinoa Salad

Prep time: 10 minutes | Cook time: 8 hours | Serves 2

1 cup quinoa, rinsed
2 cups low-sodium vegetable broth
½ cup minced onion
1 teaspoon minced garlic
½ cup corn kernels
½ cup black beans, drained and rinsed
½ cup canned fire-roasted diced tomatoes, undrained
½ jalapeño pepper, deseeded and minced
1 teaspoon ground cumin
½ teaspoon smoked paprika
⅛ teaspoon sea salt

1. Put all the ingredients into the crock pot and stir everything to mix thoroughly.
2. Cover and cook on low for 8 hours. Serve warm.

Chapter 12 Rice, Grains, and Beans | 139

Ratatouille Quinoa Casserole

Prep time: 20 minutes | Cook time: 8 hours | Serves 2

1 teaspoon extra-virgin olive oil
1 cup diced eggplant
1 cup diced zucchini
½ teaspoon sea salt
1 (15-ounce / 425-g) can whole plum tomatoes, undrained, hand-crushed
1 teaspoon minced garlic
½ cup minced onion
1 cup quinoa
1 teaspoon herbes de Provence
1½ cups low-sodium chicken or vegetable broth

1. Grease the inside of the crock pot with the olive oil.
2. Put the eggplant and zucchini in a colander in the sink. Season them liberally with the salt and allow it to rest for 10 minutes, or up to 30 minutes if you have the time.
3. Put the tomatoes, garlic, onion, quinoa, herbes de Provence, and broth in the crock pot.
4. Rinse the eggplant and zucchini under cool water and gently press any excess moisture from the salted vegetables before adding to them to the crock pot. Mix everything thoroughly.
5. Cover and cook on low for 8 hours. Serve warm.

Boston Baked Beans

Prep time: 10 minutes | Cook time: 11½ to 13½ hours | Serves 6 to 8

1 pound (454 g) dried small white navy or pea beans
½ teaspoon baking soda
1 (8-ounce / 227-g) piece salt pork
½ cup dark molasses
½ cup firmly packed light or dark brown sugar
1½ teaspoons dry mustard
1½ teaspoons salt
¼ teaspoon freshly ground black pepper
1 medium-size white onion, peeled, left whole, and scored with a crisscross through the root end
6 cups boiling water

1. Rinse the beans in a colander under cold running water and pick over for damaged beans and small stones. Transfer to the crock pot. Cover with cold water by 2 inches, soak overnight, and then drain.
2. Cover the beans with fresh water by 3 inches. Add the baking soda, cover, and cook on high until still undercooked, about 1½ hours. Drain.
3. Meanwhile, simmer the salt pork in boiling water for 10 minutes to remove excess salt. Drain and rinse under cold running water. Pat dry and dice.
4. Combine the drained beans, salt pork, molasses, brown sugar, mustard, salt, and pepper in the crock pot, stirring to mix well. Push the onion into the center of the beans and add the boiling water (it will cover everything by ½ inch). Cover and cook on high to bring to a boil, then reduce the heat to low and cook until the beans are soft, thick, and bubbling, 10 to 12 hours. Do not stir, but you can add more boiling water to keep the beans moist if you need to. Traditionally, the beans are cooked with the cover off for the last 30 minutes to thicken them to the desired consistency. Serve.

Buckwheat with Lush Mushrooms

Prep time: 20 minutes | Cook time: 5 to 6 hours | Serves 2

1 cup buckwheat groats
1 egg, beaten
1 onion, chopped
½ cup sliced button mushrooms
½ cup sliced shiitake mushrooms
½ cup sliced cremini mushrooms
2½ cups vegetable broth or chicken stock
1 bay leaf
½ teaspoon dried basil leaves
½ teaspoon salt
⅛ teaspoon freshly ground black pepper

1. In a medium bowl, mix the buckwheat groats with the egg, combining well.
2. In a medium saucepan over low heat, sauté the buckwheat mixture until the groats smell toasted, about 5 minutes.
3. In the crock pot, combine all the ingredients.
4. Cover and cook on low for 5 to 6 hours, or until the buckwheat is tender.
5. Remove and discard the bay leaf and serve.

Barley Pilaf with Dates

Prep time: 15 minutes | Cook time: 2 to 3 hours | Serves 6

1 onion, chopped fine
1½ cups pearl barley, rinsed
2 tablespoons extra-virgin olive oil, divided
2 teaspoons grated fresh ginger
Salt and ground black pepper, to taste
⅛ teaspoon ground cinnamon
⅛ teaspoon ground cardamom
3½ cups vegetable or chicken broth
½ cup pitted dates, chopped
1⅓ cup chopped fresh parsley
2 teaspoons lemon juice
Cooking spray

1. Spritz the crock pot with cooking spray. Microwave onion, barley, 1 tablespoon oil, ginger, ½ teaspoon salt, cinnamon, and cardamom in a bowl, stirring occasionally, until onion is softened and barley is lightly toasted, about 5 minutes. Transfer to the prepared crock pot.
2. Stir in broth, cover, and cook until barley is tender and all broth is absorbed, 3 to 4 hours on low or 2 to 3 hours on high.
3. Fluff barley with fork, then gently fold in dates, parsley, lemon juice, and remaining 1 tablespoon oil. Season with salt and pepper to taste. Serve.

Quinoa with Corn

Prep time: 15 minutes | Cook time: 2 to 3 hours | Serves 6

1½ cups white quinoa, rinsed
1 onion, chopped fine
2 jalapeño chiles, stemmed, deseeded, and minced
2 tablespoons extra-virgin olive oil
Salt and ground black pepper, to taste
1¾ cups water
1 cup frozen corn, thawed
1⅓ cup minced fresh cilantro
2 tablespoons lime juice
Cooking spray

1. Spritz the crock pot with cooking spray. Microwave quinoa, onion, jalapeños, 1 tablespoon oil, and 1 teaspoon salt in a bowl, stirring occasionally, until quinoa is lightly toasted and vegetables are softened, about 5 minutes. Transfer to the prepared crock pot. Stir in water, cover, and cook until quinoa is tender, and all water is absorbed, 3 to 4 hours on low or 2 to 3 hours on high.
2. Sprinkle corn over quinoa, cover, and let sit until heated through, about 5 minutes. Fluff quinoa with fork, then gently folds in cilantro, lime juice, and remaining 1 tablespoon oil. Season with salt and pepper to taste. Serve.

Tuscan-Style White Beans with Herbs

Prep time: 10 minutes | Cook time: 2½ to 3½ hours | Serves 6

2½ cups dried white beans, such as great northern or navy
2 sprigs fresh sage
1 bay leaf
1 head garlic, left whole and unpeeled
10 cups water
1 tablespoon coarse sea salt, or more to taste
A few grinds of black pepper
Extra-virgin olive oil, for serving

1. Put the beans in a colander and rinse under cold running water, picking over for damaged beans and small stones. Transfer to the crock pot and cover by 3 inches with cold water. Soak for 6 to 12 hours and then drain.
2. Add the sage, bay leaf, garlic, and 10 cups of water. Cover and cook on high for 2½ to 3½ hours. The beans need to be covered with liquid at all times to cook properly. When done, they will be tender and hold their shape, rather than fall apart. Toward the end of the cooking time, add the sea salt and remove the bay leaf and head of garlic (you can squeeze the cooked garlic back into the beans if you like or discard).
3. Let the beans cool in the crock pot for 1 hour, uncovered, then drain off all but ½ cup of the liquid. Serve, seasoned with more salt and several grinds of black pepper, and drizzled with olive oil.

Grits Casserole

Prep time: 10 minutes | Cook time: 8 hours | Serves 8

1 cup stone-ground grits
4½ cups chicken broth
4 tablespoons (½ stick) unsalted butter, melted and slightly cooled
2 large eggs, beaten
½ cup heavy cream
2 cups finely shredded mild Cheddar cheese
Nonstick cooking spray

1. Spritz the crock pot with nonstick cooking spray.
2. Stir the grits, broth, and butter together in the crock pot. Cover and cook on low for 4 hours.
3. Stir in the eggs, cream, and cheese. Cover and cook for an additional 4 hours, until the grits are creamy and the cheese has melted.
4. Serve warm.

Rice, Farro, and Barley Medley

Prep time: 15 minutes | Cook time: 7 hours | Serves 2

1 tablespoon extra-virgin olive oil
1 onion, chopped
2 garlic cloves, minced
1 carrot, sliced
1⅓ cup wild rice, rinsed and drained well
1⅓ cup farro, rinsed and drained well
1⅓ cup pearl barley, rinsed and drained well
3 cups vegetable broth
1 bay leaf
½ teaspoon dried basil leaves
½ teaspoon salt
⅛ teaspoon freshly ground black pepper
1⅓ cup grated Parmesan cheese

1. In a small saucepan over medium heat, heat the olive oil. Add the onion, garlic, and carrot, and sauté until crisp-tender, about 5 to 6 minutes.
2. In the crock pot, combine the onion mixture, rice, farro, and barley.
3. Stir in the broth, bay leaf, basil, salt, and pepper.
4. Cover and cook on low for 7 hours, or until the grains are tender. Remove and discard the bay leaf, stir in the cheese, and serve.

Basil Parmesan Polenta

Prep time: 5 minutes | Cook time: 7 hours | Makes 7 cups

5 cups vegetable broth
2 onions, chopped
4 garlic cloves, minced
1½ teaspoons salt
¼ cup butter
1½ cups cornmeal
¼ cup chopped fresh flat-leaf parsley
3 tablespoons minced fresh basil
2 tablespoons minced fresh thyme
1 cup grated Parmesan cheese

1. In a large saucepan over high heat, bring the broth, onions, garlic, salt, and butter to a boil. Turn down the heat and simmer for 5 minutes, or until the onions are crisp-tender.
2. Carefully pour the hot broth mixture into the crock pot. Add the cornmeal, stirring constantly with a wire whisk until well combined.
3. Cover and cook on low for 7 hours.
4. Stir in the parsley, basil, thyme, and cheese, and serve immediately.

Bean and Pea Medley

Prep time: 15 minutes | Cook time: 6 to 8 hours | Serves 8

1¼ cups dried black beans, rinsed and drained
1¼ cups dried kidney beans, rinsed and drained
1¼ cups dried black-eyed peas, rinsed and drained
1 leek, chopped
2 carrots, peeled and chopped
1 onion, chopped
2 garlic cloves, minced
6 cups vegetable broth
½ teaspoon dried thyme leaves
1½ cups water

1. In the crock pot, mix all the ingredients. Cover and cook on low for 6 to 8 hours, or until the beans are tender and the liquid is absorbed.
2. Serve warm.

Refried Beans

Prep time: 15 minutes | Cook time: 8 to 9 hours | Serves 6

1 onion, finely chopped
1 poblano chile, stemmed, deseeded, and minced
2 slices bacon
3 garlic cloves, minced
1 tablespoon ground cumin
1 pound (454 g) dried pinto beans, picked over and rinsed
6 cups chicken broth, plus extra as needed
3 tablespoons minced fresh cilantro
1 tablespoon lime juice, plus extra as needed
Salt and pepper, to taste

1. Microwave onion, poblano, bacon, garlic, and cumin in a bowl, stirring occasionally, until vegetables are softened, about 5 minutes. Transfer to a crock pot. Stir in beans and broth, cover, and cook until beans are tender, 8 to 9 hours on high.
2. Discard bacon. Drain beans, reserving 1 cup cooking liquid. Return beans and reserved cooking liquid to the crock pot and mash with potato masher until smooth. Stir in cilantro, lime juice, and ½ teaspoon salt. Season with salt, pepper, and extra lime juice to taste. Serve. (Beans can be held on warm or low setting for up to 2 hours; adjust consistency with extra hot broth as needed before serving.)

Lentils with Escarole and Cheese

Prep time: 10 minutes | Cook time: 3 to 4 hours | Serves 6 to 8

1 onion, finely chopped
3 tablespoons extra-virgin olive oil, divided
3 garlic cloves, minced
½ teaspoon red pepper flakes
2½ cups vegetable or chicken broth
1 cup French green lentils, picked over and rinsed
1 head escarole (1 pound / 454 g), trimmed and sliced 1 inch thick
1 ounce (28 g) Parmesan cheese, grated (½ cup)
1 tablespoon lemon juice, plus extra for seasoning
Salt and pepper, to taste

1. Microwave onion, 1 tablespoon oil, garlic, and pepper flakes in a bowl, stirring occasionally, until onion is softened, about 5 minutes. Transfer to a crock pot. Stir in broth and lentils, cover, and cook until lentils are tender, 3 to 4 hours on low or 2 to 3 hours on high.
2. Stir in escarole, 1 handful at a time, until slightly wilted. Cover and cook on high until escarole is completely wilted, about 10 minutes. Stir in Parmesan, lemon juice, and remaining 2 tablespoons oil. Season with salt, pepper, and extra lemon juice to taste. Serve.

Mexican Black Bean and Pork Stew

Prep time: 15 minutes | Cook time: 8 to 9 hours | Serves 4 to 6

1 pound (454 g) boneless pork loin, trimmed of any fat and cut into 1-inch cubes
1 teaspoon chili powder
1 teaspoon ground coriander
Salt, to taste
1 medium-size yellow onion, chopped
1 garlic clove, minced
2 (15-ounce / 425-g) cans black beans, rinsed and drained
1 (16-ounce / 454-g) can stewed tomatoes, coarsely chopped, with their juice
2 cups water
Freshly ground black pepper, to taste
For Serving:
Hot cooked white rice
¼ cup chopped fresh cilantro, for garnish

1. Toss the pork with the chili powder, coriander, and salt until coated evenly. Heat a large ungreased skillet over medium-high heat, then lightly brown the pork with the onion and garlic, stirring.
2. Transfer the pork mixture to the crock pot, stir in the beans, tomatoes with their juice, and water. Season with pepper, cover, and cook on low for 8 to 9 hours.
3. Serve the beans and pork ladled over steamed white rice and garnished with cilantro.

Molasses Baked Soybeans

Prep time: 10 minutes | Cook time: 9 to 10 hours | Serves 4 to 5

1 cup dried soybeans
4 cups water, or more to cover
½ medium-size yellow onion, sliced into half-moons
¼ cup firmly packed light or dark brown sugar
¼ cup molasses
1 teaspoon salt
½ teaspoon dry mustard
2 tablespoons toasted or black sesame oil

1. Rinse the beans in a colander under cold running water and pick over for damaged beans and small stones. Transfer to the crock pot. Cover with cold water by 2 inches, soak 6 to 12 hours, and drain.
2. Cover with the 4 cups water. Cover and cook on high until tender, about 4 hours. The beans need to be covered with liquid at all times to cook properly.
3. Drain the cooked beans and return them to the crock pot. Add the onion, brown sugar, molasses, salt, mustard, and sesame oil, stirring to combine. Cover and cook on low for 5 to 6 hours, until the soybeans are flavorful but still moist and the onion is soft. Stir gently so as not to mash the beans and serve hot.

Rosemary Lentils with Ham and Carrot

Prep time: 20 minutes | Cook time: 3½ to 4 hours | Serves 8

2 medium-size yellow onions, chopped
2 cups diced cooked ham
1 cup diced carrot or parsnip
1 cup chopped celery
2 cloves garlic, chopped
¾ teaspoon dried rosemary, crushed
¾ teaspoon rubbed sage
¼ teaspoon freshly ground black pepper
1 bay leaf
1 pound (454 g) dried brown lentils, picked over and rinsed
1 (14½-ounce / 411-g) can beef broth
5 cups water, or as needed to cover everything by 3 inches
Chopped fresh flat-leaf parsley, for serving (optional)

1. Combine all the ingredients in the crock pot, except the parsley. Cover and cook on high until the lentils are tender, 3½ to 4 hours. Add boiling water if you want soupier lentils.
2. Discard the bay leaf. Garnish with parsley, if desired, before serving.

Black-Eyed Peas and Greens and Sausage

Prep time: 15 minutes | Cook time: 9 to 11 hours | Serves 4

1 pound (454 g) dried black-eyed peas
1 large white onion, finely chopped
3 ribs celery, finely chopped
½ red bell pepper, finely chopped
½ green bell pepper, finely chopped
1 pound (454 g) smoked chicken-apple sausage, sliced ½-inch thick
1 (14½-ounce / 411-g) can diced tomatoes, with their juice
1 (4-ounce / 113-g) can diced roasted green chiles, drained
4 cups chicken broth
1 bunch collard greens
1 teaspoon fine sea salt
Ground black pepper, to taste

1. Put the black-eyed peas in a colander and rinse under cold running water, then pick over for damaged beans and small stones. Transfer to the crock pot and cover with 3 inches of cold water. Soak for 6 to 12 hours.
2. Drain the beans and return them to the crock pot. Add the onion, celery, bell peppers, sausage, tomatoes with their juice, green chiles, and broth.
3. Separate the collard green leaves and rinse well under running water. Remove the thick stems and inner ribs. Stack the leaves and roll them up, then slice into 2-inch-thick strips.
4. Add the collard greens to the crock pot. Cover and cook on low for 9 to 11 hours, until just tender. Add the salt and pepper and serve.

Herbed Black Beans with Onions

Prep time: 10 minutes | Cook time: 7 to 9 hours | Serves 8

3 cups dried black beans, rinsed and drained
2 onions, chopped   8 garlic cloves, minced
6 cups vegetable broth
1 teaspoon dried basil leaves
½ teaspoon dried thyme leaves
½ teaspoon dried oregano leaves
½ teaspoon salt

1. In the crock pot, mix all the ingredients. Cover and cook on low for 7 to 9 hours, or until the beans have absorbed the liquid and are tender.
2. Remove and discard the bay leaf before serving.

Puy Lentils with Leek

Prep time: 10 minutes | Cook time: 4 to 5 hours | Serves 8

3 cups puy lentils, rinsed and drained
1 onion, chopped   1 leek, chopped
8 garlic cloves, minced 6 cups vegetable broth
1 bay leaf
½ teaspoon dried oregano leaves

1. In the crock pot, mix all the ingredients. Cover and cook on low for 4 to 5 hours, or until the lentils are tender.
2. Remove and discard the bay leaf before serving.

Southwestern Bean and Ham Pot

Prep time: 10 minutes | Cook time: 5 to 6 hours | Serves 8

1 pound (454 g) dried Christmas lima, cranberry, pinto, or anasazi beans
7 cups water
1 large yellow onion, chopped
1 (12-ounce / 340-g) ham hock or leftover meaty ham bone
1 (8-ounce / 227-g) can or jar green chile salsa, tomato sauce, or stewed tomatoes
1 teaspoon salt, or to taste

1. Put the beans in a colander and rinse under cold running water, then pick over for damaged beans and small stones. Transfer to the crock pot. Cover with 3 inches of cold water, then soak for 6 to 12 hours, and drain.
2. Add the 7 cups of water, onion, and ham hock. Cover and cook on high for 3½ hours, then stir in the salsa.
3. Cover and continue to cook on high for another 1½ to 2½ hours. The beans should be covered with liquid at all times to cook properly, but the mixture should be thick. When done, the beans will tender and hold their shape, rather than fall apart.
4. Remove the ham hock or bone and pick off the meat. Return the meat to the crock pot and stir to combine. Season with the salt and serve.

French White Beans

Prep time: 10 minutes | Cook time: 6 to 7 hours | Serves 2

1½ cups dried great northern beans, sorted and rinsed
2 carrots, sliced   1 onion, chopped
3 garlic cloves, minced
3 cups chicken stock or vegetable broth
½ teaspoon dried thyme leaves
1 teaspoon salt
⅛ teaspoon freshly ground black pepper
2 tablespoons extra-virgin olive oil
1 tablespoon minced fresh thyme leaves
1⅓ cup grated Parmesan cheese

1. In the crock pot, combine all the ingredients except the fresh thyme and cheese, and stir.
2. Cover and cook on low for 6 to 7 hours, or until the beans are tender.
3. Stir in the fresh thyme and cheese, and serve.

Rosemary Northern Beans

Prep time: 15 minutes | Cook time: 6 to 8 hours | Serves 16

1 pound (454 g) great northern beans, rinsed and drained
1 onion, finely chopped
3 cloves garlic, minced
1 large sprig fresh rosemary
½ teaspoon salt
⅛ teaspoon white pepper
4 cups water
2 cups vegetable broth

1. Combine the beans, onion, garlic, rosemary, salt, water, and vegetable broth in the crock pot.
2. Cover and cook on low for 6 to 8 hours or until the beans are tender.
3. Remove the rosemary stem and discard. Stir the mixture gently and serve.

Appendix 1 Measurement Conversion Chart

VOLUME EQUIVALENTS(DRY)

US STANDARD	METRIC (APPROXIMATE)
1/8 teaspoon	0.5 mL
1/4 teaspoon	1 mL
1/2 teaspoon	2 mL
3/4 teaspoon	4 mL
1 teaspoon	5 mL
1 tablespoon	15 mL
1/4 cup	59 mL
1/2 cup	118 mL
3/4 cup	177 mL
1 cup	235 mL
2 cups	475 mL
3 cups	700 mL
4 cups	1 L

VOLUME EQUIVALENTS(LIQUID)

US STANDARD	US STANDARD (OUNCES)	METRIC (APPROXIMATE)
2 tablespoons	1 fl.oz.	30 mL
1/4 cup	2 fl.oz.	60 mL
1/2 cup	4 fl.oz.	120 mL
1 cup	8 fl.oz.	240 mL
1 1/2 cup	12 fl.oz.	355 mL
2 cups or 1 pint	16 fl.oz.	475 mL
4 cups or 1 quart	32 fl.oz.	1 L
1 gallon	128 fl.oz.	4 L

TEMPERATURES EQUIVALENTS

FAHRENHEIT(F)	CELSIUS(C) (APPROXIMATE)
225 °F	107 °C
250 °F	120 °C
275 °F	135 °C
300 °F	150 °C
325 °F	160 °C
350 °F	180 °C
375 °F	190 °C
400 °F	205 °C
425 °F	220 °C
450 °F	235 °C
475 °F	245 °C
500 °F	260 °C

WEIGHT EQUIVALENTS

US STANDARD	METRIC (APPROXIMATE)
1 ounce	28 g
2 ounces	57 g
5 ounces	142 g
10 ounces	284 g
15 ounces	425 g
16 ounces (1 pound)	455 g
1.5 pounds	680 g
2 pounds	907 g

Appendix 2 Recipe Index

A

Acorn Squash with Maple Orange Glaze 59
Acorn Squash with Shallots and Dates 70
Alfredo Sauce 17
Almond and Date Oatmeal 3
Almond and Peanut Butter Cheesecake 34
Almond and Raisin Granola 6
Almond and Sour Cream Cheesecake 33
Almond Cake 33
Almond Vegetable Korma 77
Almond-Mushroom Wild Rice 136
Apple and Cranberry Pork Roast 114
Apple and Walnut Pie 29
Apple Balsamic Chicken 81
Apple Cobbler 8
Apple Crisp with Oat Topping 26
Apple Crumble 29
Apricot Glazed Turkey with Herbs 87
Aromatic Vegetable Pulao 138
Asian Baby Back Ribs 101
Asian Shrimp and Rice Casserole 127
Asian-Flavored Braised Spareribs 102
Authentic Con Pollo 91
Authentic Zuppa Bastarda 48

B

Bacon and Beef Chili 56
Bacon Hash Brown Casserole 65
Baked Raisin Stuffed Apples 30
Baked Ziti with Sausage 36
Balsamic Beef with Cranberry Gravy 102
Balsamic Fresh Shell Beans with Herbs 62
Barbecue Collard Greens with Tofu 69
Barbecue Shrimp and Scallops 132
Barbecued Smokies 11
Barley and Mushroom Risotto 139
Barley Pilaf with Dates 141
Barley Risotto Primavera 139
Barley-Stuffed Cabbage Rolls 79
Basic Oatmeal 3
Basil Parmesan Polenta 142
Basil Perch with Potatoes 119
Basil Potato and Corn 71
Basil Tomato Sauce 17
BBQ Chicken Legs 92
BBQ Party Starters 10
BBQ Short Ribs 110
BBQ Tuna 124
BBQ Turkey Cutlets 97
Bean and Pea Medley 142
Beans and Couscous Stuffed Peppers 75
Beef Alphabet Soup 41
Beef and Baby Carrot Stew 98
Beef and Barley Soup 51
Beef and Cheese Dip 9
Beef and Kidney Bean Stew 53
Beef and Parsnip Soup 47
Beef and Pearl Barley Stew 54
Beef and Pumpkin Stew 48
Beef Chili 55
Beef Chili with Cilantro Cream 57
Beef Ragoût with Veggies 103
Beef Roast Sandwiches 103
Beef Roast with Stewed Tomatoes 112
Beef Roast with Tangy Au Jus 115
Beer-Braised Beef Brisket 98
Berry Sauce 16
Black and Blue Berry Cobbler 19
Black Bean and Turkey Sausage Stew 51
Black Bean Spinach Enchiladas 72
Black-Eyed Peas and Greens and Sausage 144
Black-Eyed Peas with Ham 62
Boston Baked Beans 140
Braised Butternut Squash with Pecans 59
Braised Eggplant and Lentils 78
Braised Lamb with Eggplant 106
Braised Peas with Lettuce and Onions 60
Branzino and Potato Bake 131
Brisket Braised with Dried Fruits 109
Broccoli and Three-Cheese Lasagna 36
Broccoli Dip 14
Brown Lentil Chili 56
Brown Rice and Black Bean Chili 54
Brown Rice Risotto with Starch Vegetables 138
Brown Sugar Beef Chili 54

Buckwheat with Lush Mushrooms 140
Buffalo Wing Sauce 16
Buttered Parsley Red Potatoes 61
Butternut Squash Risotto with White Wine 137
Butternut Squash Soup with Thyme 43

C-D

Cabbage and Beef Stew 98
California Chicken 94
Caponata 79
Caramelized Onion Pot Roast 38
Carrot Cake with Cream Cheese Frosting 23
Carrot Cheese Casserole 68
Catalina Marmalade Meatballs 14
Cauliflower and Zucchini Vindaloo 78
Cauliflower-Bacon Casserole with Pecans 68
Cheddar Salmon Soufflé 122
Cheese Grits with Collard Greens 4
Cheese Pulled Pork Crostini 12
Cheesy Red Potatoes 64
Cheesy Sausage Lasagna 39
Cherry and Hazelnut Stuffed Apples 27
Cherry Molton Cake 32
Chex Mix 10
Chicago-Style Flank Steaks 109
Chicken and Carrot Fricassee 40
Chicken and Red Potato Stew 37
Chicken and Turkey Sausage Jambalaya 91
Chicken and Wild Rice Soup 39
Chicken Breast with Peas 93
Chicken Cacciatore 90
Chicken Cheese Parmigiana 91
Chicken Chili 91
Chicken Olé Casserole 93
Chicken Parmesan 80
Chicken Stock 15
Chicken Tamales 92
Chicken Tetrazzini 93
Chicken Wings in Plum Sauce 96
Chicken with Apple and Chardonnay Gravy 83
Chickpea and Lentil Stew 53
Chili Dip 14
Chili Mac and Cheese 35
Chinese-Style Cumin Lamb 113
Chocolate Brownie Cake 31
Chocolate Chip Graham Cracker Cookies 20
Chocolate Fondue 20

Chocolate Snack Cake 22
Chorizo Egg Casserole 6
Cider Butternut Squash Purée 59
Cider Pork Loin 104
Cinnamon Applesauce 32
Cinnamon Glazed Acorn Squash 65
Citrus Carrots with Leek 68
Citrus Swordfish Fillets 126
Classic Bolognese Sauce 17
Classic Chicken Casablanca 90
Classic Gyro Soup 46
Coconut Curried Butternut Squash 64
Coconut Halibut with Eggplant Relish 130
Coconut Key Lime Pie 25
Cod with Garlic Edamame 122
Corn and Beef Chili 50
Cornbread Chicken Bake 82
Corned Beef Braised in Riesling 108
Country-Style Spareribs 106
Cowboy Calico Beans with Ground Beef 62
Crab Angel Hair Pasta 125
Crab Dip 9
Cranberry Swedish Meatballs 11
Cranberry Sweet Potato and Wild Rice 136
Crayfish Creole 129
Cream of Zucchini Soup 41
Creamed Broccoli 64
Creamy Butternut Squash Soup 51
Creamy Carrot and Broccoli Soup 45
Creamy Cheddar Potato Soup 43
Creamy Pumpkin Pie Pudding 19
Creamy Saffron Rice 136
Creamy Shrimp Curry 126
Crunchy Snack Mix 14
Curried Coconut Quinoa 75
Curried Vegetable Soup 51
Duck Breasts with Port and Orange Sauce 89

E

Eggplant and Potato Curry 75
Eggs in Tomato Purgatory 7

F

Fallen Chocolate Soufflé Cake 20
Fennel and Leek Soup 52
Filipino Chicken Adobo 85
Fish Congee 3

Fish Stock 15
Fish Tagine with Artichokes 123
Five-Ingredient Tuna Loaf 119
Flan 29
Flank Steak Fajitas 100
Foil Pack Garlic Butter Tilapia 128
French White Beans 145
Fruit Salsa Mahi Mahi with Lentils 129
Fruity Cake with Walnuts 20
Fudgy Brownies 21

G

Garbanzo Bean Soup 44
Garlic Braised Lamb Shanks 117
Garlic Button Mushrooms 71
Garlic Collard Greens and Kale 61
Garlic Mushrooms with Crème Fraîche 60
Garlic Squash Curry 69
Garlicky Balsamic Glazed Onions 67
Garlicky Braised Kale with Chorizo 66
Garlicky Chicken 92
Garlicky Lemon-Thyme Turkey Legs 87
Garlicky Veal Stew 112
German Sauerbraten 113
Ginger Peach Crumble 25
Ginger Peach Glazed Chicken Thighs 85
Gingerbread 33
Glazed Chicken Wings 13
Glazed Hawaiian Kielbasa Bites 10
Grape Jelly Meatballs 9
Grape-Nuts Custard Pudding 37
Greek Chicken with Potatoes 95
Greek Yogurt Mashed Pumpkin 70
Green Bean and Mushroom Casserole 67
Green Beans and Potatoes with Bacon 63
Green Chile and Shrimp Tacos 127
Green Chili Cheddar Crustless Quiche 5
Grits Casserole 142
Ground Beef Macaroni Soup 42
Ground Turkey with Potatoes 97

H

Halibut Tacos 121
Halibut with Green Bean Salad 124
Ham and Potato Casserole 37
Ham and Vegetable Soup 42
Ham Egg Cheese Casserole 7

Hamburger Chili with Beans 55
Hawaiian Huli Huli Chicken 80
Hearty Apricot Cheesecake 26
Herbed Black Beans with Onions 145
Herbed Braised Flounder 119
Hominy and Turkey Thigh Chili 57
Honey Parsnips and Carrots 68
Honeyed Worcestershire Salmon 131
Hungarian Pork Paprikash 117

I

Indian Spiced Potatoes and Cauliflower 74
Indian Tandoori Lamb 107
Indian-Style Chili 56
Irish Lamb Stew 118
Italian Beef Minestrone 42
Italian Meat Gravy 18
Italian Meatball Stew 37
Italian Pork Sausage Lasagna Soup 116
Italian-Style Braised Chicken and Veggies 90

J-K

Jalapeño Creamed Corn 65
Jamaican-Inspired Brown Chicken Stew 82
Jerk Chicken 86
Kale and White Bean Soup 48
Kedgeree (Spiced Rice with Smoked Fish) 135

L

Lamb Chops and White Beans 107
Lamb Goulash au Blanc 118
Lamb with Artichokes 99
Leafy Greens with Onions 67
Leek and Potato Soup 45
Leek and Potato Soup 49
Leeks Braised in Cream 66
Leg of Lamb and Cabbage 108
Leg of Lamb with Pinto Beans 107
Lemon Blueberry Cornmeal Cake 22
Lemon Garlic Chicken 80
Lemon Thyme Pearl Barley Risotto 138
Lemon-Dijon Salmon 130
Lemon-Dill Chicken 82
Lemon-Rosemary Beets 71
Lemony Chicken Wings 9
Lentils with Escarole and Cheese 143

Lime Buttered Salmon 129
Lush BBQ Sausage Bites 12

M-N

Macaroni Bean Stew 52
Mango Pineapple Chicken Tacos 81
Mango Yogurt with Honey and Cardamon 5
Maple Baked Beans with Bacon 63
Maple Cranberry Granola 3
Maple Pork Chops in Bourbon 101
Marinara Shrimp 134
Marinated Wings 12
Mashed Squash with Garlic 67
Mediterranean Beef Roast 101
Mediterranean Chicken with Artichokes 95
Mediterranean Lamb and Lentils 106
Mexican Beef Brisket 111
Mexican Beef Enchilada 102
Mexican Black Bean and Pork Stew 143
Mexican Corn with Pimentos 69
Mexican Pinto Beans 137
Mexican Turkey 88
Mixed Fruit Curry 28
Molasses Baked Soybeans 144
Monterey Jack Seafood Pasta 127
Moroccan Sea Bass with Bell Pepper 128
Mushroom and Bacon Soup 42
Mushroom and Tomato Mussels 133
Mushroom Chicken Alfredo 81
Mushroom Chicken Cacciatore 84
Mushroom Macaroni and Cheese 35
Mushroom Tofu Soup 46
Nacho Cheese Sauce 18
North African Pumpkin and Cauliflower Stew 77
Nutmeg Carrot Soup 41

O

Onion and Tomato Soup 49
Onion Beef Short Ribs 111
Orange Cauliflower with Herbs 68
Orange-Hoisin Chicken 85
Oregano Lamb Chops 116
Osso Buco 110

P-Q

Peanut Butter Chicken Thighs 96
Peanut Butter Oatmeal Granola 7

Pear and Chai Oatmeal 7
Pecan-Crusted Blueberry Crisp 21
Pecan-Stuffed Acorn Squash 70
Peppery Broccoli with Sesame Seeds 71
Pine Nut Pilaf 139
Pineapple and Mango Crisp 31
Pineapple Tapioca 19
Pizza Bites 11
Poached Tuna with Olives 128
Poached Turbot 130
Pork and Butternut Squash Stew 50
Pork and Butternut Stew 116
Pork Chops with Plum Sauce 100
Pork Loin with Cran-Orange Sauce 103
Pork Roast in Apricot Glaze 114
Pork Shoulder Chili Con Carne 117
Pork Tenderloin with Mango Sauce 104
Pork Veggie Soup 44
Pork Wraps with Hoisin Sauce 115
Pork-Beef Patties with Cabbage 114
Posh Fruit Compote 29
Pot De Crème 32
Potato and Beef Chili 55
Potato and Prosciutto Breakfast Strata 4
Potato and Tomato Strata 8
Potato Stuffed Peppers 73
Potato, Parsnip, and Carrot Hash 8
Pound Cake 34
Pumpkin and Mixed Berry Compote 32
Pumpkin Pie Custard 30
Pumpkin Spice Cheesecake 24
Pumpkin-Carrot Pudding 70
Puy Lentils with Leek 145
Quinoa and Cherry Porridge 8
Quinoa with Corn 141

R

Raisin Rice Pudding 19
Raspberry and Lime Custard Cake 34
Ratatouille Quinoa Casserole 140
Red Pear and Pumpkin Soup 45
Red Pepper and Lentil Soup 47
Red Pepper Chicken with Black Beans 95
Red Snapper Feast 119
Red Tofu Curry and Green Beans 77
Refried Beans 143
Rhubarb and Strawberry Compote 27

Rice, Farro, and Barley Medley 142
Roasted Cauliflower with Tomato Cashew Sauce 76
Root Vegetable Medley 63
Root Veggie Gratin with Barley 66
Rosemary Lentils with Ham and Carrot 144
Rosemary Northern Beans 145
Rosemary White Bean Soup 44
Rotisserie-Style Chicken with Carrots 84

S

Sake-Cooked Asparagus 60
Salmon and Mushroom Bake 122
Salmon with Chili-Garlic Glaze 120
Salmon with White Rice Salad 123
Salsa Mexicana 16
Salsa Verde 18
Sausage and Kale Soup 49
Sausage and Peppers in Wine 105
Sausage and Waffle Breakfast Bake 6
Sausage Cabbage Soup 45
Sausage Casserole 8
Sausage Hash Brown Breakfast Casserole 5
Scallops with Creamy Leeks 127
Seafood Medley 126
Seitan Tikka Masala with Green Beans 72
Self-Frosting Chocolate Cake 30
Shallot and Red Wine Sauce 16
Shoepeg Corn Casserole 61
Shrimp and Crab Gumbo 125
Shrimp and Ham Jambalaya 124
Shrimp Polenta 134
Shrimp Spaghetti with Marinara 125
Shrimp, Quinoa, and Corn Salad 132
Smoked Sausages with BBQ Sauce 104
Smothered Pork 38
Sour Cream Cheesecake 23
Sour Cream Chicken Enchiladas 83
Southern Brunswick Stew 53
Southwestern Bean and Ham Pot 145
Southwestern Chicken with Corn 95
Soy-Honey Lamb and Brown Rice 118
Spanish Beef and Rice Soup 47
Spanish Herbed Octopus 133
Spanish Hominy 62
Spice Stuffed Baby Eggplants 76
Spiced Applesauce Cake 28
Spicy Corn-Ham Pudding 69
Spinach and Cheese Casserole 65
Spinach Mushroom Cheese Quiche 72
Spinach-Stuffed Sole 120
Stewed Dried Apricots 21
Strawberry Rhubarb Compote 21
Stuffed Turkey Cutlets with Artichokes 89
Summer Vegetable Mélange 78
Sumptuous Chinese Vegetable Mix 79
Sumptuous Pork with Veggies 114
Super Bean Soup 40
Super Lemony Rice Pudding 30
Sweet and Savory Brisket 108
Sweet and Sour Chicken Wings 96
Sweet and Sour Pork 112
Sweet and Sour Tomato Brisket 99
Sweet and Sour Tuna 122
Sweet and Spiced Pork Loin 105
Sweet and Spicy Chicken Wings 11
Sweet and Spicy Peanuts 11
Sweet Cherry Grunt 28
Sweet Potato and Corn Scramble 4
Sweet Potato and Sirloin Stew 54
Sweet Smoked Chicken Wings 14
Swordfish with Tomato and Olive Relish 121

T-U

Tandoori Chicken 84
Tangy Carrot Bisque 49
Tarragon Chicken Marsala 86
Tea Smoked Turkey Legs 88
Tempeh and Corn Stuffed Bell Peppers 73
Tempeh and Vegetable Shepherd's Pie 73
Tender Chicken with BBQ-Soda Sauce 94
Tequila Sausage Queso 13
Teriyaki Pork Tenderloin 105
Texas-Style Pork Burritos 115
Texas-Style Smoked Beef Brisket 110
Tex-Mex Chicken and Rice 94
Tex-Mex Quinoa Salad 139
Thai Green Curry Shrimp 126
Thai Red Curry Chicken with Vegetables 38
Thai Sesame Chicken Thighs 83
Thai-Flavored Green Vegetables 71
Thyme Garlic Tomatoes 61
Thyme Onion Soup 43
Thyme Root Veggies 66
Toasted Sesame Chicken Wings 96

Tofu with Greens 79
Tomato Salsa 10
Tuna and Egg Casserole 125
Tuna and Veggie Casserole with Almonds 123
Turkey Loaf 97
Turkey Macaroni with Corn 94
Turkey Sausage and Navy Bean Stew 52
Turkey Sloppy Joes 97
Turkey Taco Salad 88
Turkey Teriyaki Sandwiches 13
Turkey Teriyaki Thighs 87
Turkey-Broccoli Supreme 97
Tuscan-Style White Beans with Herbs 141
Ultimate Chocolate Cheesecake 24

V

Vanilla Chocolate Cake 31
Vanilla Creme Brûlée 27
Vegan Garlic Pasta Sauce 18
Vegetable and Black-Eyed Pea Chili 50
Vegetable and Rice Stew 53
Vegetable Beef Soup 46

Vegetable Stock 15
Vegetarian Bean Cassoulet 74
Veggie and Brown Rice Stew 52
Veggie and Cashew Chili 55
Veggie Bulgur Wheat Chili 58
Veggie Ketchup Chicken 93
Veggie Tofu Stir-Fry 74
Vinegary Steak with Green Chilies 100

W

Warm Fruit Salad 65
White Beans with Pancetta and Carrot 135
White Fish Curry 131
Whole Roasted Mexican Chicken 86
Wild Rice and Fruit Pilaf 137
Wild Rice, Bacon, and Cherries 136

Z

Zinfandel-Braised Beef Short Ribs 111
Zucchini Stuffed Sweet Onions 63
Zucchini Tomato Casserole 64

Printed in Great Britain
by Amazon